MAKING
THE RUNNING

MAKING THE RUNNING

A Racing Life

IAN BALDING

headline

First published in 2004
by HEADLINE BOOK PUBLISHING

10 9 8 7 6 5 4 3 2 1

Cataloguing in Publication Data is available from the British Library

ISBN 0 7553 1278 3

Typeset in Cheltenham by Avon DataSet Ltd,
Bidford-on-Avon, Warwickshire

Printed and bound in Great Britain by
Clays Ltd, St Ives plc, Bungay, Suffolk

Headline's policy is to use papers that are natural, renewable and
recyclable products and made from wood grown in sustainable forests.
The logging and manufacturing processes are expected to conform to
the environmental regulations of the country of origin.

HEADLINE BOOK PUBLISHING
A division of Hodder Headline
338 Euston Road
London NW1 3BH

www.headline.co.uk
www.hodderheadline.com

To all those wonderful horses who have enriched my life.

Contents

Acknowledgements

I would like first to thank my agent, John Beaton, who had the original idea that I should write this book and who introduced me to my publishers. I would also like to thank Ian Marshall and Wendy McCance, my more recent contacts at Headline, who have put up with my tardiness at all stages.

I owe particular thanks to Heather Holden-Brown, my original commissioning editor at Headline, who was the one to realise how badly I was procrastinating in the writing task. She gave me a thorough old-fashioned bollocking that was just what I needed to get me down to the daily routine of writing and ensure that eventually – albeit late – the book got finished. How I wish she had taught me at school; I might have passed some exams!

I would like to thank my daughter Clare for her very perceptive and amusing foreword, and also for shaping the text on the inside of the jacket cover.

Immense gratitude to my editor Gillian Somerscales, who managed to cut down sensibly on my original long-winded script, and brilliantly put it all into correct English. Thanks too to Georgie Sheehan, who did some of the typing while Emma was away at the sales.

Most especially, as always, my heartfelt thanks go to the unsung heroine of Park House: my wife Emma. In spite of her reservations about the whole project, she dutifully typed up the majority of my longhand scrawl, corrected the facts and the dates – and eliminated most of the fiction.

Foreword by Clare Balding

When we were young, Andrew and I would have running races on the lawn. Arms pumping, legs straining, faces flushed with effort, we would try our hearts out. Occasionally, our father would join in. Dad would sit at the shoulder of the leader, wait until four strides before the 'winning post' and then accelerate past to win by half a length.

'Why don't you let one of them win, just once?' my mother asked him.

'Because you don't win anything until you deserve to,' came the reply. My father has lived by that dictum his whole life. It doesn't matter whether it is an egg-and-spoon race or the Grand National: if it is a competitive event then it is worth making an effort. And not just any old effort . . . Dad may not do much around the house (loading the dishwasher is beyond him), but the little things that he does bother with are done with the attention to detail of a perfectionist.

'There's no point doing anything unless you do it to the best of your ability,' he told me when I asked him why he had spent a whole hour cleaning his riding boots.

It is this near-obsessive attention to detail and fierce competitive instinct that have made my father the trainer he was for over thirty-five years and the all-round sportsman that he remains. Better than average at polo, squash, tennis, cricket and golf, he won a Cambridge blue for rugby and is acknowledged as one of the bravest and most naturally talented horsemen of his generation.

The one sport that he failed to master was skiing. Not for lack of trying, you understand, but for sheer lack of style. He would get down any mountain or cliff face that presented itself – but to see him careering down a slope towards you, controlled elegance abandoned after the first turn, was to stare fear in the face.

Dad was never afraid; it was just those around him. Similarly, despite having passed his sixty-fifth birthday, he never seems to age – but ask those who have to live every day with him how old they feel. He takes some keeping up with, my father.

'Follow me,' is his refrain, and woe betide you if you can't lay up. Second place is for losers, and there is no room for them in my father's world. There were no allowances made for my mother or myself – if we couldn't keep up with the boys then we didn't deserve to be alive. However, this exponent of equality has never quite comprehended the post-feminist world. This is the man who, shortly after Margaret Thatcher's election as Prime Minister in 1979, said to his foremost owner, 'I'm not sure I can get my head around a woman running the country.' Nothing if not honest; but when the owner on the other end of the line is the Queen, a little discretion may have been wise. To her eternal credit, Her Majesty thought it funny.

Nothing annoys my father so much as an individual who doesn't try; but give him a horse who refuses to fulfil its potential and Dad will take the challenge upon himself to discover the key. His patience with horses knows no bounds – a virtue which has borne the fruits of success with tricky customers like Lochsong and Diamond Shoal.

My father is an extraordinary individual. I have never come across anyone so self-motivated or focused. When he sets his mind to something, such as writing this book, nothing and no one will come between him and the task in hand.

For all his achievements, nothing becomes my father so much as the manner in which he has left them behind. He has stepped into the wings to offer advice and support when needed, but never once diverted the spotlight from the centre of the stage. I am proud of him for that; but most of all I'm just proud to say, 'See that nutter over there? That's my Dad.'

1

Disaster Strikes

As dawn broke I slipped quietly out of bed, trying not to disturb my wife Emma. I dressed next door and went downstairs to let the dogs out and snatch a quick cup of tea. I knew it was well before my alarm clock was due to go off, but I was unusually anxious and excited. I have always loved the feeling of being the first person around – with the one certain exception of my head lad, Bill Palmer, who would already be halfway through his early morning task of feeding sixty horses – and I nearly always woke early on 'work' mornings; but this one, the last Wednesday of August 1972, had an extra edge to it. I was anxious because there were just five and a half weeks left before Mill Reef would attempt to become the first horse since the mighty Ribot to win the Prix de l'Arc de Triomphe two years running; and I was excited because today our little superstar was to have his first serious piece of exercise for several weeks.

I had done the list the previous evening, setting out which horses were to work together, and now I clipped it to my 'slate' – the board with all the lads' names on one side and the horses they were to ride that morning opposite. Hustling the dogs into the back of my van, I drove down to the yard to drop the slate off in the tack room and to have a quick word with Bill to check that all was well. Then, as was my custom on many work mornings, I made my way up to the downs.

I had planned for Mill Reef and the others to use a piece of ground we called the 'seven'. We had not had rain for quite a while, but this gallop, which despite its name stretches for just over a mile uphill through the middle of Watership Down, was the same beautiful springy Hampshire turf on which eight Derby winners before him had been trained during the previous hundred years. I knew there would be no better grass in England on which to gallop racehorses, but I wanted to walk up the strip that our downsman Jona Holley had marked out for us, just to be certain that the descendants of Hazel, Bigwig and Fiver had not dug any holes during the night.

As the dogs and I set off on our walk I thought, not for the first time, what a wonderful way it was to start the day. I was not to know that this day would turn out to be the most traumatic of my life.

An hour later I set off for the downs again – this time sitting astride a big bay gelding called The Brigand who was my point-to-pointer and summer hack. I led the string of twenty horses with Bill Palmer at the back on Square Rigger – a very useful if temperamental gelding of Paul Mellon whom we were using as a hack to try to help him rediscover his enthusiasm.

We trotted for three or four hundred yards to a ring we used as a gathering place. From there they split into six or seven groups of twos and threes as on my work list and had a three-furlong warm-up canter. While trying to watch them all, I naturally enough never let my eyes leave Mill Reef for more than a few seconds. We had had innumerable setbacks with him ever since his last race, the Coronation Cup at Epsom in early June, when he had just scrambled home in front of Homeric. We know now, but of course had not been aware then, that he had been harbouring a debilitating respiratory virus called rhinopneumonitis at the time of the race, and this almost certainly was the indirect cause of these various problems. Still, as he moved majestically round on his first canter I could not help thinking that at last he must have put his difficulties behind him. After giving some last-minute instructions to all the riders, I cantered The Brigand up first on the twelve-foot-wide strip between the markers that I had previously walked. It was indeed perfect ground and I stationed myself opposite the two-furlong marker from where I could see both the start and the finish of the gallop.

Mill Reef followed his lead horse, Merry Slipper, at a good strong canter. Both riders had instructions to quicken into what we call a half-speed gallop from the three-furlong pole, which is at the foot of a noticeable incline. They were to go on past me and to begin easing up gradually after the one-furlong marker.

I scarcely noticed Merry Slipper, but Mill Reef, with his lad John Hallum riding, was hard held about three lengths behind as intended. I thought again how superbly he was moving and for the first time there was no sound whatever of the very slight whistle I had noticed in his breathing ever since Epsom. They were the first pair to come up, and after they had gone on past me I turned contentedly to watch the next pair, Aldie and Martinmas. As these two in turn went by, my head swivelled gradually towards the top end of the gallop – and the scene less than two hundred yards away caused my heart to miss a few beats. A few paces off to the right of the marked-out gallop was Mill Reef standing on three legs with his lad John beside him, already with the reins over the horse's head, desperately trying to control him while the next two groups of workers went by at speed.

Oh my God, I don't believe it, I thought as I moved quickly to the middle of the gallop to stop the other groups before they reached the stricken pair. I then rode over to Mill Reef and his lad. I can remember the anguish in John's voice as he shouted, 'Guvnor, I'm sure he has broken his leg – I heard a terrible crack.' With all his strength and experience he had pulled the little horse up as gently and quickly as he possibly could, but inevitably more damage had to have been done since the original sound of the crack.

I dispatched my mother-in-law, Priscilla Hastings, in her car back to the yard to summon a vet immediately and to get our box driver, Norton Jones, up to the downs in the horsebox as quickly as possible. He arrived soon after with support bandages, our blacksmith Tom Reilly, and two lads to take Bill and my hacks home. After Bill had applied the support bandages to all four of

Mill Reef's legs, he, John, Tom and I then had the difficult task of persuading the injured horse to cover the twenty or thirty yards from where he was standing to the horsebox parked in the lane next to the gallops. The lane was six to nine inches lower than the grass, so the ramp was not quite as steep as it would have been if we had driven it next to him. At this stage Mill Reef, with the adrenalin still pumping, was remarkably relaxed, picking grass and not even sweating. With gentle but forceful cajoling we pushed and pulled him on three legs those few yards across to the ramp of the horsebox. It was tough going and must have taken a good twenty minutes – and now we were faced with a still horribly steep-looking ramp. We exchanged glances, knowing that we couldn't lift him in without considerable cooperation from the patient himself.

In one of the bravest and most intelligent reactions I have ever seen from a racehorse, Mill Reef, who must have sensed the problem, jumped virtually unaided halfway up the ramp and with our assistance somehow scrambled the rest of the way. This amazing effort cost him dear, however, because now he was sweating profusely and was obviously in acute distress. The slow and painful journey down to the yard seemed interminable, but there again he helped us by coming fairly quickly down the ramp and then hopping like a veteran three-legged runner into the sanctuary of his own stable.

The vet, who was already waiting for us, was one of Peter Scott Dunn's assistants, Barry Williams. Barry, who was twenty-nine at the time and had been with Peter's practice for little more than a year, is now one of the senior veterinary advisers for the Jockey Club. He immediately gave the horse an intravenous painkilling injection, before removing the bandage from the damaged near foreleg and examining it. Happily the skin was not broken anywhere, but after very gently rocking the joint and feeling all round the leg, Barry stood up, looked me straight in the eye and made the chilling pronouncement which I have never forgotten: 'It feels like a bag of marbles.'

For the second time that morning my heart sank down to my boots; I felt what he had just described must be irreparable. He carefully applied a much better and stronger bandage to support the leg until Peter's radiographer, Mrs Grieveson, arrived to take some X-rays. Peter himself was away in Munich at that time with the Olympic three-day event team, but Barry and Tony Ward (Peter's senior partner) decided that the leg should be put in a plaster cast until such time as any further decisions could be made about a possible operation. Barry waited until Peter's secretary Barbara arrived with all the necessary equipment, and between them they carefully put the leg in plaster.

I knew that news of this nature would travel fast. Racehorses sadly break legs from time to time, and in the most serious cases when beyond repair the horse has to be humanely destroyed. Not all such occurrences are newsworthy; but here we were dealing with the best-known, probably best-loved, and certainly most valuable racehorse in the world.

I had to give his owner Paul Mellon the awful news before anyone else became aware of the situation, but he was in Virginia, USA, and therefore was five hours behind us; so I waited until midday before phoning him at his home to pass on what I realised would be one of the saddest pieces of news of even his long and eventful life. His reaction was entirely typical of the man I have always regarded as the best owner any trainer could ever have. 'Oh Ian, how dreadful, I am so sorry, but how is poor John?' His first thought, as always, was for all of us, especially for the horse's lad, John Hallum, and the horse; never for himself. Most owners could not have resisted asking, 'How on earth did it happen?'

I had no sooner put the phone down when Claude Duval, a young racing reporter for the *Sun* whom I knew quite well, rang and said, 'Ian, I have heard a rumour that Mill Reef has broken a leg – could it be true?' I found it unbelievable that the news had leaked out already, having purposely delayed informing the Press Association until I had spoken to Paul Mellon. Apparently I was remarkably polite to Claude, but inwardly I was seething to think that someone close to us all must have rung the paper.

Within half an hour of my announcement to the PA the first phone calls were coming in and photographers were already arriving at the front gates. Several of our team, such as gallop men and maintenance staff, had to become temporary security guards to prevent devious members of the paparazzi gaining access to the lower yard where Mill Reef was stabled. I answered the phone for most of the afternoon, trying to be as helpful as I could, but eventually could take it no longer and left the phone off the hook. The news bulletins on radio and TV that evening all began with Mill Reef's injury and as we went wearily to bed later that night I was aware that one or two dogged members of the media were camping at our front entrance. Our illustrious patient, however, was safely locked up with several of our lads taking turns in an all-night vigil as I tossed and turned, still unable to believe that this horse, who had raced on all those different surfaces throughout England and France, could have broken a leg going comparatively slowly on our own wonderful turf.

Next morning the *Sun*, as expected, devoted the whole of its front page to the Mill Reef story. Most of the other papers had a front-page headline with further coverage elsewhere – and the headline was much the same in all of them: 'Will Mill Reef the wonder horse survive?'

At that moment, twenty-four hours after my cheerful early morning walk on the downs, I had no idea of the answer to that gruesome question.

2

A Transatlantic Childhood

T hat fateful day of 31 August 1972 was the start of a short period in my life when all the normal considerations of family life, and even the well-being of fifty-nine other racehorses, became secondary issues. The survival of one great racehorse was the matter of all-consuming importance.

We will return to Mill Reef later; but thirty-three years previously it had all started for me on 7 November 1938 in New Jersey, USA. My father, Gerald, was at that time one of the best polo players in the world. He was then and remains today the last Englishman to have achieved a handicap of ten goals (the maximum). He captained the English team in 1939 and again after the war until very shortly before he died in 1956.

The eldest survivor of eight children, he had been born in 1903. His father, Bert Balding, was a successful horse dealer and a fine horseman. Bert and his three brothers all played polo, mostly at Rugby, and one of the brothers whom Dad knew as Uncle Billy was a nine-goal player and a talented instructor. He it was who taught Dad and his brothers and cousins to play. He was also responsible for inventing the well-known Balding gag and girth, so obviously was blessed with some brains as well as being a brilliant horseman. It is rumoured that the previous generation of Baldings were gypsies, but my sources of information can't actually verify that!

My grandfather Bert did well enough as a dealer to be able to give Dad a private education at Haileybury. Then the money ran out, so that the younger brothers and sisters had a good but much less expensive education. Their mother Florence, my grandmother, was a lovely lady and someone of whom we grandchildren became very fond in her later life, when she lived at Monxton near Andover in a charming little thatched cottage which Dad found and bought for her. She had had to put up with her husband, Bert, taking seriously to drink from middle age until his death, and Dad, as the eldest son, took over the role of father figure at a relatively young age. Their family home was Wartnaby Hall near Melton Mowbray.

Dad and Uncle Barney, the second brother, trained and rode a few jumpers in the winter months at Wartnaby and had some success with a good horse called Drinmond who won several races and finished fourth in the 1927 Grand National. Together with Ivor, the third eldest, they went to America before the war to play polo. All three were to marry American girls; both Barney and Ivor settled permanently with their families over there on Long Island, a beautiful piece of country just outside New York City.

The two younger brothers, Humphrey and Tony, stayed in England. Uncle Humphrey married Joan and they had one daughter, Sue, who later married Richard Perkins and served as Master of the Meynell Hunt for several years. Uncle Tony, the youngest, was always a very keen farmer. He and his wife Evelyn also had one daughter, Judith, who is well known in the polo world and worked with Aunt Judy for many years organising the polo for Galen Weston and Michael Butler. Uncle Tony apparently used to hunt bareback as a child, against all instructions from his father but much to the enjoyment of the members of the Quorn and Belvoir hunts who admired his riding greatly.

Aunt Judy never married and was later to play a huge part in our lives. Aunt Dide (Diana) spent most of her time caring for her mother in Florence's old age and got married to a long-time suitor very late in life. I never saw her on a horse but I am told she rode side-saddle beautifully in her younger days.

My mother Ellie was the second daughter of Joe Hoagland, a wealthy landowner from New York who virtually disinherited her after she married her English polo player. Her elder sister, Aunt Carol, married Jack Mellick, who was always a good friend to Toby and me. Her younger brother, Uncle Joe, married Kiku Millard, an extremely attractive daughter of the American ambassador to Japan. We saw quite a bit of them during the war years, and afterwards they and their three children occasionally visited us in England.

Mum and Dad were married in 1935 and my elder brother was born a year later. He too was christened Gerald but to avoid confusion was nicknamed and thereafter always known as Toby. I was born just before my father returned to England to join up in 1939, and christened Ian Anthony. I was not to see him again until after the war had ended although Toby, aged two, had a short visit to England before the hostilities made travelling impossible.

Although officially too old at thirty-six, Dad managed to get accepted into the prestigious Life Guards regiment, with whom he fought until the end of the war. Like many other professional sportsmen, he devoted what would have been his peak playing years to fighting Hitler's regime. During that war he had two injuries which affected his health seriously later. The first had nothing to do with the actual fighting: one evening he managed to dive into someone's swimming pool which was not well lit and just happened to be empty. The severe concussion he sustained caused quite a serious loss of memory and difficulty in completing his sentences which I remember well. He often seemed extremely vague and it annoyed our mother considerably. Then, when driving between the English and American camps in Germany as a liaison officer on a motorbike, he ran into an armoured car (fortunately an English one), broke all his knuckles and severely injured his right arm. He had eighty stitches in it and spent several weeks in hospital. The surgeon did a brilliant job, but afterwards Dad could never open his hand fully and his arm was very slightly bent. How he played polo to the standard he did after the war was amazing.

Our mother brought us up during those war years in a little bungalow on a large estate belonging to the wealthy and influential

Schley family, cousins of hers – the same estate, in fact, on which the Breeders Cup Chase was run some fifty years later. The nearest village, Far Hills, was only a mile away and was noted for many lovely properties and some of the best foxhunting country in the States.

Ninety-nine per cent of the male Baldings have a decidedly naughty streak in them and I was certainly not the exception. In fact my very first recollection is one of being spanked by my mother for apparently standing naked outside our bungalow, which was on the main road, waving my underpants at all the cars as the locals made their way to church on a Sunday morning.

There were various other occasions when I had done something considered to be pretty wicked – sometimes, I suspect, at Toby's instigation, but I was always the one who got spanked. I had a tricycle at one time, which I pedalled around the place as fast as I could make it go. I had been given a small American flag, which I was rather proud of, and attached it to the handlebars of my bike. Our mother told me at once to take it off as if I hit anything I could well fall forwards on to it and poke my eye out. Needless to say, before taking it off I duly had a crunch, and although the flag missed my eye it went straight into my mouth and caused a nasty cut on the roof of it, which bled profusely. I could not possibly admit to Mum how it had happened so, after hiding the flag, I gave her instead the unlikely explanation that I had swallowed some large, sharp pieces of gravel from the drive by mistake and that they must have cut my throat on the way down. I stuck to my story, so Mum had no option but to summon an ambulance and have me taken to the local hospital for X-rays. This was not a cheap exercise in America, where there was no such thing as a National Health Service. After many X-rays, all showing no signs whatsoever of the offending pieces of gravel, I eventually confessed to the doctor, who in turn gave the news to Mum. I should not have wondered why she thereafter always seemed so nice to Toby and not so pleasant to me.

When I was four and Toby six years old Mum acquired a pony for us as she knew that our father would want us to be able to ride almost as soon as we could walk. This was a skewbald gelding called Cocoa, and we both became very fond of him straight away, taking turns to ride him almost daily. At about the same time we started school at the Far Hills Country Day School, which was only a couple of miles away. We became great friends with two sets of second cousins, Reevie and Johnny Schley and John and Danny Todd. Their parents seemed to run the school during those wartime years, and all of us shared many happy times at their grandparents' nearby estate, Ripplebrook Farm. Mrs Schley senior was our grandmother's sister, and Toby and I knew her and her husband as Aunt Kate and Uncle Reeve. They were at the time an important family in local politics and that attribute was certainly passed on to another cousin a few years younger than us – Christie Todd Whitman, who later became the Republican Governor of New Jersey and until recently held the position of Secretary for the Environment in President George W. Bush's government.

Toby and I learned to play baseball in the summers and ice hockey in the winters. We wrestled constantly and got into a lot of fist fights, as they were then called, and nearly always it was the more aggressive younger cousins who got in trouble.

We were thoroughly spoiled by Granny Hoagland, who lived just up the road, and we soon learned to take advantage of her. She was an avid smoker and from about the age of six so was I. I used to steal her Philip Morrises and Toby would come and watch me smoke up to forty a day in a little shed behind the garage. Two very nice unsuspecting cooks that Gran employed were sacked for pinching her cigarettes and I still have a guilty conscience about it today.

At that time we saw a lot of an 'uncle' called Oarf Mellick who was Uncle Jack's brother. He was a tall, friendly man who seemed to spend a lot of time taking us riding or fishing, or even playing soldiers, which I loved. He was often there during the evenings when we went to bed and in fact we became quite fond of him.

Dad wrote frequently and we always enjoyed having his letters read to us by Mum. Finally there was great excitement when we had won the war – I was personally disappointed not to have played some part in that victory – and Dad was coming home at last. Our mother had told us frequently about his homecoming and proudly showed us photos of him in uniform. Unfortunately when he actually arrived it was late at night, well after we had gone to bed. Toby and I slept in a double-decker and I always occupied the top bunk. The lights went on suddenly and I recall being somewhat startled to find this very tall man in uniform right beside me as I woke up. To everyone's eternal regret my first words to my father were, 'Oh, hi, Uncle Oarf'!

Dad, Toby and I came over to England in 1946 and I didn't understand until years later why our mother did not join us until several months afterwards. It had something to do with Uncle Oarf, I guess.

Dad started to train jumpers at Down Farm, right next to the renowned arboretum at Westonbirt in Gloucestershire. His main patron was his great friend Jock Whitney, the American millionaire whose polo team Greentree had won all the major championships at Meadowbrook, Long Island just before the war. Dad, of course, had played a big part on that team alongside the greatest player of the day, Tommy Hitchcock, with Pete Bostwick, a well-known National Hunt rider, playing no. 1 and Jock Whitney himself at back.

Dad was determined to give us the kind of education which he had had but his brothers had been denied, and Toby and I were sent off to a boarding prep school near Stroud called Beaudesert Park. It had been founded around the turn of the century by the Richardson family and every member played an important part in the running of a beautiful and very successful school. Naturally we were teased about our American accents, but from the very beginning I loved every minute of the life. Toby and I had the last laugh about being 'little Yanks' when in the freezing cold winter of 1947 we were the only boys who could skate and had to show the others how to play ice hockey and to ride a toboggan. I was still naughty, of course, and not usually crafty enough to avoid getting caught. As a result I got the cane more times than any other boy in my time at Beaudesert, which in itself earned me a certain sort of notoriety, I suppose.

I soon learned that being good at games was an automatic passport to popularity with both masters and other pupils. Nearly all the masters were keen racing men and thus well aware of our connection with horses. There were always three virtual bank holidays in the middle of March for example, when all the senior masters went off to the Cheltenham Festival. At prep school level I excelled at all the sports we played, and the physical contact involved in both boxing and rugby appealed to me most of all. I played in the first XV at the almost unheard-of age of nine, mainly because I loved to tackle and did not mind how big the opposition was. One frequent punishment at Beaudesert was to be put in the boxing ring with an older, bigger boy who would 'teach us a lesson'. On one embarrassing occasion when I had been in trouble yet again and was due to be given a good hiding by a senior boy, they had to find an alternative form of penance for me as I had soon put my opponent flat on the canvas!

But there was more to Beaudesert than lessons and sport: my love of classical music was fostered here, and I cherish memories of singing in productions of *The Messiah* and *HMS Pinafore* organised by the enterprising music staff. I also learned to play the piano and, in spite of sneaking out of early morning practice sessions to join my friends at football in the playground, I won various piano prizes. I learned all my pieces off by heart but my lack of practice meant that I never learnt to sight-read properly, much to my regret in later life. Even now I still much enjoy playing many of the fairly advanced pieces that I learned then. Sadly, my repertoire has dwindled over the years and I suspect my family are sick and tired by now of hearing 'In a Monastery Garden' and 'The Dream of Olwen' in particular.

Toby moved on to Marlborough College at the age of thirteen leaving me, for the first time in my life, without my big brother's steadying influence. I missed him badly at first and realised how much I had depended on him in so many ways. In his absence I became slightly more responsible, I suppose, and in my last year at Beaudesert ended up captaining the school first teams at rugby, soccer and cricket and even became a prefect. In the summer I also carried off the Victor Ludorum at athletics. My mother came to the prize-giving ceremony in this last term and was embarrassed at the number of times I went up to receive awards.

The masters at Beaudesert were wonderful men, most of whom had been there for years, as had the senior matron Miss Pam Ward. Between them they did their best to ensure that I did not become conceited just because I happened to be good at games. I became particularly fond of the Keyte family. Two brothers, Jeremy and John, were direct contemporaries of Toby and me but went on afterwards to Radley so we rather lost touch with them. Their mother Enid was the only daughter of old Mr Richardson and taught French; her husband Vincent was one of the three joint heads all the time we were there. He was a lovely man and was a major influence in my young life at prep school. John Keyte later returned to continue the family tradition, serving as headmaster for many years.

Leaving Beaudesert was a genuine wrench – it had helped a rough, tough, ill-disciplined little Yank to grow into a slightly more responsible, well-mannered young English boy.

At that age we all had our pin-ups and heroes. My all-time sporting idol, whom I worshipped, was Denis Compton. I practised his autograph so frequently that my own version was, I felt sure, even better than his. I cared desperately about his getting runs in the test matches and even scoring goals when playing for Arsenal. Another sporting hero was the boxer Randolph Turpin. I got into trouble for sneaking a radio into our dormitory after lights out so we could listen to the big fight when he beat Sugar Ray Robinson for the world middleweight title. As for pin-ups, I considered then that Princess Margaret was even prettier than the film stars of the day and had photos of her everywhere. I would never have dreamed that in later life I would get to know both her and Denis Compton reasonably well.

During the school holidays at Down Farm Dad continued our riding instruction, and we rode out every day on our ponies at the back of his string of jumpers. Toby and I caught the racing 'bug' badly at a young age. Dad was very strict with us when teaching us to ride, but in spite of his frequent warnings not to race our ponies we just couldn't resist the temptation, and as soon as we were out of his sight we were flat out on his gallops, usually with whips up trying to imitate the champion jockey of the day. Inevitably our ponies were soon unmanageable and became decidedly dangerous to take hunting. Our local pack was the Beaufort and the two huntsmen – the Duke himself and Gerald Gundry – were both good friends of my father. Toby and I were always being run away with and on one embarrassing occasion I was carted not just through the whole field but through the hounds as well. I can recall 'Master' asking Dad to take us both home in not very polite tones.

Dad was notoriously good across country and was one of those rare people with an instinctive knowledge of which direction the fox would take. On one occasion we had left the hounds and the field for about twenty minutes on our way home when Dad suddenly told us to wait with him in the corner of the field beyond a big wood. A few minutes later the fox came out of the wood and stealthily went by us only fifty yards away. All three of us on our horses stood stationary in silence as next the hounds went screaming by in full cry, followed by 'Master' himself, who just had time to give us rather a dirty look, and finally the rest of the field. It was an exciting moment that I have never forgotten. Toby and I knew how much Dad would have loved to have hunted his own pack of hounds if he had ever been a wealthy man.

We had many similar days' hunting which were spoiled by our uncontrollable ponies. Mum came with us often too and went very well particularly on a big bay horse with flashy silver hairs in his mane and tail, called Robin Hood. Like many women I can think of she was a very good rider on her own horse whom she knew and trusted, but nervous on a strange horse, however good she might be told it was.

We had all lived at Westonbirt for only a couple of years when Dad decided he needed a larger stable and we moved to Lynes House, Bishops Cannings, just a couple of miles from Devizes and conveniently close to Marlborough, where I was to join Toby at public school. The gallops at Bishops Cannings were downland ones, a good mile-and-a-half's hack from the yard, bordering some of the more famous Beckhampton trial grounds. They were all pretty stiff and therefore perfect for training jumpers. Gradually, as Toby and I both got a bit older and stronger, we were entrusted with bigger and better ponies. We ended up with a quality brown pony called Tommy, whom Toby rode, and a smashing grey called Misty for me. They both jumped superbly and the schooling fences for our chasers were a constant source of pleasure and excitement, as were our days hunting, now with the Avon Vale. In one holiday time Dad sent us down to a riding academy in Somerset called Porlock Vale. It was run by Tony Collins, but our instructor for the week we stayed was none other than a certain Major Dick Hern. He was a wonderful teacher as well as a superb horseman himself, and in later years would often recall my 'marvellous grey pony'.

At about that time my father trained a chaser called Starlight XV who had lots of ability but did not stay two miles. Dad suggested to the owner, Mr John Baker, that the horse go to Porlock to be trained as an eventer. Dick Hern rode him and schooled him and won several small events on him. Sadly, when it came to the Olympic Games, Dick, by virtue of some archaic rule of the time, was considered to be a professional and therefore was not eligible to ride him. The horse became too good at his new job and never returned to racing, winning Badminton in 1952 ridden by Lawrence Rook.

Dad was a relatively successful National Hunt trainer, but in the summers he was still playing high-class polo, which I suspect diverted his full attention from his training job. One brilliant horse he bought for Jock Whitney, named Arctic Gold, was unlucky not to achieve more fame than he did and was certainly the best horse he ever trained. Having won the Great Yorkshire Chase at Doncaster in a canter as a six-year-old, he started to go wrong in his wind and Dad decided to let him take his chance in the 1951 National. He was extremely well handicapped at ten stone eight pounds and a hot favourite but, ridden by Tim Molony, he fell while leading at the Canal Turn on the first circuit. It was a moment of anguish for all of us.

I suppose when I was about twelve and Toby fourteen we could have been termed cheap labour for our father. During the school holidays we learned how to muck out and groom the racehorses and started riding some of the quieter ones. It was about this time that our cook, a lovely big Irish lady called Mary Roarke, asked me one day which of our many animals I liked best. There were quite a lot to choose from. We had various cats, mostly from the same family, and one of them, a male neuter tabby called Moses with a white tip on the end of his tail, was a considerable character. Toby and I had taught him to jump through our arms and occasionally when I had a nap in the afternoon I can remember waking up to find Moses curled up beside me purring contentedly. In addition, when Dad was carving the Sunday joint Moses would sit on his shoulder and wait patiently for the odd tit-bit. As for dogs, we usually had a vast pack – mostly lurchers and terriers – and although I liked them all, my enthusiasm was always slightly tempered by having to feed them and often clean up after the younger ones, not all of whom were house-trained.

But by the time I was twelve I already felt that I had a certain affinity with horses. There were plenty of times when Toby and I first started riding the racehorses that we could not hold them, and on occasions when you didn't quite know where you were going to end up it could be a bit alarming. However, I can say with certainty that I have never been scared of a horse in my life and have always loved them, marvelling at their beauty, strength and willingness. It was later in life that I came to appreciate their speed. So the answer to Mary Roarke's question was definitely horses – and at that time Misty in particular.

As soon as we had moved to Bishops Cannings, Vincent O'Brien, who was a good friend of Dad, began to send his best horses over to us from Ireland in the week leading up to the Cheltenham Festival. His younger brother Dermot would come in charge of them – a lovely, quietly spoken man who was very kind to Toby and me – along with their youngest brother, Phonsie, one of the leading amateurs in Ireland at the time. He was enormous fun and we became great chums. Vincent won the Gold Cup three years running in 1948–50 with Cottage Rake, and soon again afterwards with Knock Hard. The three times Champion Hurdle winner Hatton's Grace also stayed with us, as did many other winners of the Cheltenham novice hurdles and chases. I was thrilled when Dermot let me ride Cottage Rake one day, just walking round the yard – a momentous occasion for me. He was always exercised in a big black saddle that I could hardly lift, it was so heavy.

At Bishops Cannings Mum and Dad had a 'second' family: our younger brother Robin was born in 1947 and in 1949 our little sister, Gail, arrived on the scene and soon became the apple of her father's eye. Dad was still playing polo, mainly at Cirencester but also at Cowdray Park. He always seemed to have a wealthy patron who produced the ponies, but Dad of course would run the team. He played with Mike Holden-White at Cowdray for a few years and with Alastair Gibb at Cirencester, and also with Archie David and Boyd Gibbons, other patrons of his.

Toby and I were allowed to ride the ponies for 'stick and ball' practice; on one occasion I got my stick caught up in my pony's tail, was dragged off and had some ribs broken in the consequent fracas. We both played a lot of bicycle polo up and down the back drive. It was bordered by one of the brick-built yards, and as we hit the ball against the back wall of the stable, not surprisingly the horses within became extremely unsettled. Dad's head lad, Gerry Hamilton, frequently came out and threatened us with dire consequences. He in fact made a considerable impression in our young horse-mad lives; whatever we did seemed to be wrong. I wish I had a pound for every time I heard him say to me, 'Just because you are the Guvnor's f*****g son . . .' One of the young apprentices at Bishops Cannings at the time was Bill Palmer, who later played a big part in our lives. I recall that Toby, Bill and I all went through the unpleasant ritual of being 'greased', which was apparently a custom in all stables. It entailed being stripped by the senior lads and held while your private parts were brushed with hoof oil! At least we were afterwards considered part of the team and Dad, if he knew, certainly turned a blind eye to the treatment.

More fun for us was the excitement we had shooting rabbits at night up on the downs, with Dad driving an old Ford van and Toby and I sitting on the front with our legs wrapped round the two old-fashioned protruding headlights. Dad would drive at speed, twisting and turning to try to keep up with the rabbits in the headlights, and the van nearly turning over when it hit some old molehills. We were probably very lucky not to shoot each other. It was hilarious fun and certainly any rabbit that got hit was a very unlucky one. The few that were shot at least helped to feed the eight or so dogs which we had at any one time. Feeding the dogs, was in fact, one of my least favourite chores as it entailed skinning and cooking the rabbits and other foul-smelling meat.

One incident that occurred at Bishops Cannings has always remained vividly in my mind's eye. Dad had been sent by Jock

Whitney a horse from America named Hunter Moody. I remember his pedigree well, because he was by the Aga Khan's famous Derby winner Blenheim out of a mare called Nea Lap who was a full sister to the mighty Phar Lap of Australian fame. We had already had a beautiful little full brother three years older called Paracutin, who had won flat races and hurdles and at this time was a brilliant two-mile chaser.

Hunter Moody came to us with a considerable reputation: he was apparently incredibly vicious and as a yearling had killed a stud hand on Jock Whitney's farm where they were trying to break him in. If such an incident had occurred nowadays he would of course have been put down at once. Then, however, because the colt was so well bred he was given a second chance, and the top 'horse whisperer' of the day, a man named Hunter Moody, was summoned to Greentree and asked if he could tame the youngster. The story goes that Moody spent three whole days and nights with the colt in his stable, just being handed enough food and water for horse and man through the door. At the end of this time he brought the horse out, put some driving tack on him, and drove him away in a pony cart. The colt was named after the brilliant horseman who had tamed him and sent on his way to England, because Dad had already done so well with his brother.

Though improved, the horse was still very difficult and pretty savage, so Dad ordered that his best lad, an ex-jockey called Harry Grant, would be the only person allowed to go into his stable, whether to feed him, groom him or tack him up, and, of course, to ride him. Sadly, despite winning a race or two, Hunter Moody was not even as good as Paracutin, let alone good enough to acquire stallion value.

The day I recall so sharply was one when Dad had invited the local Pony Club to come around Lynes House for evening stables. There were about twenty children, including myself, looking round the dozen or so horses chosen by my father for us to inspect. We had virtually finished the round when we came to Hunter Moody and Dad told us all the dramatic story about his early days. We crowded into the doorway and outer part of his stable, where Harry Grant was holding the horse just on a rope and headcollar.

My father approached Hunter Moody to give him a carrot and something in the horse's mind just snapped. He reared up high, turned on his hind legs and came straight at Dad with his mouth wide open and ears laid flat on his head. My father was a big man and as he nimbly sidestepped the raging colt he hit him as hard as he could with his open hand on the side of the jaw. Jack Dempsey, Joe Louis or Mohammed Ali all rolled into one could not have timed a blow better: the horse was knocked down straight on to his side on the floor. Harry Grant quickly grabbed the rope which had been pulled out of his hand when the horse reared and we all made a very hasty exit from the box – as indeed did my father, right behind us.

It was an extraordinary incident; I suppose it may have been the unusual and sudden proximity of so many people that caused the colt to launch such an attack. Whatever the trigger, the fact was that my father could never get in the stable with that horse again. From then on, too, Hunter Moody's racecourse performance deteriorated and soon afterwards it was decided the safest thing to do was to put him down.

At that age I was incredibly enthusiastic about all our runners and listened with rapt attention to everything my father had to say about any of the horses. I was not admired for my tact, however, especially after one incident. We had a very nice National Hunt mare called Pampene, who was owned by a renowned ex-soldier, General Henry Alexander. He and his wife, Marabel, came one morning to see their lovely mare and stayed for breakfast afterwards. I could remember Dad saying the previous day that if she could be ridden by a half-decent jockey at Aintree a few days later she would win. At breakfast I repeated what my father had said with great authority – not realising, of course, that General Alexander himself was to ride his own mare in an amateur riders' race! It soon dawned on me from my father's expression that maybe I had said something I shouldn't have. Fortunately they were all great friends, so my remark did not lead to the horse being moved elsewhere.

Dad's cousin Sidney Balding, one of Uncle Billy's sons, was managing director of the Cunard White Star shipping line for several years just after the war. As a result of this we managed to get preferential treatment when travelling on any of their big ocean liners. Mum, Toby and I made several crossings in the 1950s when Dad was too busy to join us, and on one particularly memorable occasion we were woken at dawn on the enormous *Queen Mary* to watch as we sailed in eerie silence into Manhattan. It was an unforgettable sight: all those skyscrapers silhouetted against the early morning sky like some futuristic scene from a space movie.

On these various trips we visited our Schley and Todd cousins in Far Hills and also got to know well our Balding cousins on Long Island. Uncle Ivor by now had five children, all near us in age, with whom we had a lot of fun; his third daughter in particular, Sheila, became a soulmate of mine from the moment we first met. Uncle Barney ran a high-class riding school at Brookville, Long Island, where all the daughters of the wealthy local families learned to ride, and most of them seemed to be madly in love with him. His two sons, Bruce and Beaver, were never very keen riders but Beaver in particular was a good athlete and became a scratch golfer.

Uncle Barney was quite a character, but somewhat inclined to be unreliable and ill-disciplined. On one occasion just before the war, Dad told us, he was selected as the reserve for the England polo team. Like a fool he spent the whole of the very hot day before the match sunbathing, and when one of the selected players was injured and Dad was sent to find his brother and tell him he was playing, Uncle Barney had sunstroke and was so badly burned he was in no condition to play! My mother often told me in my teens that if I wasn't careful I would end up just like my Uncle Barney. I always took it as quite a compliment, though it certainly wasn't meant as such.

After the war Uncle Ivor had what my mother considered to be a much more responsible job. Before the war he had played on the Old Westbury polo team belonging to C. V. (Sonny) Whitney – Jock's cousin – and he worked for that same millionaire for many years after the war. At first he ran his farm in Kentucky, which included a big ranch of Black Angus cattle; later he became C. V. W.'s racing manager, and finally, when Sonny sacked both his trainers (he was a notoriously difficult employer), Uncle Ivor at the age of forty-five suddenly had to start training the horses himself, which he did quite successfully until retiring in 1970 to live in Camden, South Carolina.

Since Dad's death, Uncle Ivor has been my favourite older relation. He has a wonderful, naughty sense of humour and is the most successful tease I have ever met. When he is serious his wisdom is a great benefit to his children and nephews, and his company at all times has been the greatest possible fun. He was fortunate to have in his first wife, Frances Goodwin – the mother of his five children – a wonderfully understanding lady with whom to share his life. Sadly, she had a series of strokes and died after a long illness, borne with enormous courage. Almost at once and equally fortunately Ivor married Polly Sheffield (*née* Potter), who has been his loving companion in the same old house, so full of character, in Camden up to the present day. As I write Uncle Ivor is ninety-five and Polly, who would hate me saying she is the same age, is still playing golf and shooting quail in the winter. They are a remarkable couple, and Emma and I, Toby and his wife Caro, and our younger sister Gail, who lives nearby in Aiken, have all come to revel in their company on frequent visits over the years.

3

Marlborough and Weyhill

W alking through the gates of Marlborough College at the age of thirteen in September 1952 was as intimidating an experience as I can ever remember. The place seemed enormous and there were over eight hundred boys there of whom I knew precisely one – my big brother, who was not even in my house when I arrived.

I went straight into Junior House A.2, where about fifty boys, of whom half were new, were looked after by a fussy old housemaster called Percy Chapman, who was also one of our assistant chaplains. There were only two junior houses, A.1 and A.2, which stood one on top of the other on the right-hand side of the famous old courtyard. They were not very attractive buildings, externally or internally, and they were spartan to say the least. The first feature of life at Marlborough which I recall was the early morning cold bath. As we scrambled out of bed in our dormitories, about six bathtubs alongside each other were filled with cold water and the house prefects stood there to ensure that all of us in turn had a speedy but thorough dunking. It certainly woke me up and made us appreciate breakfast that bit more.

I made two lifelong friends in my very first term – David Back and Tom Cox. David, or Windy as we called him then, was a pretty useful tennis player, and in our final summer term he and I surprised everyone, especially those on the first VI, by winning the school doubles together. We still play together even now, but never as well as we did that day! Tom Cox was a more rugged character altogether and he and I spent hours wrestling together in our dormitory, probably when we should have been doing prep. Tom was as good a schoolboy boxer as I ever saw and, being a strong runner as well, was a good winger on the first XV in due course. He was also quite a ladies' man, which rather bucked the trend at Marlborough College, where (in our time at any rate) most boys seemed to be more interested in other boys than they were in girls. In our last year Tom got to know two local Marlborough girls, and he and I met up with them fairly frequently to learn a bit more about that side of life.

After three terms in A.2, Tom, Windy and I moved on to Summerfield, where Toby by now was a house prefect. It was an out college house, seven minutes' walk from the main school, and we enjoyed the new feeling of (relative) independence. Our housemaster, Leslie Coggin, known as Cogs, was a charming, elderly man – distinguished-looking, scholarly, delightfully absent-minded and easy-going – and the only old Etonian on the staff. He knew that I came with rather a wicked reputation and always looked at me in a very kindly, knowing way as if he fully expected me to get into trouble but wasn't too worried about it. His wife Mary was a doctor and was only around the house at evening meals. She too was very kind and friendly, and contributed much to the extremely happy atmosphere which existed in the house all the time I was there.

Sports played a big part in college life and they were, needless to say, my all-consuming interest. Fortunately my first term was the Michaelmas one when we played rugby, and of course I was in my element straight away. Having played scrum half for my last two years at Beaudesert I indicated that that was where I would like to play. I was told that the captain of junior colts was the scrum half and if I wanted to get on that team there might be a vacancy at full back and I should try that position. So suddenly I became a full back and as catching, kicking and tackling had always been fairly strong points I soon learned to enjoy my new role. I got on the junior colts team and a few of my chums on that side came with me all the way through the colts XV and, in due course, on to the first XV.

In the Easter term I played hockey for the junior colts, but, being less fit than usual after a bout of pneumonia and unhappy with my position at left wing, I didn't really enjoy it very much – although I did eventually play on the first XI. But I loved cricket in the summer term and again progressed through junior colts and colts to the first XI in my last year. Our coach in the junior teams was a dapper man with an American wife and a great sense of humour. His name was John (or Jas, as we called him) Maples. He was a pretty strict coach with definite ideas. The batsmen were all taught to have their left elbows up whatever the stroke, and one's head was invariably pulled into the correct position by the hair!

I went straight into the school boxing team, too, and one inter-house fight I had with a chap called Chris Jocelyn was talked about for a long time. We went hammer and tongs at each other for three rounds; at the end I just got the verdict, but we hugged each other, totally exhausted, and became thereafter the closest of friends. Tom and another good friend, Richard Coote, a very good all-round sportsman, were the two star boxers and were both unbeaten as schoolboys. They and, to a lesser extent, Chris and I used to take part in and usually win our 'four schools' boxing tournament against Sherborne, Wellington and Bryanston – home bouts taking place in the school gymnasium, which had been the town prison many years before.

I learned to play squash in the winter terms and loved it; racquets itself was always played during the rugger term, so I only ever had time for the occasional game, but I played enough to realise that it was the most exciting game one could play with a racquet. At that time Marlborough College had on its teaching staff two if not three of the best racquets players in the country. David Milford, or D.S.M. as he was known, had won a world amateur singles title and together with another master, John Thompson (known as J.R.T.), won eight or ten amateur doubles championships at Queens. J.R.T. also went on to win the amateur singles title five times. These schoolmasters were quite exceptional athletes: D.S.M. won about twenty England hockey caps as well, while J.R.T. was a superb cricketer and in the summer holidays walked straight into the Warwickshire first team as their number three batsman. He once even headed cricket's first-class averages!

Another master, the Revd J. R. Bridger, was not far behind them at racquets and opened the batting for Hampshire in the summer holidays. He was one of our assistant chaplains and greatly respected; in fact he became a great friend to me.

There was one assistant chaplain, however, whom we boys did not like, and I recall a lot of us playing rather a nasty trick on him. We organised for about forty of us – double the usual number – to go to early morning communion one Sunday, knowing that it was his turn to take the service. We had arranged that, when we all kneeled to receive our sip of wine, none of us would actually drink any. So when the assistant chaplain came to finish the wine at the end of the service before wiping the chalice clean, as is the custom, he had well over half a pint of wine to drink before he could do the 'washing up'. We all watched anxiously and giggled as he struggled manfully to swallow it all.

Unchristian as that joke was, we nevertheless took chapel quite seriously. The singing coming from eight hundred male throats in that enormous building was memorable, and I and many of my friends took a considerable interest in the scriptures. I would like to think that the urge to try to lead a Christian way of life was one of the main benefits of our privileged education at Marlborough.

For all the emphasis on sport, art and music were also prominent parts of our general education, and we all enjoyed acting in the house and school plays. The Memorial Hall, where all the plays and concerts were performed, stood just below the great chapel, and these two buildings were the most impressive architectural features of our school.

Just below the A houses there was an enormous earth mound like a mini-mountain, and it was halfway up the mound, surrounded by thick undergrowth, that all the smoking took place. As it became fashionable for boys to start smoking at about the age of thirteen, so it was that I decided to give it up. Even though I had never inhaled, I was no longer finding it any fun and thought it would be 'cool' to give it up just as my friends were beginning to take up the ghastly habit.

Having completed my O-levels fairly successfully in eight or nine subjects, my good friend Windy Back and I decided we would specialise in modern languages for our A-levels. So it was that we started on French and German and even Spanish for a term or two. Unbelievably there were only three of us in the sixth form that year – the third member, Colin Cooke-Priest, was a bit too studious for our liking and I suppose it was at this stage of my life that I truly learned the art of procrastination. Our form master – a lovely old gent called Georgie Tarleton – didn't appear to mind that we never completed our prep, or to even do too much work at all. He seemed just to enjoy our company!

So it was no surprise to anyone that I failed my A-levels. My German oral exam, however, took an unusual turn. When asked what I did in the holidays I managed to get the right word for riding, but then I tried to explain that I liked shooting also – and should not have been surprised that my examiner looked somewhat taken aback when I said '*Ich scheiss ein bisschen auch*,' instead of '*ich schiess*'. German scholars will understand the subtle difference!

My last year at Marlborough was notable for the arrival from Cambridge University of two very well-known young men, who almost straight away became junior housemasters and heroes of all the sports-mad boys. Our much-respected headmaster, Tommy Garnet, had stolen a march on his fellow heads by securing the services of Ian Beer and Dennis Silk during a raid on the Cambridge colleges.

Ian had captained the Cambridge University rugby XV and had already been capped for England before he came to Marlborough. He was not only an outstanding back-row forward but also a natural leader and therefore a very good captain, and he became a superb coach. He was tall, handsome and, if sometimes a little bit too earnest for some pupils' liking, a gifted schoolmaster.

Dennis was an impressive all-rounder: not only had he played centre three-quarter in Ian's Cambridge team, he had captained the university cricket XI, scored a century in successive Varsity matches at Lord's, and also got a rugby fives half-blue. Dennis was heavily built and very softly spoken, and possessed a great sense of humour. He was dark-haired and had a chin which some said resembled Tommy Trinder's!

Tommy Garnet allowed Ian to play club rugby in his first term at Marlborough, and Dennis immediately took over the coaching of our colts team. In what was due to be my last rugby-playing term I managed to slip and fall heavily on my right hand in virtually the first game of term. A broken scaphoid bone in my right wrist was diagnosed and I was horrified to learn that my right arm was to be in plaster for three months and the whole of the rugby season was to go by virtually without my participation. I was forbidden by the doctor to do any catching and punting, which I always enjoyed enormously, but was stupid enough not to practise my place-kicking, which I was allowed to do but for some reason I found boring.

Instead I thought it would be a suitable challenge to see if I could get my place back on the school squash team, playing left-handed. One can imagine how many hours I must have spent practising, because by the end of that winter term I had not only won our house squash tournament but managed to creep into the no. 5 spot on the school team. I remember thinking I was so clever and versatile at the time – but several years later, when my place-kicking was badly needed and could so easily have made me an automatic first-choice full back on almost any team, I dearly regretted not having spent that whole winter practising it.

My last summer term was spent playing lots of cricket and tennis, doing as little work as I could get away with in preparation for A-levels, and – most of all, it seemed – helping to organise various pranks which were designed to amuse the whole school. First of all we thought it would be fun to move a well-known stone Cupid from the fountain in the rose gardens onto the roof overlooking the main courtyard the night before Parents' Day; then we decided to redesign the sacred lawns in the same courtyard as a cricket pitch, complete with sight screens, stumps and creases (thoughtfully marked with tape rather than white-wash). Needless to say, the school authorities were less amused than our friends, and after the latter escapade we perpetrators were summoned to the Master's Lodge.

I believe it was rumoured that Jeremy Willder and I might lose our places on the first XI due to play Rugby at Lord's a few days later. Happily we didn't; instead, all of us (except one school prefect) were beaten by the Master himself. Ten strokes of the cane on one's rear end administered by a good cricketer with a strong wrist hurt one hell of a lot. It was the last time I was ever to get caned, but even now I think it was the most effective punishment that could be given to a schoolboy, and I certainly never resented it. In fact – and I am no masochist – I think my many canings at school probably did me the world of good.

A few days later our first XI assembled at Lord's to play the long-established fixture against Rugby School at cricket's headquarters. It was very exciting to be in the team and we all felt extremely honoured to be playing there; I was certainly never a great batsman as a schoolboy or afterwards, but the very slow pitch that day suited my hooking and cutting style and, batting at no. 6, I managed to get the top score of 36 not out. In a very low-scoring game, we just lost by two wickets. It was certainly one of the highlights of my cricketing career.

I had been devastated to miss the whole of what would have been my last rugger season at school and somehow I managed to persuade my father to let me go back to Marlborough for one more Michaelmas term. A lot of my friends, including Tom, had left at the end of the summer term, but we still had the nucleus of a very strong first XV. Ian Beer by now was the full-time first XV coach and even though he was still playing for Harlequins on Saturdays and therefore missing some of our matches, the difference in our team play was amazing. I don't think we actually won all our matches, but we were certainly unbeaten. I was playing pretty well at full back and enjoying all aspects of the game, especially tackling. Ian and Dennis Silk were very quickly seized on by the local county side, Dorset and Wilts, and Tommy Garnet gave them permission to go off and play in these county games which were always held midweek. After one match of the new county season the Dorset and Wilts selectors apparently wanted to remove the full back, who had had a poor game, but could not agree on who should replace him. Finally Ian, who was on the selection committee, said, 'Look, I've got a full back at school who is probably as good as any of your suggestions – let's play him.'

Being much respected, Ian got his way and took me along to play for Dorset and Wilts against Berkshire at Reading. Although I was seventeen I probably looked much younger than that, and Duggie Harrison, the team secretary, was horrified when he saw me and keen to alter the team even at that late stage. Ian and Dennis insisted that all would be well – but nevertheless, when the first high kick from the Berkshire fly half duly went up to test the diminutive opposing full back there was a certain amount of panic in our ranks. Dennis came running back from centre to cover me and out of the corner of my eye I saw Ian tearing back from his blind-side position. Lacking a bit of confidence, I thought I had better leave the high ball to the skipper and shouted at the last moment, 'Yours, sir!'

Ian was so dumbfounded to be called 'sir' on the rugby field that, not surprisingly, the ball bounced somewhere between the three of us. Luckily no harm came from the loose ball and I recovered my composure enough to play quite a competent game, even though I got a fair bit of stick from the skipper afterwards for that particular incident. I held my place on the county team for the rest of that season and in fact went on to play for Dorset and Wilts for the next fifteen years.

Another memorable feature of that last term was that our housemaster's niece, Janet Coggin, came to stay at Summerfield. To say that she caused something of a stir would be a considerable understatement. Aged twenty, she was a tall girl with an amazing figure and was beautiful in every sense – reminiscent of Raquel Welch in looks, but also incredibly nice. She had absolutely no idea of the effect she had on us older boys – to say nothing of the younger masters: Messrs Beer and Silk would appear with her on their arm on alternate weekends – and her dear old uncle 'Cogs' just maintained that same amiably acute expression on his face, no doubt well aware of the stir she was causing and not totally displeased about it.

Although officially I left Marlborough College at the end of that Michaelmas term, the rules allowed me to come back during the following term and play on the seven-a-side team. Ian Beer had of course coached the unbeaten XV the previous term, and in the spring term he supervised the sevens team that took part in the inter-school competition at Rosslyn Park. We had the nucleus of a strong side. The two props were Richard Stanton and Tony

Tanner, who was captain and had been an outstanding no. 8 the previous term. I contributed a bit of experience playing at scrum half, and in Nick Hill Norton we had a huge and very speedy winger. Ian Beer had got us very fit and to everyone's surprise we got better each round and eventually won the whole competition, beating a strongly fancied Welsh school Llandovery 19–0 in the final. In those days schoolboy rugby was often written up in the daily papers and I well remember a headline in the next day's *Daily Express*: 'Ian Beer's boys stroll it'. It was a very proud moment for him and us. All seven of us and Ian got together thirty years later at Marlborough to celebrate the win a second time at a wonderful occasion organised by Tony Tanner and hosted by the College.

In bringing Ian and Dennis to Marlborough as a new generation of games-playing schoolmasters to support the ageing D.S.M. and J.R.T., Tommy Garnet, who himself went on to be headmaster of the renowned Geelong Grammar School in Australia, had in fact discovered two extraordinary individuals. Not only did they transform the college's rugby and cricket through their coaching, they shone in their own careers both as teachers and as sportsmen. Both went on to become highly distinguished headmasters, Ian at Ellesmere, Lancing and Harrow and Dennis as Warden of Radley, where with his wife Diana he presided for twenty-three years over a golden era in the life of the school. Ian and Dennis always had a very high regard for each other and remain firm friends to this day.

For four or five years the three of us played rugby for Bath as well as Dorset and Wilts, and naturally I became great friends with them both. While at Marlborough I had been tempted by the thought of going to Cambridge University, having heard so much about it from them. But with no A-levels to my name and a riding and racing career to go into, it was never likely to be more than a passing fancy.

During my four years at Marlborough College my school holidays – and Toby's – were of course devoted to horses, and in particular to racing. Dad let us ride the racehorses more and more and was very quick to give us both opportunities to ride in races. Toby, being taller and heavier than me, was always going to struggle with his weight even as a National Hunt amateur. I was lucky enough to be smaller and therefore always the more likely to be the jockey out of the two of us. Dad was very fair to us both, though, and I can remember being disappointed when the Duke of Beaufort asked him if one of us could ride a point-to-pointer for the Queen Mother and Dad decided it should be Toby, who was eighteen at the time and riding in lots of point-to-points.

I became eligible to ride under National Hunt rules when I was sixteen, and as I had already been riding schooling and lots of 'work' I had my first ride in public almost as soon as I had passed that age barrier. During the holidays I had been riding a young horse belonging to Jock Whitney called The Quiet Man almost every day at home. Dad had purposely kept him a maiden, I suspect, so that I had a good chance of winning my first ever race in a maiden hurdle. Dad picked out what looked a weak race at Fakenham but unfortunately, never having been there himself before this occasion, had no idea how sharp the hurdle course was. We went round almost two and a half circuits for the two miles and my mount, being a long-striding horse, struggled to get round the bends and could finish no better than third. Dad had had quite a decent bet at long odds that morning – but, to be fair, as soon as we walked the course together he knew we would have problems.

About two weeks later he found a similar race for The Quiet Man and his young jockey at Ludlow. It was a two-day meeting and he and I and Uncle Jack, who was over from America and staying with us, went up and stayed in a pub in Leominster for a night. On the morning of the race Dad and Uncle Jack were chatting up rather an attractive barmaid at the hotel and I can recall overhearing Uncle Jack saying with a laugh something to the effect of 'Well, if the boy wins today *he* can spend the night with her!'

After Fakenham my father had rather lost his confidence from a betting point of view, so The Quiet Man started at 20–1. I remember getting a bit further back in the field than I had been told to, but the leaders seemed to be going very fast – probably too fast for their own good. My horse, jumping superbly, came through very late and fast to win by a couple of lengths. It was unquestionably the most exciting moment of my life so far, and from then on I was hopelessly addicted to race riding, and jumping races in particular.

That night I was sent to bed fairly early as usual, but was so over-excited that when Dad came to bed (we shared a room) I was still wide awake, although pretending to be asleep. Dad started to snore loudly as soon as his head hit the pillow, and after a while I decided that trying to get to sleep there was hopeless and I might have more chance elsewhere; so I picked up my bed clothes and pillow and went to sleep outside on the landing.

At breakfast the next morning Dad told Uncle Jack how he had woken early and, seeing my bed empty, suddenly remembered the suggestion about the barmaid and went flying out of the room to go and fetch me. He just managed to avoid falling over me on the landing outside . . .

When he returned to America, Uncle Jack left me a tie and twenty-five pounds in fivers, along with a note saying, 'Well done jockey and good luck in the future.' I was thrilled that he had called me 'jockey' because at that moment it was what I most wanted to do with my life.

It was not long after this that an incident occurred that very nearly put paid to any ideas I may have had of being a jockey, or anything else for that matter. Under Dad's tutelage I had been driving a car around the yard and on the gallops since I was about fourteen. Unusually for someone of my age, I passed my driving test at the first attempt only a month after I was officially old enough to take it. I have always found driving enjoyable and exciting and over the years my passion for speed and taking the odd chance may well have frightened the occasional passenger. The very first car I had was a tiny Austin A30 and at once I was taking chances and driving much too fast in a car that had no road-holding ability, poor brakes and not much acceleration – in other words, one that was deficient in the three factors most needed to get a reckless driver out of trouble.

I was driving one day along a main road from Stroud towards Painswick to pick up my younger brother Robin from my old prep school, Beaudesert Park, at the end of his term. As usual I was late, going much too fast and actually overtaking on a blind corner in the fog. A car happened to be coming in the other direction and although I just missed it, I skidded off the road and hit a tree rather hard. I was incredibly lucky because if the tree had not been there I would have gone straight off a bank and down a hundred-foot drop! The car was a complete write-off, but amazingly I was able to scramble out of the wreckage more or less unaided and unhurt. Some people from a house opposite kindly ushered me off the road and I realised I must look a bit of a mess when the mother said, 'Please come in and wait for the ambulance with us, but just let me go and hide the baby first.' There were no seat belts in those days and my face had obviously hit the windscreen.

I was taken to the local hospital and very well stitched up by an Indian doctor. I had over forty stitches in cuts above and below my left eye; the nastiest cut of all was on my cheek. Although odd little pieces of glass came out of my face over the next few years, I was not seriously inconvenienced by the accident. I think it slowed me down in a car for a week or two, maybe; but I did appreciate that God must have been keeping a friendly eye on me that day.

In the summer holidays when the National Hunt horses were nearly all out at grass, polo was all the rage. Toby and I did a lot of stick and balling at home – which by now was no longer Bishops Cannings but a much bigger place at Weyhill, near Andover in Hampshire. It was a yard made famous by the late Frank Hartigan and had some lovely gallops straight out in front of the house, as well as a beautiful summer downland gallop two miles away at Kimpton. Dad had tried to persuade Jock Whitney to buy Weyhill for him but it was apparently very tax disadvantageous even for very wealthy Americans to own property in this country – as I was to discover many years later with Paul Mellon. Consequently Dad next approached Colonel Bill Whitbread, head of the famous brewery firm, who was just getting into racing and with whom Dad was playing polo at that time. It seemed a very happy arrangement all round when he agreed to buy the place.

Mum organised the redecorating of Weyhill House beautifully and our family of six moved into a lovely house and garden, with a nice old stable yard for around fifty horses and a top yard of fifteen wooden boxes which was perfect for Dad's hunters and polo ponies.

Along with Weyhill we inherited a wonderful old man called Herbert Arnold who had been assistant to Frank Hartigan and a great friend to the whole Hartigan family. Herbert was well into his seventies at this stage but became for us four children the grandfather we had never known. Mum adored him, and Dad much admired his wisdom – his general knowledge of racing in all departments was incredible – and his energy. In the afternoons when, because of the very early mornings, racing people tend to have a nap, Herbert would be found either treading in on the gallops or pruning roses in the garden. He never went racing but was always the steadying influence at the yard in the absence of the boss.

Dad had collected a wonderful team of lads at Bishops Cannings and most of them – including his head lad, Gerry Hamilton – came on with him to Weyhill, where there was plenty of accommodation. In those days there was no shortage of stable staff, so at Weyhill the lads never looked after more than two horses each and we never rode more than two lots. Dad was very much a perfectionist and wanted everything done properly and the yard kept immaculate. Gerry knew this, and I was still finding it awfully difficult to please him. Evening stables, when owners often visited, were a daily ritual that happened with military precision and the horses always looked magnificent.

At that time Dad employed a secretary, Anne Wells, who became a lifetime friend of Toby and me. When she first arrived she was in her early twenties, tall and attractive with red hair; Toby and I fancied her enormously, as, I suspect, did our father as well. I recall one occasion when our parents were away and Anne, who lived in the house with us all as part of the family, took the opportunity to have a bath in Mum and Dad's bathroom. As soon as she started to run the bath and went back to her bedroom to get undressed, Toby hustled me into the large wicker clothes basket in the bathroom. I was small enough to fit in it, he said, and he was not. I was given instructions to squat in there as quiet as a mouse, watch everything carefully and tell him all about it later on. I could see out, of course, but poor Anne had no idea

I was in there – until the next day when we couldn't resist telling her all about her bath-time habits.

A week or so later she was having a bath up in the top-floor bathroom, which Toby and I shared with her. We had discovered that if we climbed up on the water tanks, which were housed in a room next door, we could get to a tiny window at the top of the bathroom where we could look straight down on our hapless secretary having her bath. Toby and I had been enjoying our bird's-eye view of Anne for several days without, we thought, our parents' knowledge, when one night, as Toby and I were stealthily clambering up on the water tanks, the door to the tank room suddenly opened and there stood the enormous figure of our father. Expecting a rocket, we at once tried to protest our innocence; but to our surprise and delight he put a finger of silence to his mouth and started to climb up beside us. In the excitement of his unexpected participation I clumsily made a noise opening the window inwards and sliding across the little curtain which covered it on the inside. Poor Anne heard the movement and, realising what was happening, sat up – covering herself as best she could with her arms – and shouted at us: 'Get out of there, you dirty little buggers – I'll call your father!' to which I replied with great glee: 'No need – he's right here!'

In those days a racing secretary was under far less pressure than now and Anne, who was a good rider, rode out two lots and even went hunting with us on odd occasions. She also went racing when it was convenient for her to help with the driving, and in every way became one of the family. We became very fond of her; but the idyll was not to last. Our mother and father were not always as happy together as we would have liked, and I suspect a lot of the tension concerned the younger children: Dad, who adored Gail, tended to spoil her, whereas Mum favoured Robin to such an extent that it really grated with the rest of us.

Anne used to wake Toby and me in the mornings, and one day she came in and said in a very sad voice, 'I'm going. I've had the sack.' Toby and I were horrified and just could not believe it. Apparently Anne had written a letter to her mother in which she had said, 'It's Gail's birthday today and they have both gone off hunting all day – selfish pigs.' Foolishly, she had left the letter outside its envelope in the office somewhere and Dad, having read it, had said, 'If that's what you think of us, you'd better go.'

Toby and I often wondered if there was more to it than that, but Anne, who has always remained a good friend of ours, would never say. She went on to marry Guy Peate who tragically died much too early, leaving her to bring up a young family on her own.

Our winter holidays were taken up with hunting, schooling the jumpers and going racing. Over the years Dad employed several top National Hunt jockeys, all of whom we got to know well. Originally there was Tim Molony, who was champion jockey for several years. Tim spoke with a deep Irish brogue and was incredibly brave and tough. He was never as stylish or as complete a jockey, however, as his younger brother Martin, who must still rank as one of the all-time great riders. Then there were Glen Kelly and Dick Francis, who rode regularly for us – both good old-fashioned horsemen rather than brilliant jockeys. After them our first jockey for a year or two was Derek Ancil, another very much in the same mould of horseman/jockey that Dad admired so much. Rex Hamey also rode for a season or two; but probably the best jockey – potentially – we had at Weyhill was the ill-fated Micky Lynn.

Micky came from Ireland as what would now be called a 'conditional'. He was the perfect build for a National Hunt jockey and worked as one of the lads in the yard, so that Toby and I got to know him extremely well. He was intelligent, brave and a brilliant all-round horseman who especially enjoyed riding all the difficult horses that no one else wanted to ride. It was in 1956 when tragedy struck. Everyone in those days always schooled either bareheaded or in just a cloth cap, usually turned around so the wind wouldn't blow it off. The skullcaps used in races were inadequate to say the least, and certainly had no chinstraps. In most cases, because at that time (unlike now) they were included in the total weight the horse would carry, the jockeys, who were nearly always struggling to make the weight, used 'cheating helmets', which looked like real ones but were made of cardboard and weighed only a few ounces.

Micky had a ghastly fall at Sandown in a novice chase, his head hitting the ground first. He never regained consciousness, and I can remember that awful feeling of shock and despair at the loss of a brilliant young talent and a wonderful Christian young man. We all felt he would soon have been champion jockey and were deeply distressed by the tragedy, as was the whole racing world.

In the summer holidays polo was everything. Dad had helped to establish the English handicaps after the war when Lord Cowdray almost singlehandedly had got the sport going again. In our biased opinions our father was still very much the best player in the country; but he reckoned that, if he had been worth ten goals just before the war, he was worth no more than six in 1947. Admittedly he was at least two stone heavier as well as quite a bit older, and had an injured right hand to contend with. Humphrey Guinness, who had played with him in the England team before the war, was also rated six, as was another old-timer, John Lakin. Alec Harper, a former soldier and now rated five goals, made up the England team in those early days after the war.

It was soon after we moved to Weyhill that Dad's sister, Aunt Judy, came to live with her old mother just down the road at Monxton, and it was she who was in charge of all Dad's polo ponies in the summer and hunters in the winter. Judy was not only tremendous fun but also a fine horsewoman and a good friend, and we all became very fond of her. She taught Toby and me how to muck out properly, and every day she, with one or the other of us, would look after and exercise twelve to fourteen ponies. She was an incurable smoker and as she was always broke I used to have a lot of fun pinching cigarettes from the house for her, especially Granny Hoagland's fag-ends which were always at least two inches long.

The first polo tournament Toby and I played in was at Henley in 1954; for some reason Dad couldn't play, but he arranged for Humphrey Guinness to take his place as the linchpin, playing at no. 3, with me at no. 1, Toby at no. 2 and Aunt Judy at back. Humphrey, who normally shouted and swore loudly at his team-mates, was incredibly kind and subdued with the three of us, and the excitement when we won the tournament was intense.

Toby, having already left school, had the opportunity of playing for one year in Colonel Billy Whitbread's team, which ended the season by winning the medium-goal tournament at Windsor. Dad played brilliantly and in the final briefed Toby, playing at no. 1, to worry and hassle the famous Hanut Singh (also a six-goal player and captain of the opposition) so successfully that the great Indian player, who had dominated the previous rounds, was rendered almost ineffective. Toby then went off to do his two-year stint of National Service in the Life Guards.

The summer of 1956, just after I had left school, was particularly memorable. Dad had arranged to play at Deauville during August. He said that I should travel with Aunt Judy and the ponies and help look after them, and that I would be able to play in the low-goal tournament while he played in the high-goal one. We travelled by train with eight ponies in two different carriages. At night I slept in the middle of one carriage with two ponies each end, facing inwards towards me lying in my sleeping bag in the middle. I remember waking in the early morning to find myself underneath two ponies who had somehow slipped out of their halters and had virtually swapped places, but needless to say avoiding stepping on me. I have always had the greatest affection and admiration for polo ponies – they have the most wonderfully kind and generous nature, and they are very brave and more willing to please us humans than most types of horses.

My two weeks in Deauville, the lovely old seaside town where the French racing and polo communities take their annual holiday during August, was as happy a time as I can recall as a teenager. Mum and Dad stayed in the very smart Hôtel Normandie, while Aunt Judy and I were in a little *pension* next to the beach with Robin and Gail, who were accompanied by their twenty-five-year-old German nanny Rosemerei. In the early mornings Judy and I would muck out and stick-and-ball eight ponies. In the afternoons we would usually watch the racing, and then everyone would move into the middle of the racetrack where the two polo pitches were and watch the polo, or in my case play as well.

The polo players, and particularly their wives and girlfriends, were as glamorous a group of people as you could ever imagine. Having studied French at school I could speak it well enough to get along with the locals, but with so many beautiful Argentinian ladies around I wished that I had taken more time and trouble with my Spanish. My German conversation, however, was being well tested. Every evening Aunt Judy and I would have a meal with Rosemerei, Robin and Gail and then, as soon as my young brother and sister and my ageing aunt were in bed, Rosemerei and I would meet up and stroll along the beach arm in arm. Luckily she seemed to take quite a fancy to her teenage companion and as she was an attractive blonde with a very sensual figure I was easily persuaded to go skinny dipping with her in the sea. This naturally led to intense passion – in fact, I have to say, the best sexual encounter of my young life – and I quickly became infatuated.

Dad had told me before we left England that the racing included an event for polo ponies which he was extremely keen to win. He had a very fast black pony called Pulpero and I was to ride it in the race. The rules stated that each pony and each rider should have played in at least one game of polo; but whereas Pulpero and I were a genuine team, the French had managed to get their leading amateur jockey to play one or two chukkas of polo and he was to ride a Thoroughbred sprinter who had taken part in literally one chukka of low-goal polo. The French had backed their main contender down to an odds-on favourite and Dad had a good bet on Pulpero and me at 10–1.

There were no starting stalls in those days, and Dad had warned me not to get left at the flag start. The race over three furlongs was on the main racetrack at the end of that day's six races and most of the crowd stayed behind to watch as it was a popular annual event. I should have known better, but I was still having my girths pulled up by the starter's assistant when the field of twelve were sent off. I was left by at least ten lengths; infuriatingly, we were flying at the finish and only beaten a rapidly diminishing half-length by the French favourite. Dad was livid at my naïvety as well as at the French connivance, and I was in the depths of despair for quite a while.

Dad, in fact, had not seemed his normal good-humoured self throughout the fortnight, and had not played as well as usual in the high-goal tournament. Toby and I had for some time been aware of the bad vibes between Mum and Dad that were, I am sure, caused mainly by the polo. Toby and I idolised Dad, as a polo player and as a father; but Mum, who was closely involved in running the business, knew just how much the polo ponies and hunters were costing and how badly the business was doing as a result. Also she annoyed us by saying that if we had ever seen our father play before the war we would realise that now he was just a poor imitation of the truly great player he once was. She was strongly against our playing as well, and as a consequence even seemed to resent Aunt Judy working with us. The tension was obvious and tended to spoil our wonderful summer sport. Later we were to understand her worries more clearly, but at the time we resented her attitude enormously.

I adored polo and felt I was bred to play it: I had quite a good eye for the ball and could ride well enough; and when we all played at Cirencester in 1955 I was thrilled to win the cup there for the most promising young player of the year. Even then, however, I realised that it was extremely difficult to mix it with training Flat horses, as Dad was trying to do. I always thought it was the one sport at which I might have reached the highest class; however, it was not to be.

4

Millfield

Not long after Deauville, Dad fell ill, and Mum, who had been going to take Robin, Gail, Rosemerei and the dogs down to the New Forest in a caravan for a ten-day break, decided to stay at home and look after him. I couldn't believe my luck when it was decided that I was responsible enough to tow the caravan and help Rosemerei look after my younger brother and sister and the two boxer dogs.

Needless to say I had an idyllic time, learning more German and much more of other things – amazingly, Robin and Gail seemed blissfully unaware of what was going on at the other end of the caravan. My father, I imagine, knew perfectly well what was happening and after we had been away for about a week he apparently said to Toby, 'I think you had better get that randy little sod of a brother of yours back home.' It may be that he wanted me back for other reasons than my moral welfare, though, because when I returned I could not believe how he had changed in those few days. He was confined to his bed and looked awful – his skin had gone a horrible yellowy colour and he had obviously lost a lot of weight very quickly. The local doctor had diagnosed jaundice, but Mum was not satisfied and soon had him moved to the London Clinic for tests.

I will never forget the moment some days later when she took Toby and me into the old playroom and, hugging us both tearfully, told us that Dad had cancer of the liver, that it was too far gone for treatment or surgery, and that he probably had only a few weeks to live. I don't think she told Robin and Gail at that time, feeling they would find it too hard to understand. I suddenly felt incredibly sorry for her because, in spite of the tensions and conflicts in which we had always supported him, she obviously still adored him and, although overcome with grief, was amazingly strong and determined to hold us together as a family.

I went to visit Dad just once while he was in the London Clinic. It was a Sunday; the previous day I had played rugby for Bath and we had managed to beat the Tigers at Welford Road, Leicester. As he had lived for years at Wartnaby, not far from Leicester, and much encouraged my rugby playing I thought an account of the match would interest him. I was deeply saddened to see that he was too ill for my story to make any impact on him. I never saw him again; he died a few days later.

It is difficult to describe now my own feelings then. I never shared them, not even with Toby, my lovely big brother and my closest friend. It is no doubt a dangerous thing to hero-worship your own father, but I did. Not only was he the finest horseman I had ever seen, he had tried so hard to pass on all he knew about horses and life in general to the two of us, and had been a wonderful father. He was always very strict with us but we respected him enormously. He had an amazing number of friends and was always kind and generous with people, especially all those who worked in the background. I never came across a gateman on the racecourse, or a porter at the hotels he stayed in, or indeed any of his own employees who didn't always greet him with respect and affection. He had, of course, died much too young and I found it hard to come to terms with this, particularly from a religious point of view. At least Toby and I had known him for eleven years and shared many happy times with him, especially out hunting or racing and playing polo. Poor Robin and Gail only knew him for the first six and eight years of their lives, and were too young really to appreciate him.

For a few weeks I retreated into my own silent little shell of depression, not really wanting to talk to people or even do very much. We were all, of course, mightily impressed by the number of people who came from all parts of the world to his funeral, and by the lovely obituaries, but inside I was devastated and suddenly did not know in which direction my life was going.

Dad had always said to Toby and me, 'I will never leave you boys any money, but I will leave you some very good friends.' He was right on both counts. Although his will officially stated that he left £500, in truth he was pretty horribly overdrawn. Happily, at the time of his death his great friend and main owner Jock Whitney had just taken up residence at Winfield House in Regent's Park on his appointment as American ambassador to London, and we were soon to learn just how good a friend of Dad he was.

Toby and I were summoned to see Jock Whitney in London very soon after the funeral. We had scarcely met him before, but obviously had been hearing all about him from Dad for years. He was a tall, well-built, kindly man with spectacles, and he was at once extremely friendly to both of us. First he said to my big brother, 'Now, Toby, if you want to take over the whole stables and continue training, I will leave my horses with you at Weyhill and support you in every way I can.' Toby was only twenty-one at the time and, having completed his two years' National Service – one of them in Egypt – had been back assisting Dad for only about six months. 'If, however,' he went on, 'you want to go now as assistant trainer to someone like Noel Murless, I will arrange that and then help you set up in, say, two years' time. You, however, must make the decision and let me know.' He then turned to me and said, 'Ian, if by any chance you want to have any further education – and it would be no bad thing to do – I will be happy to finance it.'

Toby courageously chose to stay on at Weyhill and take over all the owners and horses that were currently there. He had, however, one immediate and considerable problem. Colonel Bill Whitbread, who had bought the yard for our father a few years earlier, was very business-minded and decided that it was much too much of a gamble to have a twenty-one-year-old training his expensive horses in his stable. Consequently he not only removed his horses almost at once, but also told Toby that the whole place would have to be sold as soon as possible. Somehow, Toby and Mum had to find someone else to buy the place if we were going to stay there.

In fairness to him, Colonel Whitbread had told Dad to spend plenty of money on Weyhill refurbishing the whole place when we moved in – and the first time he came down to look around his new property he must have been somewhat miffed to find the whole place painted pink, with black and white windows and gates. These, of course, were Jock Whitney's colours; there was no sign anywhere of his own chocolate and gold. Colonel Whitbread became a great supporter of National Hunt racing, and 1957 saw the first running of the famous end-of-season steeplechase at Sandown sponsored by his company. Still, at the time our whole family and most of the other owners felt he was being pretty disloyal.

A short-term solution presented itself when some gentlemen from Hong Kong called Run Run and Runme Shaw agreed to pay Colonel Whitbread's asking price. Toby soon helped them towards recouping their outlay by landing a big gamble in the Portland Handicap with a sprinter they owned called New World who had come from Hong Kong. Toby went on to have a very good first year, in fact, and I can remember Jock Whitney on one occasion saying how proud he and the other owners were of their young trainer.

As for me, I was due to do my National Service at any moment; in fact I'd already had an interview, arranged by Dad, with Major General Sir John Baldwin, who was then Colonel-in-Chief of the 8th Hussars. His regiment was in Germany at the time and I had been assured that I would enjoy lots of racing and polo over there. But it did not take me long to decide that if I could possibly get to Cambridge University I would far rather do that than National Service. At once I consulted my older and wiser friends, Ian and Dennis, to see how I could possibly get in without a single A-level to my name. They both said that there was only one possible route: via a school in Somerset called Millfield run by an extraordinary man called R.J.O. (Jack) Meyer.

Millfield, although a public school functioning like any other, sometimes also took older boys on a crash course, and the headmaster himself had excellent contacts at both Oxford and Cambridge. Either Ian or Dennis, I suspect, arranged for my interview at Millfield, and I recall it clearly. I was hastened into Jack Meyer's study by his secretary, a fine-looking lady in her fifties called Amothe Sankey. She was not very friendly; but Jack Meyer (or Boss, as he was known by everyone at the school) certainly was.

Boss was tall and lean – unhealthily skinny, I felt – with a quiet and rather husky voice. He was grey-haired with a moustache, and had a thin, distinguished face with plenty of wrinkles. Almost permanently, it seemed to me, he had a naughty twinkle in his eye and a ready chuckle. Over the next few years I grew to revere this man almost like the father I had recently lost.

His first question at the interview was: 'Are you related to Gerald Balding?' Yes, I said, he was my father, and Boss replied, 'Well, he once knocked me cold in the boxing ring at Haileybury when I was stupid enough to get in the same heavyweight division' – and, in the same breath, 'We haven't got any room here at the moment but of course we will have to fit you in somewhere.' I guess he knew perfectly well who my father was – and that I was riding regularly in races and currently playing rugby for both Bath and Dorset and Wilts.

We discussed what subject I should read at university and decided that a veterinary course, which lasted five years, would be the most advantageous if one day I, too, ended up a trainer. It would also give me a couple of extra years in which to obtain a rugby blue if I had missed out in the first three. In fact I was really keen at that time on the thought of becoming a vet, as long as I could continue to play rugby football and ride in races. Boss said that I would have to get my A-levels in chemistry, physics and biology by the end of my two-year stint at Millfield, and that if I did he would do his very best to get me into the veterinary school at Cambridge.

So it was in the autumn of 1957 that I arrived at Millfield just before my nineteenth birthday. I had loved every moment of my time at Marlborough, but since leaving I had spent almost a year at Weyhill working pretty well full-time as a stable lad and amateur jockey, and I was not too sure if I could settle back into the more structured routine of school life.

Boss had started Millfield some thirty years before with just three Indian princes as pupils; by the time I went there it had grown to about three hundred boys and thirty girls. Millfield House itself – a pleasant old grey-stone building – only had room for about fifty boys, so over the years Boss had acquired various other houses in the neighbourhood to accommodate his growing population; the biggest was at Kingweston, five miles away, and the pupils living there had to come and go daily by bus. In managing this burgeoning institution Boss had the indispensable support of his wife Joyce who, while clearly in awe of her husband, quietly played a huge part in school life, taking responsibility among other things for the medical care of all the pupils.

It was quite typical of Boss, who was years ahead of his time in a lot of ways, that he had turned Millfield into a co-educational boarding school. The thirty-odd girls fitted into school life extremely well and at Millfield there was never a whiff of homosexuality, which had been rampant at Marlborough during my time. Also typical of Boss was his 'Robin Hood' attitude to admissions. At that time the school had pupils from over thirty different countries, including quite a few whose families were extremely wealthy, and who came to the school on the understanding that their parents helped finance the education of one local boy or girl who couldn't afford the fees – or alternatively paid for something like a new tennis court!

For my two years I was to live at a small former guesthouse in Glastonbury called Abbey Grange with five other boys. All of us were older than the regular sixth-formers and had come from other schools, trying to pass exams in a hurry to go on to university. As we were virtually unaccountable to anyone (we were nominally under the authority of a housemaster, but we never saw him), for our first year we behaved as badly as any six boys ever did at any school. I had a small car parked around the corner, which no one knew about, various attractive girls were in and out of the house frequently, and everyone – except for me – smoked and drank plenty. We cycled the two miles daily to and from

Millfield – which if nothing else was good exercise – where we then spent the day doing our lessons, having lunch and playing games in the afternoon. In the evenings we cycled back and had a meal cooked for us by our landlady – and then the fun would start. With my car we had easy access to the nightclubs as far afield as Bristol.

I did have one more serious attachment in that first year at Millfield. I was seeing a lot of a very attractive sixteen-year-old girl called Fiona Brassey, whom I would take along to race meetings and rugby matches. Her parents – Hugh, who was a fine polo player, and Joyce – were great friends of my parents, and the romance seemed to be much approved of by both Mum and Fiona's family. Then all of a sudden she was taken ill, and within what seemed a very short time was in hospital in Bath. I could hardly believe it when her mother told me one day that Fiona had incurable cancer, and would not live for more than a month or two. Joyce wanted me to go on seeing her daughter as often as I could, as apparently it was the only thing that made the rest of Fiona's life bearable. Coming so soon after my father's death from the same ghastly disease, this news hit me hard. I was deeply depressed by the unfairness of it all and once again seriously questioned my Christian faith. How could a loving, caring God allow this beautiful young girl to die in such a horrible way? Fiona was brave and lovely to the end, and for quite a while thereafter I was broken-hearted.

My official housemaster, known as 'Brom', who taught me chemistry, was also the athletics coach and was more preoccupied in the afternoons teaching Mary Bignall (later Mary Rand) the long jump. Mary was at Millfield on a 'sports' scholarship and she was as natural an athlete as I ever saw. She was immensely attractive also, and always had boys pursuing her. Her virtually free education at Millfield – her parents lived locally and had very little money – was typical of Boss's generosity.

Boss himself had been no mean athlete in his heyday: a brilliant cricketer, he had played regularly for Somerset, and on one occasion captained the Gentlemen against the Players at Lord's. He was apparently rather an eccentric captain, however, and when he opened the bowling in that match with an orange rather than the new ball it did not go down at all well with the powers that be!

Boss told me that during the term time he wanted me to train and play with the school rugger team, but that if we had no matches, or we were playing a school who objected to my playing, I would be free to go and play for Bath, or Dorset and Wilts. He had also said that I could go and ride in races, but only if I got his permission first. The first time I asked him was when Toby had said I could ride a horse at Taunton one weekday afternoon. As it was a local meeting I thought that Boss would have no objection, but when I told him the name of my mount, to my amazement he said, 'Isn't that the horse that fell last time out, unseated its rider the previous time and ran out the time before that?' When I confirmed all this, he said, 'Well, you tell your brother: no, sorry. I will let you go when he offers you a decent ride.' It had not escaped my notice in my first visit to Boss's office that the *Sporting Life* and *The Times* were the only two newspapers in evidence. He very obviously gave plenty of attention to the former. I had several rides that year, including a few winners, and Toby noticed more than I did that they were always well backed if I had told Boss we thought they had a decent chance.

On one occasion I did not ask Boss if I could go and ride. Toby had rung and said that if I could get myself up to Fakenham on a Saturday I could ride Winter Gale, who had an outstanding chance. He had runners far and wide that day and was short of jockeys, so he badly wanted me to go. I knew Boss would say no, as to get to Norfolk I would have to leave the previous day and I assumed he was unaware that I had my own car. I told Toby that if he put down no jockey on the horse in the morning paper we would probably get away with it. I fixed it with my teachers, who were easy to silence with a decent tip, and took the whole day off lessons. The horse duly won – and although I naturally made certain I was not mentioned in the write-up in the *Sporting Life,* they could not avoid printing the result. Among the many weekend results the next day, there was Winter Gale as winner of the 2.30 p.m. at Fakenham ridden by Mr I. Balding.

I took care to avoid Boss for a few days, but when eventually I did bump into him he just said with a smile, 'It was lucky I had a tenner on Winter Gale at Fakenham the other day. Although you said nothing about it I thought he had a pretty good chance and guessed he might be ridden by some obscure amateur!' I felt very embarrassed and was never less than honest with him again.

Given episodes such as this, it came as a huge surprise when, at the end of the summer term, Boss said to me, 'Ian, I want you to be my Senior Prefect next year.' Having been used all my school life to treating prefects as the enemy and knowing how badly I had behaved in my first year at Millfield, I thought he could only have been following the old theory of 'setting a thief to catch a thief'. I was still to live at Abbey Grange, so I plucked up courage to ask if perhaps I might keep a car nearby, as it would make life a lot easier. He said with a knowing smile, 'Yes, that's fine, but don't let's tell everyone about it, shall we?'

When I told Toby I was to be Senior Prefect he merely said, 'Well, I should bloody well hope so, you must be the oldest schoolboy in England by now!'

At the beginning of the next term, Boss called me in and told me about my first duty. He had just accepted a rather wayward boy called the Hon. Peregrine Eliot, the heir to the Earl of St Germans, who had recently failed O-level maths at Eton and was coming to Millfield to get it. I was to take this scion of the aristocracy under my wing, have him in my house and 'make a man of him'. Perry was a desperate smoker, so I immediately forbade him – or anyone else in our small house – to smoke. He had been in the Combined Cadet Force at Eton and possessed some heavy black corps boots; so, for the first two weeks of term he and I walked the two miles to and from Millfield every day, and for the next two weeks we jogged both ways – he always in his corps boots, me in my gym shoes. By then Perry was reasonably fit and I allowed him thereafter to cycle in and back with me. He had played the Wall Game at Eton, but now I saw to it that for the first time he played rugby football most days – in the second row of the scrum, so that he would get well roughed up in the thick of the action.

Perry soon settled into Millfield life and did not bear me any grudge for my sometimes draconian efforts to 'make a man' of him – they even seemed to amuse him. And he passed his maths exam. In fact, he became the one really good friend that I have kept from Millfield since those days.

My more mundane duties as Senior Prefect included organising the rota for all the rugger matches, and even arranging the referees for those games. Sometimes this entailed politely having to ask certain masters if they would alter their timetables in the afternoons. In addition I had the other school prefects to organise. I was also making speeches here and there to various societies in the school, and even to local organisations in Street and Glastonbury with which Boss felt the school should be friendly. I found all of this fascinating, and it certainly helped me to acquire some much-needed diplomatic skills. Unfortunately, I was only too happy to allow my duties as Senior Prefect to distract me from the work I should have been doing, of which there was plenty: in this final year I was supposedly cramming two years' work into one in order to pass my A-levels. I was also playing every sport I could – boxing, squash, rugby in the winter terms – and was still going off to ride in races. In the spring term I suddenly discovered the joy of point-to-pointing. The local farmers were aware that there was a promising young amateur rider living locally in Street and I was soon having rides at Kingweston and other nearby tracks. George Small, John Daniels and Michael Tory were three of the best West Country amateurs at that time, and I was much enjoying the experience of riding against them.

In the winter and spring holidays I was still playing rugger regularly for Bath and Dorset and Wilts. Bath Rugby Club was not then the force nationally that it became in the 1990s, but it had an amazingly strong fixture list and played against all the top teams in England and Wales. When Ian and Dennis were first persuaded to play for Bath they took me along with them, and I played a few games in the second team before becoming a regular on the firsts for the next ten years or so.

There were some wonderful characters helping to run the Club. John Roberts, club captain for my first two or three years and later chairman for a long spell after he retired from playing, personified Bath rugby for me. His team talk before we went out on the pitch was legendary and didn't vary much. After a few choice words about the opposition, he would suddenly look serious and say,

'Now remember, boys, no bloody shinanicking' (Ian, Dennis and I never dared ask what that word meant), and then, looking in my direction, 'and you, ya young bugger – no runnin' up your own arse: just hoof it into touch.' John was a hard man who had mixed it with all the best prop forwards in England and Wales and we all respected him enormously. Jack Arnold was the team secretary then, and he too did amazing favours for the three of us and became a great friend.

Our local derbies against Gloucester and especially Bristol were the games that mattered most. In those days we rarely beat Bristol but Ian and Dennis, who were then at their playing peak, made an enormous difference to the quality of our side and when they were both playing we had a chance against even the best teams. One time the three of us were selected to play for the Southern Counties against the Wallabies team from Australia at Brighton and Hove Albion football stadium. I was delighted to read that my opposite number at full back for the touring side, Terry Curley, was also only nineteen years of age. When we met before the game, however, I found to my horror that he was about six foot two and at least three stone heavier than me – and he made a point of shaking my hand so hard it took me a minute or two to recover! As expected, our makeshift team from several different counties were hopelessly outclassed by a touring side who in their first match on English soil were determined to make a good impression.

There were a few occasions in my teens and early twenties when I rode in a race and played rugby on the same day. My friends at Bath were always keen to get the latest tips from the Weyhill stable and even then I was a lousy tipster, frequently putting them on to losers and, even worse, failing to mention the odd long-priced winner! One Thursday afternoon I had won a steeplechase at Wincanton on my old favourite, The Quiet Man, and had gone on afterwards to play for Bath at the Rec against a local team, Clifton, in the evening. My horse had won at 100–8, and of course the previous Saturday I had failed to mention he was even running. I didn't dare say anything to my team-mates about riding that afternoon and was unobtrusively changing into my rugby kit in the corner when suddenly I heard our captain,

John Roberts, saying in his lovely deep Somerset accent from the other end of the changing room, 'Hello, there's a very *quiet man* changing over there in the corner.'

One incident in my second spring term at Millfield was not only memorable but probably unique in the life of the school. My brother Toby was not slow to realise that my headmaster, sadly, was a gambling addict – something of which I had been naïvely unaware. So it was no surprise to him that Boss could not resist the offer of actually owning his own racehorse. Toby sold him a smashing little grey gelding called Milk Shake, who was about eight years old at the time and a son of the extremely successful National Hunt stallion Doubtless II. This beautiful black Argentinian-bred horse, whom our father had trained successfully for Jock Whitney, was standing at stud in England. Milk Shake, like all Doubtless's progeny, was a brilliant jumper and, being also very sound, he ran frequently.

As you would expect, Boss took an enormous interest in his horse, and when Toby asked me to ride Milk Shake one Thursday afternoon at Wincanton he became extremely excited about the whole occasion and took along about thirty pupils who were unoccupied that particular afternoon. When his Senior Prefect arrived in the paddock in his colours there was Boss, in his dirty old mackintosh, *Sporting Life* tucked under one arm and fivers falling out of both pockets, wanting to give me the instructions himself. Toby looked on with great amusement. Happily, between us we didn't get it too far wrong as Milk Shake duly won comfortably. The scenes of celebration in the winner's enclosure afterwards were hilarious. Boss led his own horse in, ridden by his Senior Prefect and surrounded by joyful Millfield pupils. He then couldn't decide whether to give a press conference first or rush off to collect his winnings from the bookmakers, whom he was convinced would welch on him.

In my final summer term at Millfield I was well aware that I was not going to pass my A-levels – simply because I had not done enough work. During the spring holiday I had been anxious enough to go to Ian Beer and persuade him, as a biologist, to give me some extra tuition in his subject. This had certainly helped me a lot, as he had a gift for making a subject I thought extremely complicated seem relatively easy. Nevertheless I knew I was still hopelessly short of A-level standard.

I was not helped by the headmaster himself, who had persuaded me not only to play on his school polo team but also to help coach the other players. Needless to say, Millfield was the only school in the country at that time with a polo team of its own; all the school horses and polo ponies were run by Captain Roy Hern (Dick Hern's father). Polo was a very expensive extra on the bill normally, but when I told Boss that on no account was polo to appear as an extra on my bill to Jock Whitney, he said: 'No, no, of course not – you will have a polo scholarship!'

During that last year I got into the habit of going to see Boss on his own every evening after our meal, by which time his ever-faithful secretary had gone home. We would discuss everything happening at school before inevitably moving on to racing and what might be going to win shortly. Being away from home I had no idea what was going on with the horses at Weyhill, so my information was probably even worse than usual. Still, he never seemed to mind backing losers, and our horses were in any case usually doubled up with England to win the current test match. What I did learn was how much serious gamblers care when they are not on to a winner!

One evening I have always remembered. As usual, I knocked softly on the study door and quietly let myself in. Boss was on the phone at the other end of the room, so I thought I would stand unobtrusively just inside the door until he had finished. I couldn't help hearing the conversation and it became clear that he was talking to an admissions tutor at a university. After a short while I suddenly realised, to my horror, that he was talking about me and almost certainly had no idea I was in the room. Embarrassed, I did not know whether to risk making a noise by going back out of the door or just stay quietly and pretend afterwards I had heard nothing.

I opted to stay and listened to him extolling my virtues as a rugger player, boxer, polo player, jockey and anything else he could think of to disguise my limited potential as a veterinary student. Then suddenly he paused for a moment and, in an even softer tone than usual, said: '– and of course, he is one of God's own.' I was puzzled by this unusual description. Although I was a regular churchgoer and would like to think I have always been a Christian, I was never one to publicise my faith in God. I knew that what he had said must be flattering – but it was not until I retired from training forty-odd years later that I finally worked out what I think he meant that evening.

Before I sat my A-level exams towards the end of that summer term, Boss organised for me go to Cambridge for two interviews. First of all I went to Clare College, where I had a perfectly pleasant interview with the Senior Tutor, Dr Northam. Unfortunately I was asked to sit a three-hour general science exam as well. After about an hour I had written all I knew on the subject, whether it was related to the questions or not, and I think I actually slept with my head on the desk for the last hour. I was not surprised to hear later that I had achieved less than half the mark of the next lowest person taking the exam and that Clare College could not help me.

A week or two later Boss sounded quite excited when he told me I was to have an interview with a Dr Pratt, the Senior Tutor at Christ's College. He said that this man was very keen on sportsmen, but that I must convince him that I intended to give to his college as much as I could, rather than just take. Boss also warned me that my interview might just be a trifle unusual.

I was glad that I had been forewarned. When I knocked on the door at the appointed hour there was a very loud and gruff 'Come in!' Dr Lucan Pratt was seated behind his desk on the left of the room. His glasses were disconcertingly thick so that I could not really see his eyes, and the coloured patch on his face, which I was told was the result of an explosives accident in the war, was very evident. After a few awkward scientific questions in which I felt sure I scarcely covered myself with glory, he suddenly said, 'Well, if you are serious about being a veterinary student you will have to read this book in your first year.' With this he pulled a very large volume from the shelf behind him and hurled it across the room at me. I caught it comfortably and put it down on the table in front of me, saying, 'Yes, of course, I will look forward to reading it,' or some such drivel. Then his voice softened and he said, 'Well, Ian [my Christian name for the first time], let's get down to important matters. Do you kick with both feet?'

'Yes, sir, I do!' said I quickly, with satisfaction.

'Well, you won't get on the university team this next term because a certain Mr K. J. F. Scotland is still in residence. You won't get on the Sixty Club [second team] side either, because Chris Howland is still up and was the full back of that team last season; and I doubt if you will even get on our college team, because our skipper is a full back and I doubt if you are even the best freshman full back coming to Christ's next term! However, if you pass your A-levels I will keep you a place on the veterinary course.'

I tried to explain how I felt I had a lot to give to the college, one way or another, and on leaving felt quite up-beat, rather than in a deep depression as I had after the Clare College experience. To me it had indeed seemed a most unusual interview – but I gathered later on that it was pretty much the norm for would-be full backs or fly halves!

I ended my last term at Millfield by making a significant speech on Parents' Day in front of the whole school and many parents, as the Senior Prefect was expected to do. My confidence had risen through the year with Boss giving me more and more responsibility, and I felt that I got on really well with nearly all the members of his Common Room. He had collected some amazing teachers and real characters, including some older ones who had been pensioned off by other public schools, and I became very friendly with many of them.

My exam results came about three weeks after the end of that last summer term, and needless to say I had failed comprehensively in all three subjects. Boss could hardly have been surprised, but seemed disappointed all the same. However, he told me I might still have a chance with Dr Pratt at Christ's College. I was certainly not hopeful myself, as I knew I had no chance of getting on to the veterinary course. Then, a few weeks later, to my surprise and great delight I heard that Christ's would take me and that I could read rural estate management. The only qualifications for this degree course apparently were five or six varied O-levels, which I had. I gathered that it was very similar to agriculture, but even more suitable for someone whose future almost certainly lay in the world of horse racing.

My gratitude to Millfield, to my excellent teachers and in particular to Boss was immeasurable. Ian and Dennis had been right – it was the only possible way I could have got to Cambridge University – and they had somehow done it. I fully realised how incredibly lucky I had been, and that my final year as Senior Prefect had in addition given me wonderful experience and confidence in dealing with people and difficult situations. My appreciation and affection for Boss could not have been greater. Nevertheless, although sad in a way to leave, I had had more than enough time at school and was ready to move on.

At about this time my mother told me that a Mr Herbert Blagrave, who had been a good friend of my father, would like to see me. I knew that he trained about twenty horses of his own at Beckhampton, and I was very interested to meet him and hear what he had got to say. He had the reputation in the racing world of being a rather eccentric but extremely wealthy owner, trainer and breeder. He and his wife Gwen, who was about seventy at that time, lived in a very nice house called The Grange, which was close to the A4 and about a hundred yards away from the charming old stable yard with its twenty or so thatched boxes. Just down the road was the much bigger and better-known yard belonging to Jeremy Tree, where the great Fred Darling had trained.

Herbert told me that he had been a friend of my father for years, knew all about my riding and rugby prowess, and would be keen to give me a job. I told him that, financed fortunately by Jock Whitney, I was committed to doing a three-year course in rural estate management at Cambridge. Herbert explained that, quite apart from his twenty flat horses which he trained himself, he had a stud farm near Kintbury in the Newbury area managed by a nephew of his wife, Michael Forsyth-Forrest. He also had some property in Reading which was currently run by an estate agent. Herbert seemed delighted that I was to read rural estate management and said that when I had finished my course he would like to give me a job which would involve assisting him in all three departments. It sounded just perfect, as he also seemed very keen for me to continue riding and playing rugger. In fact he was extremely keen himself on all sports and happened to be president of Southampton Football Club at that time. My mother was a little bit wary of my committing myself totally to Mr Blagrave, but at the same time she was relieved that I might have a ready-made job waiting for me as soon as I had finished my course.

Leaving Millfield certainly didn't mean the end of my contact with Boss. He was frequently on the phone to Toby – I think that by now he had realised that, not being interested in betting at all myself, I was a pretty poor source of information for him – and also came to visit his horse on occasion. He took a great interest in my career, not only at Cambridge but also much later on when I was training at Kingsclere. Dick Hern had also been a pupil at Millfield for a year or two before me, so at the time that we were both training for the Queen and had each trained a Derby winner our photographs were put alongside those of Mary Rand and Gareth Edwards among the more renowned Old Millfieldians.

I know that Dick too used to get various phone calls from his old headmaster congratulating him on some big winner and asking should he now take the 10–1 that was currently on offer about that horse for the Arc de Triomphe? When Mill Reef won the Derby, Boss had of course backed him – but had also put him in a treble with Gareth Edwards scoring a try for the British Lions in the current test match in New Zealand and Mark Cox, another old Millfieldian, winning the men's singles title at Wimbledon: one of those typical bets of his that never quite came up!

Boss was kind enough to take my younger brother at a considerably reduced fee for all his four years at Millfield, and Robin enjoyed his time there enormously. He was in the first XV at the same time as Gareth Edwards – an outstanding and unbeaten school side. My little sister was another Balding not entirely without a naughty streak. She had gone to school at Hatherop Castle, but was expelled after being caught sunbathing nude with another girl on the squash court roof. Boss was also happy to take her at Millfield at a reduced fee for two years. She got her two A-levels there and met up with her first serious boyfriend, Mike Burns – whose grandfather happened to be Noel Le Mare, owner of the famous Red Rum.

Many years later, Boss came to visit Emma and me at Kingsclere one day. Our son Andrew was about seven at the time. We were aware that he was quite seriously dyslexic and, although he could play football well enough, it irritated me considerably that he could not hit a cricket ball to save his life – especially as his godfather, Tony Lewis, had captained England at cricket and had given him a much-treasured bat. I told Boss that I had tried for ages without success to teach him how to hold the bat and strike the ball, and felt that his inability to do it was probably something to do with his dyslexia. Boss said, 'I doubt that very much. Why don't you let me have twenty minutes with him in the garden with his bat and ball?' I was only too pleased, but excused myself from watching as I had things to do in the office.

About half an hour later he came to find me and asked if I could spare a few minutes to come and bowl at my son. I went out and found to my utter amazement that Andrew was suddenly hitting the ball beautifully. Boss just said quietly, 'He's a natural, you know – must be in the genes.' To me it was just another example of his magic with young people.

My old headmaster went through a difficult time as soon as he retired. He personally picked his own successor, Colin Atkinson – but perhaps unwisely had a bungalow specially built for himself and Joyce only about two hundred yards away from Millfield House, and of course he could not resist interfering in all matters to do with school life. Eventually the governors had to make the difficult decision to move him and Joyce out to a new bungalow near Wells, further away from the school. Boss was frustrated and hurt, feeling that his governors, whom he had appointed and most of whom were close friends, had turned their backs on him. He heard of an opportunity in Greece and went off there for a couple of years to build another school very much on Millfield lines. When he returned he lived with Joyce in the bungalow in uneasy retirement until his death a few years later.

I was honoured to be asked to read a lesson at Boss's memorial service at Wells Cathedral – a notable occasion attended by about a thousand people, at which Gareth Edwards gave a moving and impressive address. As I started to read my lesson there was suddenly a loud rumbling noise, which sounded to me like some heavy furniture being moved at the bottom end of the cathedral. It ended more or less as I finished reading. When we made our exit from the cathedral after the service the sun was shining brightly but the ground was saturated with rain. I realised that, rather eerily, there must have been a short sharp thunderstorm just as I began reading the lesson.

Many years later, not long before I retired from training, Peter Johnson, the third headmaster after Boss (Chris Martin had followed Colin Atkinson), invited me to come down and address the school and parents as their guest of honour on Prize Day. I was very flattered to be asked and only too happy to accept. I told the pupils and their parents about the founder and former headmaster of their wonderful school, and how my life and the lives of many hundreds of others before them had been altered for the better by this genius of a schoolmaster. I had seen how extensively the whole estate had been developed, with beautiful new brick classrooms in place of the old Nissen huts I remembered, and wonderful new indoor tennis courts. The redevelopment had all been started, of course, by Boss's own precious 'building fund', which I hoped had been topped up a tiny bit by Milk Shake's memorable win at Wincanton. It was not easy to talk about this legendary man to whom I had been so close, but I just about got through it without choking up.

Before that, I had been only too pleased to serve as a committee member of the Millfield Diamond Jubilee Appeal, with Joyce Meyer as a very active patron and Gareth as chairman. It was the very least I could do for the school that had altered the whole course of my life. I was thrilled that it funded the Meyer Theatre, an outstanding building and a fitting tribute to the great man who founded the school and developed it so skilfully over all those years. His genius, envied by many establishment figures, lay in his humanity and skill in bringing out the very best in the young people in his care.

5

Cambridge

I suspect that I was probably the last person to be allowed entry to Cambridge University without an A-level to my name. It was not something I was proud of, and I tended to try and impress my friends by telling them how many O-levels I had passed – without necessarily stressing that the last three came at the age of twenty! All the same, I soon learned that the rural estate management course had quite a few sportsmen on it and was certainly not noted for the intellectual capacity of its students.

Most students spent two of their three years at Cambridge in digs organised by their college, and one year in rooms actually in college. My first digs were handily just across the road from the beautiful and renowned gates of Christ's College. I shared them with four other Christ's College freshmen, including a big, rough, slightly uncouth Yorkshireman called John Brash. Our landlady, Mrs Southgate, was a nightmare of a woman – not just ugly to look at but extremely unpleasant as well. She was a middle-aged widow with a live-in lover we called Alex ze Pole who spoke hardly a word of English but seemed to support her in every way she could find to make our lives a misery. Being a well-mannered lad, I tried the more tactful approach of trying to charm her, which got me precisely nowhere. John was just as rude to them as he could be and had far more success in getting some of the things we needed.

Almost at once I was part of a little clique of seven or eight rugby players who became great friends. Dr Pratt had been quite right about the level of competition for getting into the university first XV and I was grateful just to play in the freshmen's trial. I performed well enough in that and managed initially to get on the university first team. However, in about our third match I had a disastrous game against Bedford playing at fly half. Not only was I not fully fit, stupidly playing with a damaged hamstring, but also the opposing open-side wing forward was none other than Budge Rogers, probably the best player in the British Isles in that position. Not surprisingly, after such a poor game I was dropped, and I did not get back into the side until my great friend and arch-rival at that time, Tony Lewis, was injured. In that first term of mine there were two current British Lions up – Gordon Waddell, who would have played at stand-off half if fit (which nearly all that term he wasn't), and Kenny Scotland, who would of course have played full back but was versatile enough to direct operations from fly half. This left the full-back berth open, and Tony and I had a desperate struggle to claim it. Tony got the nod in the end, and though I can still remember my huge disappointment at not getting on the team in that first year, I have to say that the future England cricket captain was the best catcher and kicker of a rugby football that I have ever seen. Neither of us, however, could hold a candle to Kenny Scotland's all-round genius as a rugby player.

Apart from Tony, the only other freshman to get a blue was my companion in digs, John Brash, who was the open-side wing forward. The night he was awarded his blue he came home very late and, as one would expect, the wretched Mrs Southgate had locked him out. John very noisily climbed in through her bedroom window, two floors up, and still somehow managed to get away with it.

My other great mate who came up at the same time and has been one of my very closest friends ever since was Roger Dalzell. Rogie had been the scrum half on the Bedford School first XV, but such was the competition at Cambridge that he scarcely played even in our Christ's College first XV. He was, however, a superb gymnast as well and soon got a half-blue in that sport. He also boxed often enough for the university to be awarded a second half-blue. The two of us somehow met up with two extremely attractive girls who were only sixteen and from a local school at Shelford called Kirby Lodge. Rogie went out with Linda Dorman, who lived very near the school, and I was taking out Sue Coriat, whose elder sisters had been at Millfield at the same time as me. Sue had neglected to tell me that she was a ward of court, so soon after Rog and I had got the girls back to school late for about the third time, I was rather startled to receive a very strongly worded letter from her guardian. He was a solicitor, and told me that if it happened again I would be in contempt of court and liable to face legal action!

Sue was slim and dark and beautiful in the same way as the Argentinian ladies at Deauville. So, being somewhat captivated, I went on taking her out and bringing her back late. The next episode was a formal meeting with her solicitor/guardian, who asked me bluntly what my intentions were towards this very young lady. I thought I had better not confess that, like any other university student, my main objective was to get his ward of court into bed with me. I very innocently just said that I was very fond of Sue and that if all went well with the relationship I hoped we might one day get married. The next riposte was an irate letter from her father, who I was told was the illegitimate son of Spanish royalty and was renowned to have a particularly foul temper. He said in the letter that he was horrified to hear that I had proposed marriage to his daughter and if I didn't stop seeing her at once he would organise for me to be gelded fairly quickly!

There was one last incident which convinced me that maybe I should forsake my young girlfriend. Towards the end of that first term a lot of my Cambridge friends came down to Fyfield House, where Toby and my mother were now living, for my twenty-first birthday party which Toby had kindly organised. My old friend from Millfield, Perry Eliot, was going out with Sue's elder sister Jenny, and we were firmly told that both sisters had to be home by midnight – they lived in a village only about four or five miles away. Needless to say the party was still going well after midnight so I suppose it was about one in the morning by the time Perry and I got the girls to their front drive.

Sensibly we drove up quite quietly, dimming our lights as we got close to the front gates. From there we could see their father illuminated in the front porch where he stood looking menacingly in our direction with a double-barrelled shotgun in one hand and a big hunting crop in the other! Perry and I assumed from his expression that the shotgun was meant for us and the hunting crop for his daughters, so rather unchivalrously we let the girls walk in on their own after we had rapidly driven away!

On the rural estate management course we had exams at the end of each year, which had to be passed to continue on the course. As I had failed to get my rugby blue in our first year I was determined to stay at Cambridge at least until I had another chance; consequently I worked hard enough actually to pass those exams at the first time of asking – a great relief, as they were the first set of exams I had passed for quite a while. However, things could so easily have gone the other way. Our crop husbandry oral exam was at the University Farm, and I had some difficulty in finding it as I had not been to the few lectures that were held out there. Arriving late and flustered, I eventually found my fellow students and our examiner. He welcomed me by saying, 'Good afternoon, Mr Balding – nice to meet you at last – now would you like to tell me, please, what this is I have in my hand?' He held out a handful of grain and, knowing that the three cereals that we had been studying were oats, wheat and barley, I at least realised it had to be one of them. Having been brought up feeding oats to horses, I knew that sadly it was not that one. Now the desperate fifty-fifty decision had to be made – and I had no idea which of the other two it was. So with all the confidence I could muster I gambled and blurted out, 'It's wheat, sir.'

Our examiner looked at me contemptuously and retorted, 'Of course it is wheat, Mr Balding – which *variety* of wheat is what I am asking you!' God was with me yet again, as I felt that had I gone for the other option, barley, my career at Cambridge would have ended there and then.

In that first year I used to take the odd day off to go and ride in a race for Toby. On one occasion he had asked me to go all the way to Devon and Exeter to ride a horse called Come To Charlie. He was a fierce puller and rather a chancy jumper as well, but I enjoyed the challenge of riding him more than our other jockeys did.

It was a long drive from Cambridge, but a great friend of mine called Dave MacSweeney wanted to come and keep us company. Dave was an amazing character: a medic and probably the oldest student at Christ's College at the time (he later became a psychologist of some note), he was also a very skilful rugby player and had already been capped for Ireland. And, being Irish, he loved racing.

I rode Come To Charlie that day in a double bridle, complete with curb chain, at Toby's suggestion—the only time I can remember a horse being so bitted in a race. It wasn't too hard to convince the other jockeys that they could quite safely let me go off in front and would do better not to take me on, because up to that day I had fallen four times in three races on this horse (once I had been stupid enough to remount, only for him to fall again at the last fence!). By the time we had gone half a mile I was almost a fence in front, and to my surprise Come To Charlie gradually settled and jumped superbly. He kept going well and we won by about twenty lengths. Dave had backed him at long odds, and the drive back to Cambridge seemed a lot shorter than the drive down.

Dave was by no means the only one of my Cambridge rugby-playing friends who used to like to come racing with me, and often I'd wangle badges for them as visiting amateur riders – and very implausible jockeys they made too! The memory of Brian Thomas, a six-foot-four Welshman weighing in at something over sixteen stone, carrying my saddle and bending double to get past the gateman still makes me chuckle.

During the Michaelmas term of my second year at Cambridge I probably played the best rugby of my career. Tony Lewis, having got his cricket blue, had injured a knee quite severely and had more or less given up playing rugby. However, Gordon Waddell, though still playing only occasionally, was much fitter than the previous year, so with Kenny Scotland still up and skippering the team I had no chance of getting a blue. However, I was playing a lot in the first XV. There was not the same pressure as I had felt in my first year, and the outstanding Cambridge team played and mostly beat all the top club sides in the country. We trained every afternoon and consequently were much fitter than the average club side in those days.

Two of our close group of friends who got into the university team that year were Mike Lord and Alan Godson, both of whom had been at William Hulme's Grammar School in Manchester. Mike was a strong-running centre three-quarter and a skilful passer of the ball. For some reason he had not been christened as a youngster, and I was proud to act as his godfather at that ceremony which was held in the college chapel. Alan Godson, a very speedy side-stepping centre three-quarter who eventually got into the team on the right wing, was also a fervent evangelical Christian who never gave up trying to convert us all to a more active and positive Christian life. In the Varsity Match that year we beat Oxford handsomely by three tries to nil – two of them scored by Mike and one, after a dramatic scissors movement with Kenny Scotland, by Alan.

Mike Lord, who has remained a close friend, much later became MP for Bedford and Deputy Speaker of the House of Commons, and very nearly achieved the prestigious role of Speaker itself. Alan Godson also became a lasting friend to our whole family. He served as vicar of Edge Hill in Liverpool for almost thirty years and was well known as one of the original inspirations behind the Christians in Sport movement.

In the spring term, when rugby was taken a little less seriously, I did more race-riding – and had one particularly eventful Saturday when Toby had asked me to ride a horse called Pure Whiskey in the 2.00 p.m. (a novice chase) at Huntingdon. I told him that I couldn't be late for a 2.45 p.m. kick-off for the university XV at Grange Road, and if I was to have any chance of doing the two I would have to borrow his very speedy MG sports car. This was somehow arranged and, having won the novice chase and weighed in rapidly, I drove furiously the fifteen miles to Cambridge. Five minutes before the kick-off time the Cambridge full back was seen running into the dressing room in his racing breeches and boots. We won the rugby too – and when I cried off boxing for the university later the same evening (I had as usual lost quite a few pounds to do the weight on Pure Whiskey and by then didn't feel too well) my friends all said I was behaving like a real wimp!

I had also discovered that riding out for Willie Stephenson at Royston was far more fun than lectures, and I managed to convince myself that it was probably more important for my future career as well. Willie was married to Frenchie Nicholson's sister Bobbie and they had five daughters, all of whom worked like mad for their father. Willie was an amazing character and I was delighted to get to know him and his family well. He, of course, was one of the few trainers to win both a Derby (with Arctic Prince in 1951) and a Grand National (with Oxo in 1959). He seemed to take a liking to me and gave me several rides in amateur races and hunter chases. Surprisingly, because he was unreasonably strict about who took his daughters out, I was even allowed to take Gillian, who later married Bruce Raymond, to a nightclub or two. Willie was tough on all his daughters, but I became very fond of him and admired his shrewd business brain enormously.

All through that second year Rogie and I shared a lovely room in Second Court on the edge of the college gardens. It was large and convenient and became the general meeting place for our group of rugby-playing friends – and the site of many tea parties there after training or college games. Our social lives flourished in other directions, too. Rogie was still going out with Linda Dorman and cementing what was to prove a lifelong love affair. My lovely cousin Sheila, who was an exceptional girl, was spending a year in England and she was my constant companion at this time. Attending lectures and studying for the inevitable exams became more and more difficult, and to no one's great surprise I once again found myself on the wrong side of the exam results at the end of term. Dr Pratt said that I should do a long vacation term and retake my exams in September – and that if I wished to remain at Cambridge I had to pass them this time. Faced once more with the awful possibility of having to leave before I had got my rugby blue, I eventually buckled down and managed to pass at the second attempt, securing my place at Christ's for the third year.

In the first term of that third year I looked to have an outstanding chance of cementing my position as full back on the first XV, and was playing well enough until our match against our own 60 Club, which was always pretty vicious. Falling on the ball, I didn't get off it quickly enough, and a well-directed boot broke three of my ribs. I missed the next six weeks and during all that time watched the games in anguish. We kept winning but our deputy full back, Bob Evans, was performing ominously well. Fortunately our skipper, Mike Wade, selected me again as soon as I was passed fit, and I came in for the crunch match against Micky Steele-Bodger's XV which, with fourteen internationals on it, was as strong a scratch side as could be mustered. Amazingly, we scored a handsome win, and one incident in particular will always remain in my memory. The great British Lion Tony O'Reilly, playing for Bodgers, broke through the centre, went clear and had just the Cambridge full back to beat before scoring. He could so easily have run round me on either side, but luckily for me opted to try to go straight through me. I could still tackle, and he came down with a dramatic thud. That night Mike Wade awarded me my blue.

Many years later I met Tony on various occasions at Ascot races when he was chairman of Heinz, which sponsored races there. He would always chuckle and ask in his deep Irish brogue, 'Now, how is that old Cambridge full back?' I would tell him how grateful I had always been that he had chosen not to make a fool of me that day at Grange Road!

Our 1961 Cambridge team, having won all its matches, came to the big fixture against Oxford played, as always, at Twickenham on the second Tuesday of December, in front of 60,000 spectators. With Gordon Waddell back to his best still playing fly half, future internationals Mike Wade (our skipper) and Geoff Francome in the centre and a very strong pack, we had a formidable side. However, playing for Oxford were Richard Sharp, England's brilliant outside half and John Willcox, their captain and England full back. They also had a former American footballer, Pete Dawkins, on the wing who was strong and fast and could throw the ball accurately one-handed any distance up to about forty yards.

In a very tight contest, described by the press as one of the best they could remember, we won 9–3: two tries and a drop goal to a Richard Sharp drop goal. We thus became the only Cambridge side ever to win every match including the Varsity Match. The euphoria experienced in the dressing room afterwards was something akin to how I felt after Mill Reef won the Derby ten years later – which perhaps indicates just how much it meant to us all. There were six members of Christ's College on that team – which says something for Dr Pratt's judgement – and nine future or current internationals. One or two of our victorious team played in the final England trial and one or two others, including myself, received travelling reserve cards – but that was as close as I was ever likely to get to the pinnacle of rugby success.

Forty years later both teams met up at a memorable dinner hosted by the former Cabinet Secretary, Robin Butler, who was Master of University College Oxford and had played in a previous Varsity Match. Even more recently some of us were excited to be able to watch a video of that 1961 match – but were more than a little deflated to see how slow and cumbersome we all looked compared to the players of the modern professional era. If that match was considered a good one to watch, I dread to think what the bad ones were like!

Having now got my long-desired blue at rugby, I devoted the rest of my time at Cambridge to other activities. The boxing club were as friendly a group of sportsmen as one could find, and I had been persuaded to don the gloves once already in my second year. On that outing, at London University, I had somewhat fortuitously knocked out their tall and rather lethargic middleweight. Thereafter I had vowed never to fight again and thus end my boxing career on a winning note – but now found myself due to enter the ring against the formidable Belsize Amateur Boxing Club on a Saturday evening at the Corn Exchange in Cambridge.

As usual I had played rugger in the afternoon and already had some misgivings about the impending encounter. My faithful friend Rogie was my second, and as soon as we saw my opponent warming up in the corner of the dressing room in his long black boxing boots and smart silk dressing gown I had an eerie feeling that it might prove an uncomfortable evening. It did: I received the boxing lesson and biggest hiding of my life. At the end of each round Rogie kept telling me to lie down the next time I was hit or he would throw the towel in. Somehow I managed to survive the three rounds but my face was in some state at the end and my head was spinning to such an extent I couldn't sleep that night. The following morning I recall walking past Dr Pratt in our college grounds and was surprised he didn't stop to chat as I said 'Good morning, Sir.' A few moments later I heard him stop and say, 'Ian, is that you?' He came back to talk and, not having realised that I was boxing the previous evening, gave me a severe reprimand and told me to stick to rugby football!

I had met and become very friendly with Andrew Wates, from the well-known family building firm, who was at Emmanuel College. He had been coming with me to ride out at Willie Stephenson's, and we thought it would be fun to have a point-to-pointer to run at local meetings during the Easter term. Big brother Toby decided that we could have an unraced five-year-old mare that he and Mum had bred. She was called Carellie, and we stabled her locally at a livery yard in the care of Liz Pickard, together with a retired old chaser of ours called Winter Gale for company. I persuaded my old chum from Marlborough, Windy Back, to take a third share in our venture.

The deal was that Andrew and I would train the two horses together, and when it came time to run Carellie I would ride her the first time, Andrew the second, and so on, continuing to take turns. There were local point-to-points three Saturdays running. The plan was for me to give her a quiet run the first time at Cottenham and for Andrew to do the same the second Saturday at Moulton. Then the third week, back at Cottenham for the university race, when I was back in the saddle and the competition shouldn't be too hot, the big money would be down.

Windy came up for all three races, and in the paddock for Carellie's debut the three of us decided that as I was merely giving her an educational run we might defray expenses by having a few quid on the hot favourite. We had only schooled our mare once over fences, courtesy of Willie Stephenson, and that had not gone too well, so we weren't surprised when she jumped very sketchily early on; but gradually she warmed up and, to my horror, about three fences from home I realised I was going better than the favourite. Being a little competitive anyway and feeling that we might never win another race, I decided to go for it, and to our amazement she finished well and won decisively. In the winning enclosure afterwards, in spite of losing our money, one might have thought we had won the Grand National. I still count it as my first training triumph!

The next Saturday Andrew rode her in a confined race at Moulton. The point-to-point course here sadly no longer exists, but it was notable for some biggish black fences and one particular downhill open ditch that was especially unappealing. It was to be Andrew's first ride, and when walking him around the course beforehand I could tell he didn't much fancy that obstacle; but in the race, though they lost a lot of ground, he and Carellie stayed together and finished well to be sixth of fourteen runners.

On the final Saturday of term we had Carellie entered in most of the races at the Cambridge University point-to-point at Cottenham. Largely for the selfish reason that I had rides in all the others, we eventually opted to run her in the race confined to current or former members of the university. Robin Collie, a well-known owner and rider, had brought a good-class hunter chaser called RUCD down for this particular race and it was a long odds-on favourite. Carellie was about 10–1 and I advised all my friends, including Windy, on no account to waste money backing her. I had chosen the wrong race, I said; we couldn't possibly beat RUCD. You can imagine the inevitable outcome: I sat on Robin Collie's tail all the way round and to my surprise Carellie found a devastating turn of foot to go by him and win by a length. This time the mood in the winner's enclosure was somewhat muted as we impoverished students rued the missed opportunity in not supporting our own horse at 10–1.

That same term our college rugby XV was in the Cuppers Final (the inter-college competition), and I was due to play at full back. Unfortunately, it clashed with the National Hunt Chase at Cheltenham (the amateurs' Grand National) where I was supposed to be riding the favourite, a brilliant little mare called Spinning Coin on whom I had won a couple of open point-to-points. I persuaded all my friends that if I could win this race it would not only considerably augment their pocket money but also help my future career immeasurably. They all said, 'Yes, yes, *we* believe you – but just you go and try and get permission from Dr Pratt, who brought you up here mainly to play rugby.'

My Senior Tutor was wonderful. He let me really struggle for about five minutes on how this could make all the difference to my future career in racing etc., and even spin the unlikely tale that if I won it might just bring reflected glory to Christ's College and so on. He knew all the time that we had at least two full backs in college who could comfortably take my place. Eventually he took a five-pound note from his pocket and, with a smile, said, 'Go on, bugger off to Cheltenham then, Ian, and put this fiver on the wretched animal for me.' Apparently there was a pretty big gamble on Spinning Coin with the Cambridge bookie and to my lasting regret the little mare fell with about a mile to go when she was cantering. My late arrival at the victorious college rugby dinner that evening was greeted, not surprisingly, by a deluge of buns and abuse – but at least we had won the Cuppers Final.

At the end of term Carellie went home, and Toby insisted that I ride her in all her races. In spite of Andrew not getting the rides that we had agreed, we remained good friends and in the Easter holidays went off together on a short trip in his car to Spain. The main purpose of this holiday was for us to run in front of the bulls at Pamplona – a popular dare-devil escapade practised mostly by students. Being pretty fit, we had no trouble keeping up with the leaders and well in front of the bulls and the majority of the two or three hundred young men taking part. As we got to the ring, however, there was suddenly a crush as we all tried to get through the relatively narrow gates at the same time as the bulls approached. I would not have wanted to get pushed over at this point. Once into the ring we had considerable difficulty in actually getting up and over the wall, as all the spectators were leaning over it watching and not really wanting to help us escape as they were there for some gory action. I confess I didn't look too hard to see where Andrew was, or if I could help him escape!

We watched a bullfight the next day and I cannot say that I enjoyed it much. Some of my friends consider it to be a noble sport, and certainly the matadors have to be brave and skilful, but somehow I cannot relish a contest where the bull has to end up losing his life.

As the end of my final term at Cambridge loomed near, I simply could not force myself to do the work I knew needed to be done if I was to get a degree. It did not help knowing that I had a job with Herbert Blagrave to go to whether I got a degree or not. I sought solace by frequenting the town's cinemas, trying to take my chums with me, arguing that a little relaxation was very good for the brain. Everyone tried to persuade me to work harder; Tony Lewis's fiancée Joannie, who was a frequent weekend visitor to Christ's, even copied out in her superb handwriting other people's notes and diagrams for me to study. It was all to no avail. I failed my exams – albeit narrowly enough to have a second crack at them a couple of months later, mainly, of course, because I felt very badly for my lecturers, who had all tried very hard to help me, and especially for Dr Pratt and Boss Meyer, both of whom had put their faith in me and knew I was well capable of getting a degree. Sadly I failed them at the second attempt too.

Over thirty years later Emma, Andrew and I witnessed Clare being presented with her degree in English at the very formal and old-fashioned ceremony at the Senate House in Cambridge. It had naturally been described to me in detail many years before by Rogie, Tony and the others, who had made certain that I knew what I had missed out on. As the gathering cleared following Clare's graduation, I rather irreverently made Andrew stay behind, and as I knelt he tapped me on the shoulder, as the Vice-Chancellor had just done to Clare, and uttered the famous words 'Te admitto' etc.

At the end of term I went to Gibraltar on a sporting tour organised by one of the more entrepreneurial undergraduates at Christ's called Mike Brufal. The main event was to be boxing, but we were also to play the locals at six other sports – and I was to take part in five of them, as well as boxing in the middleweight class. A few days before we left one of my wisdom teeth got infected and I rang Mike to break the news that although I was still OK for the other sports, including the cricket, for which I was captain, I would not be able to box.

The boxing match was enthusiastically attended by what looked like most of the local population. The ring was floodlit and high up with a gladiatorial atmosphere, not unlike a bullfight. My place had been taken at the last minute by an old Etonian boxing enthusiast called Dudley Savill, with me now acting as his second. Poor Dudley – up against a very tough local who had boxed in a European amateur team – took a terrible pounding. As I picked him up at the end of each round, vigorously sponged his face, applied ice and smelling salts and sent him out again, I could not stop myself giggling hysterically and thinking how it should have been me out there in the ring taking this awful hammering. I was so full of admiration for Dudley's courage on that occasion that I am still a sitting duck for his annual appeal for funds to keep the Amateur Schools Boxing going. I can hardly wait to send him my cheque!

We lost not only the boxing but all the other sports as well, and my only partial success on the tour was managing to persuade a particularly attractive girl from a titled Spanish family whom we had met at a reception to go out with me. Her name was Inmaculada. I should have known that even that skirmish was doomed to failure: my lady companion and I were accompanied the whole time by a rather ferocious-looking Spanish chaperone!

Cambridge University, and Christ's College in particular, had meant a huge amount to me – and they still do. I made most of my closest friends there, and I hope and feel that we contributed to college life in many ways, not just on the rugby field. I certainly nurtured my love of classical music and went to many concerts. I also always enjoyed going to chapel (and many years later coincidentally met our college chaplain Michael Mantelow, when he was Bishop of Basingstoke and I had taken on the less likely role of churchwarden at Kingsclere). Thanks to the benevolence of my father's great friend, Jock Whitney, my three years at Cambridge University are a privileged memory. I will always think of them with a warm glow of pleasure.

6

Beckhampton and Fyfield

I started my job with Herbert Blagrave almost immediately after coming down from Cambridge in the summer of 1962. I had already organised my own digs in Marlborough, where our old matron at Summerfield, Miss Kaye Merritt, had retired and leased quite a large house. Here I occupied a very small flat, alongside three other tenants in similar flats, and she looked after me like a doting grandmother.

Herbert was in his sixties and although always very friendly was a strange man. No one seemed to know how and where he had acquired his wealth, but I soon learned about the old adage that rich men usually know how to stay rich. When I eventually got around to asking him how much he was going to pay me, he explained that his wife Gwen's nephew Michael Forsyth-Forrest, who managed his Harwood Stud, was not paid very much, and as I was new to the job I couldn't be seen to be getting even that; so therefore he would prefer to pay all my expenses, such as the rent for my flat and petrol for my car, and then just give me cash at regular intervals with a bonus when the stable had a winner. I didn't really mind this system as I had never had any money to speak of and it was nice to have some ready money; but my mother, who was expecting me to earn a regular monthly salary, was furious about it.

Gwen, somewhat older than Herbert in her mid-seventies, was a delightful lady and was always extremely kind to me; and Herbert's secretary, Diana Hastings, who lived in a little cottage in the yard, was the greatest fun. I spent many happy tea or coffee times in her kitchen. Most of Herbert's lads had been with him for a long time and seemed to know how to get by without working very hard – with the one exception of his head lad, Colin Richards (a younger brother of Sir Gordon). He couldn't persuade the other lads to do any of the odd jobs so he ended up doing them all himself!

Herbert was keen for me to pursue my career as an amateur rider and with that in mind had brought a promising young chaser of his own called Milo back to Beckhampton from Bob Turnell's, where he had been trained as a novice hurdler. I rode him out every day with Herbert's small string of Flat horses and soon we got to know each other well. He had a lot of ability and was a lovely ride, but in the stable he would bite or kick in quite a nasty fashion if given half a chance. Toby was giving me rides whenever he could and I was notching up quite a few winners here and there. I had plenty of time for racing; I never seemed to be asked to go either to Harwood Stud or to Herbert's office in Reading, and my boss was of course training the horses himself. I rode Milo in his first two novice chases, which he won quite impressively, and it was evident that he was good enough to target one of the races at the 1962 Cheltenham Festival. I was hoping that Herbert would choose one of the novice chases, where he would carry enough weight for me to ride, but realised that the horse would now be qualified for one of the handicap chases as well.

I remember we had a very cold January and February that year, and in the frost and snow exercise was confined to a large straw ring in the field just outside the yard. I would wait for Herbert's Flat horses to go in after two or three long trots, and then Milo and I would canter several circuits in either direction. About two weeks before Cheltenham the weather broke and at last we could get on to the lovely Beckhampton downs to do more serious exercise with our one jumper. Herbert explained that he wanted

Milo to have his one major gallop exactly a week before the race. He said the horse didn't need much work and I was to come up a four-and-a-half-furlong gallop to finish well at the top where he would be standing.

Herbert was notorious for training his Flat horses very lightly; he loved them to look big and well and have several runs before they were fully fit, by which time they were usually well handicapped too. Our one chaser had not run for six weeks, and all he had done in the meantime was to canter steadily around our straw ring. I could not believe that this one gallop over four and a half furlongs could possibly get him fit enough for a two-and-a-half-mile chase the next week. On the morning of the gallop it happened to be foggy and I took a desperate chance, completely disobeying my orders, and galloped him a mile on a circular gallop down below in the fog before heading up the four-and-a-half-furlong climb to Herbert who was waiting at the top. He remarked afterwards that it seemed to have taken me rather a long time and I said that I had just got a bit confused in the fog as to where I should set off! The following week Herbert decided to run Milo in the Mildmay of Flete Handicap Chase over two and a half miles, in which with ten stone four on his back he looked to be extremely well handicapped even for a novice. I was desperately disappointed, however, as eleven stone was the lightest I could do and Johnny Haine, who had ridden him over hurdles, was booked for the ride. All went well and amid great excitement Milo won his race impressively. I had of course told Toby about my secret gallop in the fog, but never dared let on to Herbert. In any case, who could ever know if it made any difference or not?

As the months passed, my mother was getting increasingly anxious that I didn't have a proper job with regular payment, and eventually persuaded me to tackle Herbert about it. Once again he managed to avoid complying, saying rather shrewdly that because I was riding in races so often – which he had encouraged me to do, of course – he couldn't really put me on a fixed salary. Still, I was happy enough, and he had been very generous with a cash present after Milo's victory at Cheltenham.

Herbert had some lovely Flat horses, all home-bred, and I was sent to saddle them at the more distant meetings. My boss, like a proper gentleman trainer, didn't really like to go racing unless he could be home in time for tea. As a result, our horses frequently ran at Newbury, Salisbury, Bath and Chepstow, our four nearest tracks, and occasionally went to Warwick or Wolverhampton. Ascot, Sandown and Kempton were fair game also, but only usually for the big handicaps when we had a good chance. The yard had a pretty good season that year, with more winners than usual – but I doubt it had anything to do with my influence.

It was certainly a great experience to be working at Beckhampton. Herbert at that time owned the whole place, leasing the famous old yard down the road where Fred Darling had trained to Jeremy Tree. The five hundred acres of downland gallops were superb and, taking into account the trial grounds on the other side of the Devizes road near where we used to be at Bishops Cannings, the training facilities were as good as anywhere in the country. Ironically, perhaps, given the quality of the training grounds, if I learned one thing from Herbert about training racehorses it was how little work a horse could do and still run well. I was frustrated, though, because I felt that these lovely big home-breds were just not getting enough graft to do themselves full justice on the track, and also I myself did not have enough work to keep me satisfied. In addition, he never really took me into his confidence about the entering and placing of the horses.

Towards the end of the summer I was asked to have a serious chat with Toby and Mum, and they persuaded me that I should give up my job at Beckhampton and come back to join them at the family yard, where there was more than enough work for all of us. Weyhill by now had been sold and a new yard built at Fyfield Stud, a small estate my mother had had the foresight to buy quite cheaply a few years earlier, only a mile down the road from Weyhill and exactly a mile from the Kimpton gallops. While the new yard there was being built Toby had spent a very successful year about five miles away at Park House, Cholderton. Herbert did not seem too put out about my decision – I told him it was much more to do with my ambition to become the leading amateur rider than with any disappointment in my job with him: obviously by living and working with Toby I was going to get far more riding opportunities. We parted on the very best of terms, and only my old landlady Miss Merritt took it badly when I said I was leaving.

Throughout my time with Herbert Blagrave and the subsequent year back at Fyfield, and even for a short while at Kingsclere, my constant companion and dearest friend was Tony Lewis's younger sister Heather, to whom he had introduced me just after we had finished at university. Tony himself, apart from being multi-talented at sport, was also a fine musician and had played the violin in the Welsh National Youth Orchestra. To Heather, music meant everything. She was a fine concert pianist and when we first started going out together, in my attempts to impress her I couldn't wait to play her my pathetic little forty-minute repertoire. She was kind enough to tell me what good touch I had, but when I asked her to play for me I was seriously embarrassed by the contrast – I felt it could have been Ashkenazy himself playing.

For most of the time I was at Beckhampton and Fyfield, Heather was teaching music at Westonbirt girls' school, very near where we had lived just after the war, and thus conveniently close. She often came to watch me play rugger and especially to ride in races; although she had never had any experience of horses before, she thought that they were very beautiful creatures and that race riding was an art form of its own which she enjoyed and appreciated considerably. It was a very happy time for both of us.

By the time I returned to the family fold, ready for the 1962–3 National Hunt season, Toby was married to Carolyn Barclay; they lived in Fyfield House itself, while I moved in with Mum, Robin and Gail in the bungalow she had had built on to the far end of the house, which she called Fieldcroft Farm.

Toby had gathered a marvellous team of helpers together at Fyfield. Buddy Sayers was his head lad, John Price his travelling head lad, and Owen McNally and Bill Palmer – together with the new full-time amateur Mr I. Balding – rode all the horses in their races. Clive Bailey (who is still at Fyfield, albeit now toothless) was then a promising young apprentice. Our secretary was the very efficient Margerite Willis, assisted after a fashion by Tony Jakobson, a former Oxford cricket blue. Fyfield somehow seemed to collect 'characters' and Tony, or 'Jak' as we all called him, had taken over from one of them – a certain Michael Kauntze who, together with his extremely ignorant boxer dog, Dempsey, had just departed to a more important role as Vincent O'Brien's assistant at Ballydoyle. Later, of course, he went on to train successfully himself. In his time at Fyfield 'Kauntzie' had been responsible for the book-keeping. This turned out to have been one of my big brother's less shrewd appointments: there was rather a nasty tax inspection almost as soon as I arrived when it was found that the books (the few that could be found) were in considerable disarray. As Toby wanted to be free of this sort of problem and to concentrate on training the horses, he felt that with my very long and expensive education I should at least be capable of organising the monthly bills to the owners, which I duly did. Our mother also took a close interest in the running of the business. Nevertheless, I wanted to be riding, not stuck in the office, and we clearly needed some expert help. We had heard that the former National Hunt jockey Lionel Vick had become a skilful accountant after a career-ending fall and specialised in helping trainers. This was just what we needed and we asked him to come and see us.

Lionel was a truly remarkable man. He had broken his back in a ghastly fall at the age of thirty just as he was getting near to the top of the tree as a jockey. With the help of the brilliant specialists at Stoke Mandeville hospital he had regained the will not just to live but to get qualified to do something that might assist his friends in the racing world. Having left school aged fifteen to go into racing, and knowing barely more than how to read and write, he now resumed his education from scratch and qualified as an accountant. After only a year with another firm he was brave enough to branch out on his own.

Despite being paralysed from the waist down, Lionel used to drive himself down from his bungalow at Wendover in his specially adapted car to see us, and was always thrilled that he did the journey inside an hour and a quarter (even I had to drive quite fast to do it quicker than that!). He completely revolutionised our whole business, and on his advice we formed two companies – Baldings Racing Ltd and Fyfield Stud Ltd – with Mum, Toby and me as the three directors of both. Suddenly we were not just paying no tax at all but even getting repayments from the Revenue on overpayments in the past few years! Tragically, Lionel was killed a few years later – in a car accident, which in fact came as no great surprise to us. A steeplechase named in his honour is run at Newbury to this day.

Although I was still struggling with my weight Toby was determined that I should try to win the National Hunt amateurs' championship. It seemed a realistic goal: I had finished fourth the previous year, and now he was giving me a lot of good rides. I won races on some of Jock Whitney's good horses, such as Green Light and Belgrano, and a home-bred of our own called Ande R was a particular friend to me. I won four races on him that season, including his final one around the Mildmay course at Aintree. He looked every inch a Grand National horse in the making and I was already excited at the thought of riding him in it. At that same meeting, riding Belgrano in a valuable two-and-a-half-mile handicap hurdle race, I had come from a long way back and just managed to get up and win. As he was leading me in, John Price turned to me and said, 'You'll make a jockey one day, you know!' From him that was praise indeed, and I knew I must have done all right.

The best horse we had in training that season was a gelding called Caduval, whom we had taken over from the brilliant Australian rider Laurie Morgan. Toby had persuaded a new owner, Arthur Owen, to buy him and also insisted that my style of riding would suit the horse better than that of one of the stronger professionals. He was a tall, dark brown horse with a lot of ability; though he was not really a bold enough jumper to win a Cheltenham Gold Cup, he was certainly in that sort of class.

Our partnership did not have an entirely smooth start; one of my first rides on him, at Wincanton, was extremely embarrassing. We were leading as we came in to the water jump – at that time right in front of the stands – at which point Caduval suddenly put the brakes on and I went straight over his head and into the water – which was a good deal deeper in those days than it is now! He was a hot favourite, so I got quite a bit of stick from the crowd when I eventually emerged, drenched from head to foot. I certainly got no sympathy from the trainer, and you can imagine my feelings when Toby said the horse's next race was to be an amateurs' chase at – Wincanton. Again he was a hot favourite and

I was told to be certain to get a lead going into the water jump this time. In spite of my fellow amateurs trying to arrange for me to be in front coming into the fence, we managed to negotiate it safely and to go on and win comfortably.

Next time out Caduval and I came back victorious in the prestigious Rhymney Breweries Handicap Chase at Chepstow, carrying top weight. This was the most important race against professionals that I had won, and if Arkle and Mill House had not been around Caduval would certainly have been considered just about the best chaser in the country. He had been favourite for the Whitbread Gold Cup towards the end of the previous season – but here we had a great disappointment: after I had struggled to get him jumping fluently early on, we were brought down at the downhill fence on the second circuit just as he was beginning to warm up.

Toby then decided that as the horse was French-bred anyway and just beginning to thrive in the warm weather, we would have an early summer campaign in France and try to win the Grand Steeple de Paris at Auteuil. I was sent over on my own with Caduval, and we arranged to stay with a French trainer, Paul Peraldi, whom we knew well as he had ridden for a full season for our father at Weyhill. Paul was as good a horseman/jockey as I ever saw, and a charming gentleman to boot. My French at the time was good enough to get by, and the month I spent there looking after just the one horse was as interesting and enjoyable as anything I had done. Paul's yard was at Mesnil-le-Roi and we used all those beautiful tree-lined sand gallops at Maisons-Laffitte. I fed Caduval early in the morning and late at night. I groomed him meticulously and of course rode him each morning and took him out every afternoon for a long walk and pick of grass. Obviously I was in touch constantly with my big brother, but for those few short weeks I reckoned I was the trainer as well as the jockey, and I loved every moment of it.

About two weeks before the Grand Steeple I rode Caduval in his first race at Auteuil which was a prep outing – and disaster struck. At the water jump on the far side of the course Caduval stood off too far, touched down on the edge of the water and toppled over. He was cruising at the time and I was mortified. Toby quite rightly decided it would not be fair to run him in the

Grand Steeple after this débâcle but suggested we have a crack at the Grande Course de Haies (the French Champion Hurdle, over three miles) instead. The runners in that event all carried ten stone, which was much lower than my bottom limit, so Josh Gifford was engaged to ride. Although I was disappointed, in a way I felt it was time he had the benefit of a top-class professional on his back. On the day he jumped the last hurdle (actually, like all French 'hurdles', an attractive little green hedge) in front, but was just run out of it by three French horses and finished a very close and honourable fourth.

I would have to say that Caduval was the most talented chaser I ever rode, and like all the very best ones he had as much speed over five furlongs as our best sprinters at Fyfield. If a few of his races were somewhat disappointing for me, I still had a pretty successful season.

Willie Stephenson had asked me to ride a young horse of his called Time in the National Hunt Chase at Cheltenham in 1963. This race was known as the amateurs' Grand National and I was very keen to win it, not just because of Spinning Coin's untimely fall a couple of years before but also because I had a few years previously won the 'amateurs' Derby' on the flat at Epsom, on a lovely horse belonging to Jock Whitney called Playroom, and wanted to have a crack at getting the double.

I had a dream ride on Time. In those days this particular race over four miles took us way out behind the grandstands, where the car parks are now (ridiculous, really, as no one could see that bit of the race), on a unique circuit where I don't think we jumped any fence more than once. The leaders went rather too fast early on, as often happens in amateur races, and I was a long way back in a large field of well over twenty runners. But the further we went, the better my big bay gelding jumped and the stronger he got. I knew a long way from home that barring a fall the race was ours, and happily there were no disasters this time and we won comfortably. It was the only winner I ever rode at the Cheltenham Festival, and it was a moment of great excitement. Time was favourite for the Grand National the following year, ridden then by Michael Scudamore, but made a bad blunder early on and never featured.

A few days after that Cheltenham victory Willie Stephenson, who had had a good bet on his horse, gave me a big envelope with three hundred pounds in it. For me that was like winning the pools. Amateurs were not officially supposed to be paid, of course. However, earlier that same season I had won quite a valuable hurdle race at Wincanton on a good horse which Toby trained called Satchmo. He was owned by the Earl of Ilchester, who was not just chairman of the racecourse and a local steward, but a steward of the Jockey Club also. Toby had told him that the normal custom was to give the winning amateur a few quid by way of a present. I would love to have a photograph of the scene as the Earl of Ilchester took me round behind the weighing room and furtively handed me a few fivers, hoping desperately that no one was watching!

At about this time my old pal Dennis Silk had told me that a very good friend of his, the famous poet Siegfried Sassoon, was mad keen about horses and apparently anxious to meet me. At that stage I had not read any of Siegfried's work but naturally I was well aware of who he was, and flattered that he would like to make my acquaintance. I arranged with Dennis that I would drive to Heytesbury House, where the great man lived, and promised to be there at four o'clock one particular afternoon.

As usual I had been trying to fit too much into one day, and eventually arrived at the big house, a shade flustered, almost an hour late. As I drove up I saw an old man in a dirty old overcoat with a woollen beret on his head walking about, picking up sticks. Thinking it was the gardener, I went over to him and was just about to ask him where I might find Mr Sassoon when the old man smiled at me and said, 'I see that on this occasion you are not on *Time.*' Much too slow-witted to comprehend the brilliant pun straight away, I looked at my watch and mumbled some feeble apologies for being late before finally realising what he had meant.

Siegfried was a treasure, as Dennis had said he would be. Although vastly different in age and certainly in intellect, we somehow hit it off straight away and became the best of friends. He knew the names of most of the horses I had been riding that season and wanted to know all about their races and even their characters. I was enchanted, and could happily talk about horses with him for hours, which is what he seemed to enjoy most. I took Heather to meet him a couple of times. She played the piano for him and very cleverly set a couple of his poems to music which I know gave him enormous pleasure.

On one occasion he invited me to go shooting at Heytesbury. I have never been a great lover of shooting, but Dennis was going that day as well as some other interesting friends, and Siegfried was very keen for me to meet his man who ran the shoot, a character called Armytage. Apparently he was a real student of the form book and was the main source of the old boy's 'information' on the horses. It was a hilarious day from which it was obvious that our host got great pleasure – though Dennis and I were never too sure that Armytage was the most reliable of Siegfried's friends. Dennis gave me a copy of Siegfried's semi-autobiographical *The complete memoirs of George Sherston*, which both Dennis and Siegfried had inscribed for me, and it is one of my most treasured possessions. From time to time I love to go back and reread the first part of it, 'Memoirs of a Fox-Hunting Man'. Not only does it always lift my spirits, it also reminds me of the very special man who wrote it and whom I was proud to have known in his last years. How I wish that Siegfried was with us now, with his brilliant literary wit, to taunt and embarrass this current government over their pathetic obsession with abolishing fox-hunting.

My riding that season had been going well enough to put me right in the hunt to be the leading National Hunt amateur. Toby was having a lot of winners; Bill Palmer rode most of the hurdlers, but Owen McNally and I shared the rides on the chasers. I also won a couple of hunter chases on a lovely grey mare called Megsbridge for Willie Stephenson. The best amateurs I had been riding with and against during the previous few years were Bob McCreery, John Lawrence (later Lord Oaksey), Gay Kindersley, Edward Cazalet and, when he came over from Ireland, Alan Lillingston. The Biddlecombe brothers, Terry and Tony, were very good young amateurs too, but they were soon made to turn professional by the Jockey Club. (The authorities did not encourage amateurs to take rides from the professionals in normal races open to both, and if this was happening too often they usually persuaded the amateurs in question to 'turn'.) Of all those fine riders I always felt that Bob McCreery was the best. He had no wish to turn professional and thus had to accept some arrangement with the Jockey Club whereby he could only have a certain number of rides with and against the pros.

This particular year my battle for the title was not with any of them but with a wealthy young man newly on the racing scene called Sir William Pigott-Brown. William had been perceptive enough to select Frank Cundell as his trainer and tutor, and Frank of course was one of the wisest of all the NH trainers. William owned probably a dozen of his own jumpers, all of which he rode, and he was going so well that Frank put him on a few of his other winners as well. One day at Plumpton, riding Ande R, I managed to beat William on a much more highly rated chaser of his called Superfine. This looked as if it might be a crucial step to victory in the title race. However, towards the end of the season when I was one winner ahead, William bought two or three more horses which just turned the tables in his favour, and he narrowly beat me for the title – I rode about twenty winners, I think, and he had a couple more. I was disappointed, but felt that I would have more chances.

Life at Fyfield was good. Toby and Caro entertained the owners superbly in the big house, Mum, Robin, Gail and I were happy in the bungalow next door, and the horses were running well. There was no racing on Sundays then and our stable soccer team played every Sunday in the very hotly contested Lambourn stable lads' league. We had a very competitive team and virtually everyone played. With the trainer himself and Buddy Sayers at full back providing the brawn, Tony Jakobson (who had played for the Oxford University second team) and, to a lesser extent, me the stable amateur, produced most of the skill upfront. We took it incredibly seriously, and a football win on a Sunday did as much for stable morale as a couple of winners over jumps during the week! By the end of that season we had won the coveted league title, and Toby and 'Jak', who had had the foresight to back us early on at 10–1, landed quite a good touch!

My father Gerald Balding, a ten-goal polo player, in 1938

Below: Me on the left aged eight, Dad and Toby

Robin and Gail on the beach in Deauville with their German nanny, Rosemerei

My mother, Ellie, at my wedding to Emma in 1969

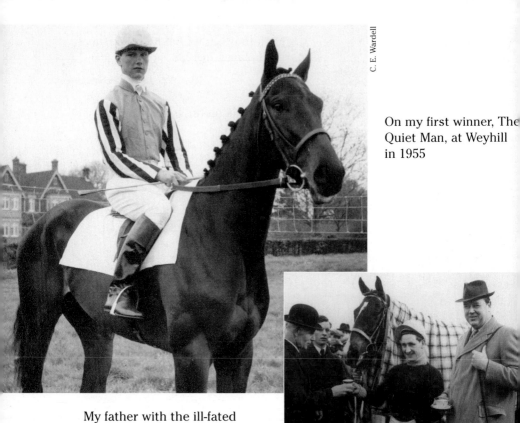

On my first winner, The
Quiet Man, at Weyhill
in 1955

My father with the ill-fated
jockey, Micky Lynn, and Son Of
Marie at Worcester

The best chaser I ever rode – Caduval winning at
Wincanton in 1963

Winning the Amateur's Derby at Epsom on Mr Jock Whitney's Playroom

Two old-timers, Ross Poldark and me, leading the field over Bechers Brook in the Foxhunters at Aintree in 1983

The record-breaking 1961 team – the only Cambridge University rugby XV to win all its matches. The full back top left

Emma and I at our wedding on 25 August 1969

My mother-in-law, Priscilla, with Emmsie Jane, at the wedding

Emma's father,
Peter Hastings-
Bass, on his
hack, Pat

Below: My
favourite
cousin, Sheila,
with her
youngest
daughter, Flora

My Uncle Ivor
with his wife,
Polly

Keystone Press Agency

Uncle Ivor's only son,
David Balding

My whole family at Gail's wedding. From left to right:
Emma, my step-father Martin Quirk, Robin, my mother,
me, Gail and David, Sue, Caro and Toby

John Hallum leading in Mill Reef after the Derby in 1971

Below: Mill Reef (ridden by G. Lewis) beating Linden Tree and Irish Ball in the 1971 Derby at Epsom

Queen Elizabeth The Queen Mother with myself, Paul and Bunny Mellon after Mill Reef's victory in the King George VI and Queen Elizabeth Stakes at Ascot in 1971

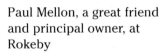

Paul Mellon, a great friend and principal owner, at Rokeby

Mill Reef and Geoff Lewis winning the King George VI and Queen Elizabeth at Ascot. 'Daylight was second'!

Clare just before her
second birthday,
with Mill Reef as a
patient after his
injury

Clare on Frank, me on
Paintbox and Andrew on
Raffles at a Berks and
Bucks Draghounds meet
at Kingsclere

The memory of one incident that happened that winter still amuses me; somehow it was typical of life at Fyfield. Our Uncle Barney had rung Toby (a very rare occurrence) and said that one of his very favourite girls was coming over from America for a short holiday with her parents, and he had told her that she must stop in at Fyfield and have a ride. Her name was Anne Lapham; Uncle Barney said she was one of his better riders and as she was 'special' would we please look after her really well! I think that my big brother had forgotten about her wanting to ride until she arrived dressed in breeches and boots and a very smart tweed jacket, together with her parents. Old Milk Shake, who was now retired but used daily as a hack and a general schoolmaster, was quickly saddled up for her and I was told to go with her, look after her and give her a good time.

The only problem was that the horse I was to ride was recovering from leg trouble and I had firm instructions that I was not to go out of a trot. Anne, who was about eighteen, was certainly not unattractive and was good company; I noticed that she rode, as many Americans tend to, with both stirrup leathers and rein rather too long – too long, at least, when riding a racehorse. I had decided we would go to the summer gallop at Kimpton Down, which was no more than a mile away, and then go trotting and hacking up on the army land just beyond our boundary. We trotted all the way up the road and just before we got to the gallop I got Anne to stop and pull her leathers up two or three holes, explaining that she would find it easier like that to hold Milk Shake at a canter. As I was going to be following up slowly behind her I told her in detail exactly where the gallop went and what she should do if by any remote chance Milk Shake was too strong for her.

As soon as we got off the road on to the grass, dear old Milk Shake knew he was in charge and took off at a fairly good gallop. I had told Anne to swing right at the top of the hill, where she would have about five furlongs in which to pull him up before the end of the gallop if by any chance he was going too strong. Meanwhile, with some concern for the young lady I was supposed to be looking after, I obediently trotted to the top of the hill and then right-handed towards the far end of the gallop. We used to have a chain about three to four feet high which went the full width right at the end of the gallop to divide it from the army land, and I was hoping to see them waiting for me there.

When I got to the chain and there was still no sign of Anne or Milk Shake I began to worry seriously. I undid the chain, went through, got back on my horse and in dread went searching for them. Still at a trot I went a good mile and a half into army land before I finally spotted our lovely old Milk Shake stationary, head down, picking grass; but at that distance to my horror there appeared to be no sign of his rider. I now began shouting for Anne and at last, about a hundred yards before I got to Milk Shake, I heard her voice – coming from the middle of a big gorse bush! To my amazement she was laughing rather than crying. I got off and pulled her out. Apparently Milk Shake had jumped the chain at speed and looked like jumping this large gorse bush as well when at the last moment he had ducked out and sent Anne straight on to land on her back in the middle of the bush!

Once I had them reunited – Milk Shake by now looking very pleased with himself – I took no chances and we walked nearly all the way home. Then, as we passed our schooling field, only about three hundred yards from the stable, I stupidly said to Anne, 'Look, he is such a brilliant jumper – and you haven't really had much fun – if you would like to just jump three hurdles you can do so – and there is an enormous hedge only seventy yards beyond the last hurdle, so if by any remote chance he is going too fast just steer him straight at the hedge and he will have no option but to pull up!' Anne could not resist the challenge. Milk Shake jumped the three hurdles brilliantly, never looked like pulling up at the big hedge and swerved sharply left-handed to avoid running into it. Anne went straight on over his neck and once again ended upside down, this time in the hedge. I was so concerned that Milk Shake should not arrive back at the yard riderless that I made sure I caught him before attending to my young companion. Happily Anne was unhurt and to her credit was still laughing as I legged her up for a second time.

We arrived back at the yard, no less than two and half hours after we had set off, to find her parents waiting anxiously at the front door; even Toby looked concerned. As Anne ran up to them beaming with pleasure and telling them what a fantastic time she had had, I suddenly noticed the green stains all down the back of her jacket and breeches. She turned round and gave me a big kiss and profuse thanks. As she did so, her parents also must have noticed the stains and as horror spread all over their faces I could see exactly what was going through their minds! And for once in my life I was innocent . . .

Towards the end of that winter of 1963–4 Herbert Blagrave telephoned me to say that Peter Hastings-Bass, who was a nephew of his wife Gwen and a well-known Flat trainer at Kingsclere, would like me to get in touch with him. I had actually met him – after a fashion – once before, and not in the most propitious circumstances. I had ridden a point-to-point winner on a useful mare called Landrail belonging to Mrs Joan Makin (Peter Makin's mother), who lived in the village of Kingsclere. The one time I had been to ride her beforehand I was late as usual and came flying over the top of the hill in my car a mile south of the village doing about eighty miles an hour – to see straight ahead of me a string of racehorses walking up the track beside the main road with the trainer on his hack out in the middle of the road desperately waving me down. I was going so fast I thought I would do less harm by keeping going than by braking suddenly. As I went by at speed, I was just able to recognise Peter Hastings-Bass and to hear the oaths that were coming in my direction. Once past, I looked in my mirror and saw to my relief that none of the string had even whipped around.

It was only a couple of weeks after this that I responded to the summons. Fortunately, he had not remembered the incident or even recognised me, and now just said, 'Don't worry, it happens all the time.' Then he explained why he'd wanted to see me. He had not been well, and his doctor had advised him to get an assistant who could do most of the work for him during the summer months. He had given it a lot of thought, he said, and having talked to Herbert Blagrave had decided that he wanted me; how soon could I start? This was a bombshell. I quickly explained my current circumstances and said I would discuss it with my family and let him know as soon as I could.

Initially I was very excited – here was a serious trainer with a big Flat stable and some of the best owners in the land as his patrons. I explained to Toby and Mum that it was only for the summer months in any case, and that this was an opportunity for one of us to get experience with high-class Flat horses, and that in time it might benefit us all. Toby said I shouldn't go until the end of the National Hunt season and we all reached an uneasy agreement that I would go to Kingsclere towards the end of March, at the start of the 1964 Flat season.

I was not to know that this would turn out to be the most important change of direction in my life.

7

Kingsclere

I arrived at Park House feeling excited but a bit anxious about my new challenge. Peter Hastings had been a godson of the wealthy baronet of brewing renown, Sir William Bass. This gentleman, who had no son or other direct heir, had told Peter that if he took on the name of Bass he would inherit a good deal of his money. Peter very sensibly assumed the name of Hastings-Bass by deed poll and in 1953, with his godfather's legacy, bought the whole of the fifteen-hundred-acre estate at Kingsclere. This comprised Park House itself, the stables (two yards, with fifty-five boxes), approximately ten cottages, about two hundred acres of farmland on the eastern side of the road near the stables, an eleven-hundred-acre farm on the other side of the road, and finally two hundred acres of summer downland gallops a mile away at the top of the hill.

Peter Hastings-Bass himself had been an outstanding all-round athlete, distinguishing himself particularly at rugby: he had been good enough to get a couple of wartime caps for England playing at fly half. He had been too big to ride in races himself, but his father Aubrey Hastings had been a supreme jockey/trainer at Wroughton and had trained three Grand National winners, one of which (Ascetic's Silver) he had ridden himself.

Peter's wife Priscilla (formerly Bullock) was a grand-daughter of the famous owner, the 17th Earl of Derby. (She rather stubbornly refused ever to assume her husband's full name, insisting that she had married Peter *Hastings*.) They had four children: William, the eldest son; Emma, their only daughter; then Simon, and finally, a few years later, John. Peter's mother Win Hastings – an absolute gem of a lady and the younger sister of Gwen Blagrave – lived in a fine house at the top of the hill called the Lynches, which overlooked the whole property. Park House itself was enormous. The family's lovely old nanny (Minnie Fuller) lived in the house, as did Mrs Paddy the cook, in a flat on the top floor. There was also a butler we all called 'Stampy' (Jack Stamp), who lived with his family in one of the many cottages on the place. There were two full-time gardeners and a couple of daily ladies who came in to clean every morning: the whole place was immaculate. Overall, it was a very different and rather smarter set-up than I was used to. I was at once flabbergasted by the beauty of the place and rather surprised that I had never heard about it.

Peter insisted that I live in the house as one of the family and everyone was incredibly kind and welcoming. Even Nanny Fuller and old Mrs Paddy – the widow of a former travelling head lad at Wroughton – seemed to accept me. The children were all away at school when I arrived – William and Simon at Winchester, Emma at Downe House and John still at prep school. The only member of the family I had previously met was Emma, who was my little sister Gail's best friend. They had become great mates at a girls' prep school owned and run by Lady Tryon at Great Durnford near Salisbury. Emma had visited Gail on several occasions and even stayed with us at Weyhill, and I had noticed then that she was a girl of considerable character.

Peter Hastings-Bass employed a lot of lads (hardly any girls); rather like in my father's day at Weyhill, they only looked after two horses each. There was a serious round at evening stables when the trainer inspected every horse closely and the lads almost stood to attention as they presented their horses. At Fyfield we were not used to that sort of formality. The old head lad Charlie Moore was very much the boss's man and not unnaturally was never over-friendly with me, but with most of the others I got on extremely well.

Peter was meticulous in his planning. On the evenings before work mornings (always Wednesdays and Saturdays) he would spend at least an hour and a half on the 'list', arranging all the horses to gallop in twos and threes, always keeping the same age groups together and the colts separate from the fillies. He knew the exact weight of every work rider, and was very particular about the weights the horses carried in their workouts. Having looked through the racing calendars beforehand and planned where each horse was going to run, he then organised the work accordingly. Mostly he liked to give a horse its main gallop about ten days before its race, and in that gallop it would cover pretty well the same distance it was going to run over. As the race got nearer, so the horse would cover a shorter distance but go a little faster.

All of this was new to me and fascinating. Both Herbert Blagrave and Toby had work mornings rather at their own whim and organised the gallops, with the various races just in their minds, each morning as the horses were walking around. If I had to put a finger on the difference, I would say that Peter Hastings-Bass trained his horses according to a highly regulated and sound method, whereas Herbert and Toby did it more by instant flair. Training racehorses, however, is not a precise art, and the end result was probably the same.

I am sure that some trainers are very good at preparing a horse for a particular race. Others may excel at choosing the right race in the first place. What is certain, however, is that unless a horse is right in itself – that is, free from any respiratory or other problem – it will not perform at its best. When the horses in the yard are all well in themselves, then the trainer should run them as often as he can.

I watched everything Peter did very carefully and he explained to me in detail why he did certain things. Priscilla drove him out to the gallops every day, but having been told by him exactly what all the horses were to do, I would then give the lads their instructions. (On work days, of course, there was a written list with every detail on it which went out with the slate, so that the lads knew not only what they were riding but who they were paired up with and what distance they were going before they even saddled up their horses.) Peter was getting progressively less mobile, and almost from the beginning of the season I was driving to all the race meetings, saddling the horses and dealing with the owners who were present. Except for the big races which were shown on the BBC there was no television then, so each time I got home I was required to give Peter a detailed report on the race and how I thought our jockey had ridden, and even the state of the ground. After we had talked, he would ring the owners himself and give them the news. Sometimes if he was not feeling well enough Priscilla would do this, and occasionally he would even ask me to.

It was not long before I realised that Peter must be seriously ill. I was never told anything about his condition, but I recognised that ghastly yellow colour of his skin and drew my own gloomy conclusions. I had been at Kingsclere less than three months when, in early June, Peter died. Once again I could scarcely believe how quickly the dreaded cancer had done its deadly work. Naturally I was shocked and saddened, because in the short time I had known Peter I had come to admire and respect him enormously. Above all, I felt intense sympathy for Priscilla and their young family. Ironically, Peter was forty-two – the exact age at which his father had died, from a heart attack after a game of polo.

I had no idea at the time, and certainly Priscilla never told me, but I rather suspect that even when Peter first interviewed me he was probably aware of what was wrong with him and that he might not be with us for very long. The manner in which he explained everything he did so precisely to me, and also encouraged me gradually to talk to some of the owners myself, suggested that perhaps he hoped I would be there for more than just the summer months we had agreed upon.

I had come to a place with a long and distinguished racing pedigree, and already I was taking great pains to get acquainted with the whole property, especially the gradient and contours of all the many different gallops up on the downs. I was still playing regular first-class rugby for Bath, and by running up all the various gallops I was keeping fit as well as getting to know them. On a less energetic level, I read the book written by John Porter himself – the great trainer who initially made Kingsclere famous – and became fascinated by the history of the place.

Sir Joseph Hawley, a colourful figure of the Victorian racing era, had been the first owner of the property. He had a stable built out of converted farm buildings up on the hill at nearby Cannon Heath Down, where he employed the young John Porter as his private trainer. Porter himself found the location too cold for the horses to flourish and in 1867 persuaded Hawley to build a new stable in the valley below, about half a mile outside the village of Kingsclere. This small yard of thirteen boxes, with a hayloft above and a tiny trainer's house attached to one side, is now known as the John Porter yard.

Eight years after appointing Porter as his trainer, Hawley died and – no doubt partly in gratitude for Blue Gown's triumph in the 1868 Derby – generously included a clause in his will giving the young trainer an option to purchase the estate for £4,000 – half of what it had originally cost. The ambitious John Porter, who was rapidly becoming the leading trainer of his day, exercised the option and set about transforming the yard into a model of its type. Over the next twenty years the two main yards, which exist almost untouched today, gradually came into being. Park House itself was built in 1887, and the superb hostel for the lads, attached to the main yard, was completed two years later.

John Porter's success as a trainer is legendary. By the time he retired in 1905 he had trained the winners of twenty-three Classics, including seven Derbies, and three of those had won the Triple Crown. In 1885 he sent out a two-year-old called Ormonde belonging to the Duke of Westminster to win the Dewhurst Stakes in his final start that season. He won the Triple Crown the following season and remained unbeaten throughout his career. Ormonde and his regular jockey Fred Archer are two of the greatest names in the history of the Turf – as of course was the trainer himself. John Porter must have been a man of great vision because besides carving out a beautiful new winding uphill gallop through a valley on Cannon Heath Down especially for his Derby horses, he also founded Newbury racecourse, where a race named in his honour is run to this day. The hostel he built for the lads and their special mess room (now our renowned colour room) showed how much he cared for his staff. St Mary's Church has a window in his honour as well as a magnificent gravestone, so no doubt he was also a regular churchgoer.

The Prince of Wales (later King Edward VII) was one of his many illustrious owners, and John Porter built in brick and tiles a small building in the garden, inside which was a toilet, in case his eminent owner should need the use of it on his journeys around the stables and gardens. It is still with us today, as are many other reminders of my most exalted predecessor.

In 1948 the property was bought by Evan Williams and his wife Gill. Evan, who was to be Emma's godfather, had been the secretary to Ivor Anthony and Win (Granny) Hastings at Wroughton, and had ridden the 1937 Grand National winner Royal Mail. He was a great all-round horseman and as a trainer won the inaugural running of what is now the great midsummer showpiece, the one-and-a-half-mile King George VI and Queen Elizabeth Stakes at Ascot, with a horse called Supreme Court.

In 1953 Peter Hastings, who was a very close friend of Evan, bought the whole property from him and Evan and Gill went to Ireland, where they ran a successful breeding operation at their Knockaney Stud – and where Evan, as Master of the Tipperary Hunt for many years, became renowned as one of the all-time great huntsmen.

By the time he took over at Kingsclere in 1953, Peter Hastings had benefited from a long and thorough apprenticeship at Wroughton under Ivor Anthony (affectionately known as 'the old trainer') and his own mother Win, who played a big part in the set-up. They had had many fine horses there under both codes, including of course the immortal Brown Jack. Over the following decade until his untimely death Peter had established himself as one of the rising talents in the training ranks, winning major handicaps such as the Cambridgeshire, the Royal Hunt Cup and the Stewards Cup. He had also won the July Cup at Newmarket with the flying grey filly Secret Step.

That spring of 1964 our campaign had started well enough and Priscilla told me that all the owners had indicated that they would like me to stay on at least until the end of the Flat season. The Jockey Club issued me with a temporary licence and suddenly the horses were running under the name of I. A. Balding as trainer.

This made me responsible to some illustrious people. The previous autumn, the Queen had for the first time sent six yearlings to Park House, and happily Peter had trained one winner for her before he died – a little chestnut filly called Planta Genista. Even apart from Her Majesty, Peter's list of owners read like an international *Who's Who*. There was Paul Mellon, the American millionaire philanthropist; the Earl of Sefton, who had been the Senior Steward of the Jockey Club; Colonel the Hon. Julian Berry, whose family owned the *Daily Telegraph*, the Earl Cadogan, another member of the Jockey Club who owned a sizeable portion of London; Mrs John Rogerson, a member of the famous Joel family; and certainly not least, the wealthy and influential Canadian business mogul Bud McDougald.

And then, of course, there were the horses. Peter was well aware that there was one very high-class two-year-old in the yard that he would be passing on to my care. Silly Season, a son of the great Greentree stallion Tom Fool, had been bred by his owner Paul Mellon and in a first run full of promise he had finished second in the Salisbury Stakes over five furlongs in May. His next target, I knew, was always going to be the Coventry Stakes at Royal Ascot, so there we duly went. I was lucky enough that we had two or three other horses good enough to run at the Royal Meeting, and to everyone's astonishment we had two winners there less than three weeks after I had taken over the licence! Silly Season won the Coventry Stakes narrowly, and Linnet Lane, a six-year-old mare bred and owned by Priscilla herself, won the Bessborough Stakes. Our young stable jockey Geoff Lewis, with whom I had already become very friendly, rode them both.

It was, of course, a dream start – but if I had any delusions of grandeur I was soon put in my place by a senior trainer called Ryan Jarvis whom I knew to be also a great rugby enthusiast. He said to me, 'I hope you realise just how bloody lucky you are. I have been training for over twenty years and never managed so far to have a winner at Royal Ascot, and here you are – been doing it for ten minutes and you've had two!'

Almost at once Priscilla was saying that I would have to stay on at Kingsclere on a permanent basis. When I replied that I still had family obligations at Fyfield she simply said, 'Well, I will just have to sell the place then at the end of the year.' This led to some difficult conversations with my mother and brother. I knew that Toby, though possibly annoyed, could manage perfectly well without me, and that once I had finished riding there probably wouldn't be room for both of us at Fyfield in any case. My mother, however, gave me a much harder time. She said that if I didn't come back it would mean not only breaking up the two newly formed companies, but more importantly her selling up and moving back to America – in which case she would take Robin and Gail, then aged seventeen and fifteen, back there with her. I realised that there was perhaps a touch of emotional blackmail going on, but at the same time I was genuinely concerned for Robin and Gail, who as far as I knew had no real wish to live in America.

From a personal point of view I knew that if I stayed on as the trainer at Kingsclere it would mean the end of my riding career. The Jockey Club had rather an archaic rule at the time which stated that a professional trainer could only ride as an amateur on a horse he owned himself. To ride as a professional was acceptable, but mainly because of my weight I had never wanted to do that. So embarking on a training career now would mean the end of my ambition to be the leading amateur rider, and especially to ride in the Grand National. This to me was a major negative.

Race riding of any kind is still the most exciting sport in which I have taken part. For a steeplechase jockey there can be no better sensation than coming into a fence at speed on a good jumper knowing you are meeting it on the right stride. Squeezing your horse to stand off and passing others in the air before landing way out the far side of the fence is a joy that would be difficult to surpass. Riding a winner over fences is extra special because not only has one savoured the thrill of jumping all those fences, one's competitive instinct is only truly satisfied by winning. I knew I was quite good at it; and the thought of losing all that, before I had even reached my best, was a private agony.

I had never been very good at making decisions. Here was the most important one that I had ever faced, and I was already prevaricating. Finally, Priscilla said that I would have to make a definite decision by the end of August, as the owners needed to know by then what they would be doing with their yearlings.

For the Glorious Goodwood meeting at the end of July, Peter and Priscilla had for many years stayed with the Duke and Duchess of Norfolk at Arundel Castle. I had got to know their four daughters and had ridden a point-to-point winner for Anne, the eldest, at Larkhill a year or two before then. Nevertheless I was pleasantly surprised when I was invited to go with Priscilla and stay at Arundel for the five-day meeting that summer.

It was the custom at that time for the Queen and Prince Philip to stay during the Goodwood meeting with the Norfolks at Arundel one year and with the Duke and Duchess of Richmond at Goodwood House the next; and it happened that in 1964 they were staying at Arundel. Although I was training six two-year-olds for the Queen I had not yet met her, and I guessed that Priscilla and Lavinia (the Duchess), who were close friends, decided that it would be an ideal opportunity. I found the Queen to be delightful and very easy, and somewhat to my surprise Prince Philip was also particularly friendly. At tea one day he took me aside for a chat and casually said to me, 'I gather you have rather a tricky decision to make very shortly.' I replied that it was particularly difficult because while I realised what a great opportunity and tremendous challenge it would be to take over at Kingsclere on the one hand, I had a potentially serious rift with my whole family to face on the other; and he encouraged me to explain the whole conundrum to him in detail. He listened with great understanding and even sympathy, but ended up by saying: 'It would be very sad for our country if all our bright young men failed to accept the challenges that come their way.' It meant a great deal to me that he had taken the trouble to discuss the whole situation with me; and judging from his final sentence, I had to assume that the Queen herself was keen for me to stay on.

We had a winner at the meeting – my very first, of course, at Goodwood – when a very useful gelding of Paul Mellon called Early To Rise won the Chesterfield Cup. It is a strange fact, but one that all trainers will recognise, that sometimes a single opportune winner can appear to make all the difference to one's life! This for me was the one; together with Prince Philip's advice, it tipped the balance, and I made my decision there and then to stay on at Kingsclere. Later that year, when Silly Season won the Dewhurst Stakes at Newmarket, I knew we had a potential Two Thousand Guineas horse and that I would have been foolish not to have accepted my challenge.

My first full year in 1965 went so well, in fact, that I might have been forgiven for thinking that training racehorses was an easy business. With no more than fifty-five horses in the yard we ended the season with forty-three winners and over £70,000 in prize money – which meant that I finished second in the trainers' table behind only Paddy Prendergast, the Irish maestro.

Geoff Lewis had ridden well over thirty of those winners, and a young apprentice we had called Ernie Johnson had impressed even Lord Sefton by winning a nice race at York for him. We notched up ten victories for the Queen, including one at Ascot in the autumn, and a certain four-year-old gelding of Paul Mellon called Morris Dancer won on no fewer than seven races.

Our star, of course, was Silly Season, who got us off to a good start, comfortably winning the Greenham Stakes at Newbury in April to become favourite for the Two Thousand Guineas. At Newmarket he finished an unlucky second to Niksar, and I feel that if Geoff could have ridden the race again a few years later he might well have won it. Silly Season was entered in the Derby and Paul Mellon, never having previously had a runner in the premier Classic, was understandably keen to run. The horse patently did not stay and finished in midfield behind the great Sea Bird, but Geoff wisely looked after him and he did not have a hard race.

Silly Season next ran in the St James's Palace Stakes at Royal Ascot, and Geoff asked me beforehand if I minded if he let the colt bowl along in front rather than struggle to hold him in behind. I encouraged him to do so and he made all, just holding on to win in a photo-finish. After a couple of disappointing races Silly Season came back to his best and under a brilliant waiting ride from behind Geoff won the very valuable and prestigious Champion Stakes at Newmarket, with the Two Thousand Guineas winner Niksar well behind him in third place. Paul Mellon was over from America to see him triumph; and we also won the premier two-year-old fillies race the Cheveley Park Stakes with a temperamental lady of his called Berkeley Springs. It was only her second start.

For an absolutely top-class horse, which Silly Season was, he was inconsistent, and I am certain now that in some of the bad races he ran he was in considerable pain. We knew that he was a 'rig' – a colt one of whose testicles has not fully descended into the scrotum – and sometimes, particularly when that errant ball (which is often much smaller than the other) is trapped in the canal just above the scrotum rather than being right up in the abdomen, it can be pinched when galloping and cause severe discomfort. Nowadays vets know much more about the problem and can easily remove the offending organ – with dramatic results, as was proved with Selkirk many years later.

It did not help Silly Season that he was looked after by one of the worst-tempered lads I have ever employed – and that I did not have enough nerve at that early stage to change this lad as soon as I should have. Like most high-class horses, Silly Season was keen to get on with the job and pulled hard. His lad had poor hands and, whenever I wasn't looking, would yank the horse around; when cantering, he always had the colt's head pulled over to one side so he could hold him. Much too late – with hindsight – I asked Reg Corfield, one of the best horsemen in the yard, to take over the riding of our 'star'. Reg couldn't hold one side of him, and I had no option but to put his original lad back on him. All this made the colt a very tough ride on the course for Geoff.

Silly Season's four-year-old season started with an impressive win in the Lockinge Stakes at Newbury, but that was followed by near misses at Royal Ascot and in the Sussex Stakes, and another comfortable victory at Newbury, this time in the Hungerford Stakes over seven furlongs, was his only other visit to the winner's enclosure in 1966. His career ended with another frustrating second to the highly regarded ex-American colt Hill Rise, superbly ridden by Lester Piggott in the Queen Elizabeth II Stakes at Ascot, after which he went to stand at Richard Stanley's New England

Stud, where he was a pretty successful stallion, particularly of broodmares.

Silly Season was a brilliant miler but a difficult colt to train and ride. My feeling now is that if he had come along later in both Geoff's and my careers, when we had more experience, he could have been a great horse. I remember saying to Paul Mellon something about how sad I was that we had not achieved with Silly Season what I felt we should have done, and that I doubted if I would ever have a better horse to train. I recall his emphatic reply quite clearly: 'Oh yes, of course you will.' Beneath the man's gentle modesty I could glimpse a touch of ambition and determination!

After that golden start in 1964, my second year soon taught me about the ups and downs of racing. Apart from Silly Season's near misses, Berkeley Springs was narrowly beaten in the One Thousand Guineas and was second again in the Oaks. There was, however, one gelding of Paul Mellon's who was fast becoming a Kingsclere legend. This was Morris Dancer, who in 1965 and 1966 won a total of thirteen races and in both years acted as Silly Season's main lead horse on serious work days as well. Then in 1967 he himself became the yard star, winning at Royal Ascot and going to France a month later to win the Prix Messidor. Morris Dancer was perhaps the prophet for what was shortly to be Paul Mellon's and Kingsclere's messiah.

I got on very well with Priscilla, who devoted all her time and energy to trying to help and generally make life easier for the young trainer. She would share the driving to the races and the phone calls to the owners. While she never interfered with the actual training of the horses, she was always out watching what went on, especially on work days, and would discuss with me at length running plans for all the horses. It probably did my relationship with her no harm that over the next couple of years two more good horses that she had bred herself were to win at Royal Ascot. Sharavogue won the King George V Handicap and then, only four years after Silly Season, we won the Coventry Stakes again with Murrayfield – a very useful dark brown colt by Herbert Blagrave's good stallion Match III who stood at Harwood Stud.

Over these first few years, too, I was getting to know all the owners much better, and apart from being somewhat in awe of Lord Sefton, who was never very cosy, I found them very pleasant and simple to deal with. They all seemed to accept me much more readily than I had expected.

Life was made a good deal more interesting for me when in 1966 Herbert Blagrave actually gave me my old friend Milo. After I moved to Fyfield, Herbert had sent him back to Bob Turnell's and, while winning the odd chase, he had never really fulfilled his potential so Herbert decided he should come to me. In fact, it was probably the right move for Milo as he enjoyed the few days of qualifying we did with the Vine and Craven Hunt, and when I started hunter-chasing him in 1967 as a twelve-year-old he thrived on the excitement.

The gift of Milo was not only a very kind and generous gesture from Herbert, who had taken personal pleasure in the part he had played in getting me to Kingsclere and was much enjoying my early success; it also made all the difference to my riding prospects. Suddenly I owned my own horse and could thus continue my amateur career, albeit in just three or four races in the spring before our Flat season really started. Milo never really stayed three miles and at that time there were several decent two-and-a-half-mile hunter chases. We won such a race at Sandown in February 1967 and went on three weeks later to win another hunter chase over that distance at Ascot. There was a price to be paid for this fun, of course: with my enforced temporary break from race riding I had put on quite a bit of weight, so I now began the unpleasant ritual of losing a stone or more each spring for the hunter chase/point-to-point season. This was to go on until I finally hung up my breeches and boots twenty years later in 1987.

Priscilla and I had been back to stay at Arundel each year for Goodwood and I had got to know the family well. They were all superb hosts, and I was very fond of all four of the daughters – in fact, I had fairly serious romances with two of them, first Mary and then Sarah. So I probably deserved the somewhat embarrassing challenge the Duchess levelled at me one day in Goodwood week 1968. All the members of the house party, including the Queen and Prince Philip, had returned to the castle from the races and were having tea in the lovely drawing room, which sits high up in the castle looking south over the River Arun. There were probably twenty-five people in the room – everyone important names in the world of racing – and suddenly all of them heard above the chatter the somewhat shrill tones of Lavinia, Duchess of Norfolk. With a big smile on her face she said, 'Well now, Ian, come on – which of my four daughters are you going to marry? I don't mind which one, but hurry up and get on with it!'

She was not to know, of course, but a more lasting romance had been budding at Park House: I had fallen in love with Emma, the young daughter of the household. More than that, I had been to America to see my mother, who had returned there in 1965, and had warned her that a marriage could well be on the cards shortly. My younger sister Gail in particular was extremely excited at the prospect of her best friend marrying her older brother. Only one small problem remained: I had not yet asked Emma! Fortunately, when I returned from my travels and eventually posed the all-important question, she consented. Although only twenty, she already had wisdom well beyond her years; but I doubt if she realised then just what she was taking on!

Our wedding, on 25 August 1969, was probably as much fun as anyone's own wedding can be. The service was at St Mary's, the lovely old Norman church in the village, and Emma's eldest brother, William, guided her up the aisle. A lot of my old Cambridge chums came – including the Revd Alan Godson, who assisted at the service, which was conducted by the Bishop of Winchester. Toby, of course, was my best man, as I had been at his wedding. I had decided that we would fly off after the reception from Newbury racecourse, in a little plane lent to us by Dick Francis. Piloted by Alan Biltcliffe (who later flew Willie Carson everywhere), it would take us to our honeymoon destination – unknown, naturally, to my bride.

Being something of a cheapskate and also obsessed by not wanting to miss too many days' racing (it was, after all, the middle of the season), I had asked my old friend Perry Eliot if he had any ideas about a suitable and secluded spot in England where we could stay for three or four days. Straight away he had come up with the perfect solution by inviting us down to Port Eliot as his guests. In fact, he had arranged for us to take over the top floor of his local pub, feeling it would be more private for us than actually staying with him – and he even had the kindness to have a large double bed moved in for us. We had access to his private beach, which was beautiful, and the three-day break in Cornwall would have been entirely blissful had I not got pretty seasick when we were taken shark fishing. Perry's large estate at St Germans was lovely, and it was refreshing to see how popular the young landlord was with all his tenants. Precisely three days later we flew back and landed at Bath racecourse in time to saddle our first runner there.

A wedding of a different kind had played a major part in the life of the Balding family a few months earlier that year. My big brother Toby had trained his first Grand National winner – a fine old chaser called Highland Wedding. We had all hoped he would win the great race in both the two previous years, when I had made a point of going to Aintree. This time, however, I had decided to play rugger for Newbury that particular Saturday afternoon in April. Once the race had started, every time I could get my hands on the ball I booted it miles into touch so that before the game continued I could stop for a few moments and listen to the commentary that one of the spectators on the touchline had going on his radio. As soon as I could after the game I dashed up to Aintree to join Emma and the others in the post-race celebrations, feeling guilty that I had not been there for the race itself. It was a momentous occasion for Toby and his family. The horse himself was a special friend who had been at Fyfield for five or six years and had always threatened to win this great race; he was ridden by the trainer's good chum Edward Patrick Harty; and one of the owners, Charles Burns, was also a long-standing friend. Toby, of course, was to have a second Grand National winner twenty years later when Little Polveir, ridden by Jimmy Frost, won in 1989.

Emma had been left some money by her father and fortunately it was just enough to buy The Lynches, where Granny Hastings had been living. She was only too happy to move down to a much smaller house just across the garden from Park House. The

Lynches, built in the 1930s, was certainly not aesthetically beautiful – but what was special about it was that it was high up on the hill with a stunning view south over the whole stable, the gallops and the stud complex. It was also very private, with quite a large garden. Emma always loved it up there, and it was certainly a wonderful place to have dogs and ponies and to bring up young children.

We soon bought the twenty acres behind The Lynches between us and the village. It was grassland owned by a local farmer, and I inherited his six young bullocks at the same time. The land was poorly fenced at that stage and these wretched cattle seemed to get into more people's gardens than one would have thought possible. Once we had sold the cattle – who in a very short time had made the local trainer a very unpopular farmer – I decided with my vast agricultural knowledge that it would do the old grass the world of good to be burned off. I started the fire at the far eastern end of the land, thinking it would burn better with the wind behind it, heading downhill towards the road. Once again my farming know-how and even my common sense were slightly at fault because before we knew what was happening the smoke and fire were heading rapidly down to the main road. Almost at once, it seemed, there was mayhem just outside the village, with cars screeching to a halt in the dense smoke – and suddenly the fire alarms were going and police arriving at our front door. I was extremely lucky there was not an accident and that no official action was taken – but again farmer Balding was not the most popular man in the village!

Having already spent what money she had on our new house, Emma often reminds me that my most generous wedding present to her was my old horse Milo, whom she much enjoyed riding – on the few occasions she was allowed to. She reckons that it was indicative of how our marriage was to be when the next time he ran in a race she found that, somewhat to her surprise, he was still running in my name and colours. Naturally he was also to be ridden by Mr I. A. Balding!

In the short time that I had been at Park House I had already started a love affair with the place. Although there was later an opportunity to move, I knew then that I would never want to train anywhere else. I had also made up my mind that any money earned from the training business would be rapidly ploughed back into the property in order to maintain and improve it. I secretly longed to be able to buy it one day.

I knew that we would never have the use of the millions of pounds that were to be spent on places like Manton, Ballydoyle and Jackdaws Castle, but Kingsclere for me has always been the finest place that a racehorse and his trainer could live. And for some strange reason its beauty has always remained one of the best-kept secrets of all.

There have been countless times when horses have run badly or been injured and I have come back from the races thoroughly depressed. On these occasions I would always hurry the dogs into the back of the car and drive up the hill to Watership Down. We would go for a walk on those gallops and very soon I would be forgetting my worries and thanking God for the privilege of living in such a beautiful place and realising how incredibly fortunate I was.

8

Mill Reef and Paul Mellon

There was something exciting about the way Paul Mellon had corrected me quickly when I had suggested we might never get a better horse than Silly Season. I was aware, of course, that he had already bred champions in the USA of the quality of Quadrangle, Arts And Letters and Fort Marcy, and I felt it was perhaps only a question of time before he would supply us with a star. As is so often the case in racing, however, no one could have guessed that the small bay colt who arrived in the draft of yearlings from America in the autumn of 1969 would turn out to be the one. By the speedy and popular stallion Never Bend out of a mare named Milan Mill who had not won a race, he possessed the remarkable Nasrullah/Princequillo nick which had already been so successful in North America. Mill Reef was the name Paul Mellon had chosen for him, after the luxurious club next door to his winter home in Antigua.

Of our many good stable lads in the yard at that time there was one who had not been with us as long as some of the others but had already impressed me enormously. His name was John Hallum. He had served his apprenticeship with Peter Nelson, but after a spell out of racing he and his wife Audrey had fortunately picked Kingsclere as the place to pick up the threads again. I had particularly admired the way John had handled Morris Dancer, who was far from easy either to ride or to groom, and so gave him the choice of the three colts arriving from Paul Mellon's Rokeby Farm that November. Happily for all concerned, John chose the small bay rather than the much bigger and superbly bred chestnut called Quantico whom Elliot Burch, P.M.'s American trainer, had been particularly sad to see go to England. Mill Reef and John were to forge a partnership between man and horse which was as happy and intimate as any that I have known in my lifetime with horses.

Another piece of good fortune came my way that autumn. Peter Hastings-Bass's old head lad, Charlie Moore, was retiring and my search for a replacement would go no further if I could persuade my big brother that a move for Bill and Anne Palmer from Fyfield to Kingsclere would benefit everyone involved. Bill, of course, had been with our family back at Bishops Cannings, where he was one of Dad's apprentices. Now he had recently retired from race riding for Toby and, as the head lad and travelling head lad jobs at Fyfield were already filled by good men in Buddy Sayers and John Price, Toby considered that there was really no suitable role for Bill there any longer. So it was that at this key moment Bill and Anne, with their three children, came to Kingsclere.

Bill and I had virtually been brought up together at Bishops Cannings, and had ridden together for years at Weyhill and Fyfield; so we were old friends. We thought the same way about horses, about feeding, even about the lads and girls we employed at Kingsclere. It was a happy and successful partnership that was to last until Bill's retirement in 1998. Even now he and Anne live in Troutbeck bungalow; Bill comes in every work day to ride out, and our current head lads are not slow to seek his advice on problems of all kinds.

There are some two-year-olds who straight away impress at home in their early gallops. Sometimes they go on to give great performances on the racecourse, but all too often they turn out to be 'morning glories', never achieving on the racetrack what they show on the gallops. There are others – and I can think of several, with Selkirk in particular springing to mind – who at first look complete goons at home but eventually become champions.

There is only one horse I have handled who at once looked a champion at home and then turned out to be that and more on the racecourse.

We usually start doing a strongish canter with the youngsters who have just turned two in late January or early February, weather permitting. By then they have all done lots of figure-of-eights on their own in the field, walked quietly through the starting stalls and done plenty of 'baby' canters in threes and fours, with one leading one day and another the next.

One such day in February 1970 all the two-year-olds were being exercised in our 'starting gate' field, where the gallop alongside the schooling fences is about four furlongs long. It goes gently uphill for about two and a half furlongs, bears right-handed and finishes slightly downhill by a gate in the corner of the field. I had told John Hallum, who was riding Mill Reef, to lead his group and to go just that 'half stride' faster. I watched him carefully and noticed the beautiful easy action as the horse lengthened his stride effortlessly up the hill and, hard held by John, gradually eased slightly as he came down towards the gate. I looked back and suddenly noticed the three colts behind him being pushed along fairly vigorously by their riders and seemingly getting further behind the leader. When John came back to me I rather harshly rebuked him for going too fast, repeating that I had told him just to *canter*. I will always remember his reply, 'Guvnor, I *was* only cantering.' That was my first inclination that we might have amongst us something pretty special.

The next auspicious occasion I recall was when Mill Reef did his only serious gallop before his first race at Salisbury in May. We had not had a two-year-old runner yet this year and Mill Reef, being much the most precocious, was to be the first. Both Silly Season and Murrayfield had used the Salisbury Stakes in May as their warm-up before winning the Coventry Stakes at Royal Ascot, and I had decided to take the same route with this colt. He needed one proper gallop on the downs beforehand, so about ten days ahead of the race I arranged to gallop him over four and a half furlongs with another colt of the same age. This was a grey of Paul Mellon called Red Reef, who looked at that stage our next most forward two-year-old. He was to lead, with Mill Reef sitting a couple of lengths behind and joining him at the bend with just over two furlongs, slightly uphill, to run. Joe Bonner, Red Reef's lad, was riding him and John, who was well over a stone heavier, was as usual on his own little colt. The pair joined at the corner and I had asked John at that point to give his horse a good kick in the belly or even a slap down the shoulder for the first time to get him to really stretch out just this once before his race. The result was astonishing: I had never seen anything like it. Mill Reef opened up a gap that widened with every stride he took and at the top, with John struggling to pull him up, he must have been at least twenty-five lengths clear of his galloping companion. It was not just the wide smile on John's face afterwards that delighted me but the grim look on Joe's as he said, 'This one must be bloody useless or else that is a flying machine.' This was a defining moment.

There were eleven runners in the Salisbury Stakes, which was surprising because a horse of Charles Engelhard ridden by Lester, called Fireside Chat, was an odds-on favourite and looked unbeatable. He had been massively impressive in winning his first race at Newmarket. We had told no one about the gallop with Red Reef, and Geoff had never sat on his back, so Mill Reef started at 8–1 that day.

We had only put him through the starting stalls once beforehand and he had come out very slowly. So I said to Geoff in the paddock beforehand: 'This fellow will be slow to start, but we think he is a nice horse, so please look after him. Don't be too surprised if you bustle up the favourite towards the end.'

When the stalls opened Mill Reef flew out and neither Fireside Chat nor the others saw which way he went. He won unextended by four lengths and on dismounting our jockey said to me, with a few of his usual stammers, 'This is for sure the best horse you have had, and I rather suspect he might be the best horse you will ever have!' What a prophetic observation from G. Lewis that was.

After Salisbury Mill Reef did one serious piece of work before Ascot, up our famous Valley Gallop – John Porter's old Derby gallop – which is now six furlongs long. His companion on this occasion was our old warrior Morris Dancer, now aged nine. My remark on the work list in red ink afterwards read 'Mill Reef easily best', and as they were off level weights I knew we had a far better two-year-old than even Silly Season had been at the same stage.

At Royal Ascot Mill Reef looked magnificent. I am sure that John Oaksey will not mind if I borrow here some words from his masterly book, *The Story of Mill Reef.*

> No lover of horses or indeed of beauty in any form will easily forget his first sight of Mill Reef at Royal Ascot. With the possible exception of the 1971 Eclipse I do not believe he ever again came quite so near physical perfection. Though always superbly balanced and with quality etched in every line he often tended afterwards to run up light behind the saddle in hard training. At Ascot his middle piece was so deep and his quarter so round that no lack of scope was apparent. Under the gleaming mahogany coat the muscles of his forearms and second thighs rippled like sleepy snakes and as he danced light-footed round the tree-lined paddock, long ears cocked to the unfamiliar sights and sounds, the blend of explosive power with easy natural grace was unforgettable.

In my view this was as beautiful and accurate a description of our horse as I could imagine – and to think that we had the pleasure of looking at him every day!

The race itself takes little description. Geoff Lewis let his partner bowl along in front, and without ever coming off a tight rein he easily went eight lengths clear at the end – Geoff's only problem was pulling him up afterwards. On fast ground and unextended he was only just outside the track record, and until the Gimcrack two months later I couldn't recall seeing a high-class two-year-old race won so easily.

History relates how My Swallow beat Mill Reef by a short head in the Prix Papin at Maisons-Laffitte a month later. Geoff had felt that the rain-softened ground that day had not helped us. My view was that a restless journey to France and the unfavourable draw on the outside were more contributory factors in the horse's first defeat. But he was nothing if not tough, and despite looking to have lost a lot of weight after a long journey and a hard race, he soon came bouncing back.

I was keen to run him in the Gimcrack Stakes over six furlongs at York just a month later. Not only is it one of the oldest and most prestigious races in the calendar, but I was aware that the owner of the winner is required to make a speech at the celebrated Gimcrack Dinner in December, and P.M. had connections that would make this prospect particularly inviting. He was an old and close friend of Charles, the 2nd Earl of Halifax, chairman of York Racecourse, whose wife, Ruth, was Priscilla Hastings's half-sister. P.M. had moreover hunted with the Middleton, of which Lord Halifax was Master, and had stayed more than once at the Earl's ancestral home, Garrowby. So it was for the Gimcrack that P.M. came to England to see his little superstar run for the first time.

In those days the Gimcrack was run on the third day of the York August meeting. The ground was already on the soft side on the Wednesday and it poured with rain all that night. I went to walk the course on the Thursday morning with some foreboding. As I had feared, the deep hoofprints from the previous day had filled with water, and the turf was as soft as I have ever seen it for Flat racing.

I went to find P.M., who was having lunch with Lord Halifax and the other stewards. I explained that I felt the ground was as deep as I had ever seen it and, bearing in mind Geoff's concern after Maisons-Laffitte, I thought that it was totally unsuitable for our potential champion. I could see the disappointment on his face and so added quickly that as Geoff was riding in the first race we could delay a decision until after that and have a discussion then among the three of us. We would still have time to withdraw the horse if necessary.

I will never forget that three-way discussion. There was Geoff, saying he had never ridden on heavier ground and if by any chance we decided to run he would not in any circumstances pick up his stick. Then there was the trainer, saying that under these conditions he would not even consider running a horse of Mill Reef's quality if he ever happened to own one! Finally, having patiently listened to both of us, P.M. said: 'Well, I appreciate enormously how much you both obviously care for this horse and please don't think it is because I am over to see him for the first time, but I have this funny feeling everything will be all right and that we should run.'

Never was I to be more grateful for an owner's decision. I know that if P.M. had not been there we would have pulled out and almost certainly never run Mill Reef on heavy ground again. Thank God for his presence, because what we saw next will never be forgotten by anyone who was on the Knavesmire that day. Mill Reef led from the start, as was his custom, and as Geoff asked him to pick up the pace from halfway the race quickly became a procession. He forged further and further ahead and was going so strongly at the end that, as at Ascot, it took quite a while to pull him up. I happened to see the judge, John Hancock, afterwards and jokingly said, 'Well, that didn't test you too much' – to which he replied that strangely enough it was a difficult margin to assess because at the post our horse was going so much faster than the others that in another half-furlong he'd have won by twenty rather than the official ten lengths. Our colt's opponents were no slouches, either: Green God, who was second, went on to be champion sprinter the following season and was always happy on soft ground; and Kings Company, who finished a long way back, went on to win the Irish Guineas and the Cork and Orrery on soft ground at Royal Ascot the following year.

A month later Mill Reef won the Imperial Stakes at Kempton narrowly by a neck from a very good filly called Hecla in his least impressive performance to date. I had always believed he was an out-and-out two-year-old performer – judging from both his pedigree and his compact and mature shape – and so his race-a-month programme was to end with the Group I Dewhurst Stakes over seven furlongs at Newmarket in mid-October. This would be his first race over further than six furlongs and both Geoff and I, thinking ahead to his three-year-old season, felt that we should try on this occasion to tuck him in behind during the early stages. In the race, Mill Reef not only settled comfortably in behind his two opponents but went by them down the hill from the Bushes to win easily and impressively by four lengths. He looked every bit as impressive as Nijinsky had in the same race the previous year.

Mill Reef, of course, was not the only rising star of his generation. My Swallow was unbeaten, and because he had won the Prix Papin by a short head was rated a pound above Mill Reef in the Free Handicap. And I was also well aware, of a third top-class colt that season: the unbeaten Brigadier Gerard, who had been rated one pound lower than Mill Reef by the handicapper. To this day, however – biased as it may sound – I still feel that Mill Reef, both in the Coventry on firm ground and in the Gimcrack on heavy ground, was the best two-year-old I have ever seen.

In the 1960s and 1970s all our horses, including the youngsters just turned three, used to do a serious amount of road work for about a six-week period during January and February before we started cantering. Brought up with jumpers, I was a firm believer that the young horse's bones, joints and tendons were all hardened up considerably by this form of exercise. We had a seven-mile circuit that took us up three steepish hills and through the picturesque village of Ecchinswell. It may have seemed a needless risk to take with the Two Thousand Guineas and Derby favourite, but he wore knee boots and we had a hack out in front of the string to slow any traffic virtually to a standstill; and we had no alarms that I recall. With the horses trotting up all the hills and walking down the other side, the whole exercise took about an hour and a half, and in my view put a lot of muscle and hard conditioning on the horses before they started cantering.

Mill Reef then had about three weeks of cantering before starting faster work. My feeling at this stage – which I had, of course, conveyed to P.M. – was that we should make every effort to have him 101 per cent fit for the Two Thousand Guineas. He was naturally entered in the Derby, but whether he would stay a mile and a half or not at that stage was pure conjecture. I was actually telling myself that if we did not win the Two Thousand Guineas with Mill Reef I doubted whether I would ever train an English Classic winner. My plan was to run first in the Greenham Stakes at Newbury over seven furlongs, for which I hoped to have him 95 per cent fit as it was only two weeks to the day before the first colts' Classic. If all went well we would need to do very little with him then to have him spot-on on 1 May.

All did go well, and with Geoff and Mill Reef winning the trial at Newbury comfortably, we were a pretty hot favourite for the big race. But the 1971 Two Thousand Guineas was the most eagerly awaited Classic I can ever recall. My Swallow had also won his trial convincingly over the full mile at Kempton, and the word buzzing around from West Ilsley was that the Brigadier had done a fantastic home gallop with Joe Mercer riding. Apart from the big three, there was Nijinsky's much-heralded full brother Minsky. This colt, also trained by Vincent O'Brien and ridden by Lester Piggott, was unbeaten so far in his two races and he was to be fitted with blinkers for the Guineas. The other two runners, Indian Ruler and Good Bond, were quality horses but rank outsiders in this company.

When P.M. and I looked at our horse in the Links stables at Newmarket at noon on the day of the race he looked stunning. I next saw him in the pre-parade ring, and at this point he looked unusually stirred up. Minsky was walking around behind him and behaving as if he was ready to cover the first mare or anything else he could find. Our little horse was very sensitive and I guessed it was this that was upsetting him. Certainly when I saddled him up he was in an unusually nasty frame of mind and even sweating a bit. But by the time of the parade, even with Minsky directly behind him, all seemed well and although he had 'tucked up a bit' he moved to post quite beautifully as usual.

We were drawn no. 1, on the rail, and My Swallow and Frankie Durr were on the outside at no. 6. I had suggested to Geoff that he stay on the rail; that way, not only would Mill Reef and My Swallow be less likely to take each other on, but Joe on the Brigadier wouldn't have an easy choice as to which of the big two to track. As it happened, after a furlong Geoff drifted over to My Swallow in the middle of the track and Joe was able to settle nicely behind the pair of them. In hindsight our only chance of beating Brigadier Gerard that day would have been to go as fast as we could up the stands rail and hope that over the mile we might outstay our rival or at least dull his great finishing speed. As the race was run, I think that Geoff and Frankie were too concerned about cutting each others' throats, and as a consequence did not go fast enough. The Brigadier went scorching by both of them coming down the hill and came away to win impressively by three lengths. We stayed on up the final hill to beat My Swallow by three-quarters of a length with the other three way behind. On perfect ground the time, although respectable, was nowhere near a record, which it should have been had there been a really strong gallop all the way.

I am not in any way detracting from Brigadier Gerard's brilliant victory. He turned out to be probably the best miler in British turf history, and Mill Reef would almost certainly never have beaten him at that distance. Tactically, however, I feel we played into the opposition's hands. I can recall being more disappointed afterwards than at any other time in my life – I simply could not believe that Mill Reef had been beaten so easily.

I was in much better shape than our jockey, however, who had a crushing fall in the last race of the day which put him in hospital with a pinched nerve in his spine that was causing partial paralysis to both his hands. Geoff had quite rightly accepted the juicy offer of a retainer to the leading trainer of the day, Noel Murless, at the beginning of 1971 – the top job at the time; but he had also managed to negotiate the right to ride Mill Reef in all his races first and foremost. When I visited him in hospital he was able to put on a grin of sorts and said, 'We'll win the Derby, you know – the way he stayed on up that hill – he'll get a mile and a half all right.' I wasn't so sure.

Neither Brigadier Gerard nor My Swallow was ever entered in the Derby, as one mile was clearly felt to be the limit of their stamina. Thus Mill Reef was the only truly outstanding colt that we knew of who was heading for the Epsom Classic. He had come out of the Guineas in his usual way – with no problems, and eager to get on with his next challenge. My dilemma now was how to train him for the most important race of his life so far. Should I gallop him over the full distance at home, to get some idea of whether he would stay or not? Or should I just have him fit and fresh on the day and *hope* that he had sufficient stamina?

I decided to seek advice from the two truly great trainers of the day, both of whom had plenty of experience with Derby horses. First I phoned Noel Murless and asked if I could come and talk to him at Warren Place. He was extremely gracious and helpful. He said that when he had been at Beckhampton as assistant to Fred

Darling (who had trained seven Derby winners) they always galloped their Derby horses over the full mile and a half on their Derby trial ground on the Saturday morning just four days before the big race. To my next question, 'What did you do with them then?', he replied, 'Nothing – just shut them up.' I didn't like to ask exactly what that meant, because I am sure they must have been walked and trotted at least on those next three days. Noel said that he had always followed that same practice in his time at Newmarket.

I didn't go to Ireland, but I had a long phone conversation one evening with my idol and Dad's old friend Vincent O'Brien. In Sir Ivor and Nijinsky he had recently handled two brilliant US-bred Derby winners who were similar in a way to Mill Reef. His method was to gallop them no more than one mile about ten days or a week before the race. He aimed to have them 100 per cent fit, but did not really want to know beforehand if they stayed or not: that he would leave in Lester Piggott's more than capable hands on the big day.

Most of the Fred Darling/Noel Murless Derby horses had been big, strong home-breds with classical English pedigrees who probably went on to run in the St Leger. Mill Reef, I felt, was by contrast much more an O'Brien type of horse; so I decided that we would have our main gallop ten days before the race, as Peter Hastings-Bass would also have done. We have a beautiful round gallop up on Cannon Heath Down, where the mile and a half has similar contours to Epsom. I considered that a mile and a quarter was about the right distance to go, as this had a stretch downhill and a left-handed bend which would give the colt experience over something other than a straight track,

Paul Cook, a fine horseman, had taken over from Geoff as our main jockey that year and Philip Waldron was our up-and-coming apprentice. For this key gallop, Philip was to lead on the useful five-year-old grey gelding Aldie and Paul was to sit second on Bright Beam – a very good ex-Newmarket horse we had bought as a pacemaker for our star. Geoff was to tuck Mill Reef in third a few lengths behind and not join the other two until the final corner with about a furlong and a half to run.

I set them off at the ten-furlong marker and pushed my stop-watch before cantering across to the finish of the gallop on my hack The Brigand. It happened to be a very foggy morning and we could hear the horses coming long before we could see them – the tension was almost unbearable. At last, suddenly I could see one horse on his own only about a hundred yards from us. For a split second my heart sank, because in the fog the horse looked to be grey and I just had time to think, 'Oh God, it's Aldie!' Then to my great relief I saw it was Geoff on Mill Reef – and he was about eight lengths clear of Aldie, who in turn was clear of Bright Beam.

I timed them at two minutes twenty-two seconds, which of course is slow by racing standards, but quite a few seconds quicker than we usually go round that particular gallop. Geoff was more than ever convinced that our horse would get the trip, but there were plenty of good judges still saying that he had too much speed to be a true mile-and-a-half horse. Paul Mellon's closest friend in America, Jimmy Brady, was adamant that Mill Reef would not stay and apparently even went as far as saying, 'Over my dead body will any son of Never Bend win over a mile and a half!' P.M. told me much later that unbelievably Jimmy Brady had died a few days before the 1971 Derby!

All went smoothly leading up to the race. On the big day I sent our lovely old Irish blacksmith, Tom Reilly, in the horsebox with John Hallum, Norton Jones the driver and the travelling head lad Bill Jennings. Winter Fair, one of Mill Reef's many galloping companions, was running in the valuable mile-and-a-quarter handicap – the race just before the Derby – and he was the only other horse on the box, together with his lad Paddy Heffernan.

Emma, her mother Priscilla and I left with plenty of time for what should be just over an hour's journey. However, the police in their wisdom had redirected all the traffic, even from the London area, to come in on our route, so that as we got to within two miles of the course the traffic gradually became very slow and then ground to a halt. After about ten minutes of this I could take it no longer and said to my passengers, 'I'm off – one of you had better drive.' I suppose my two-mile hike in top hat and tails took me just over twenty minutes – I was still quite fit then and jogged most of the way, refusing plenty of friends who offered me lifts, knowing that I would reach the racecourse long before they did.

I got there, in fact, just in time to saddle Winter Fair, who ran pretty well to finish fourth. In the parade for the Derby, Alec Head's contestant, Bourbon, behaved so mulishly that the race was about ten minutes late starting – which just gave my wife and mother-in-law time to get to the stands and watch it after their horrendously slow journey.

Geoff, whose bad hand had mercifully recovered in time for him to ride at Epsom, had only one anxious moment, halfway down the hill towards Tattenham Corner; but Joe Mercer gave him a yard or two of daylight when it was most needed and Mill Reef was able to turn into the straight perfectly placed in fourth behind Linden Tree, Lombardo and Homeric. From there the race was predictable: Mill Reef never for a moment looked likely to be beaten or not to stay, and quickened well to score a clear, albeit not massively impressive, victory. Linden Tree battled on bravely to be a worthy second and Irish Ball came late and fast to finish third.

Geoff had given Mill Reef a perfect ride – and as he also won both the Oaks on Altesse Royale and the Coronation Cup on Lupe, it could be said that he had a pretty successful Epsom meeting! In fact Geoff, with the help of Noel Murless's many class horses, had rapidly become not just Lester Piggott's main challenger as champion jockey, but a top-class rider on all the big occasions.

There was, of course, a feeling of euphoria immediately afterwards; but to be perfectly honest my main sensation was one of intense relief. I was thanking God that between us we had managed not to screw up! The winner's enclosure at Epsom is unique. For those who have never seen it, it is a small circle right under the main grandstand with its own entrance off the racetrack. The placed horses stay on the main track just outside it, with the also-rans further down. In the marvellous film made later about Mill Reef entitled *Something to Brighten the Morning* there is a brief shot from high on the stands roof of him returning to this prized spot. The script written by Hugh McIlvanney and read by Albert Finney calls it 'an oasis of pleasure in the memory' – and I can think of no better description. In fact I have thought about it on each occasion I have been there since that great day.

When the horsebox came back to Kingsclere that evening Norton Jones drove very slowly through the village and Mill Reef's many friends and admirers ran and walked beside it for the half-mile to Park House to welcome our Derby winner. Mill Reef strolled nonchalantly among them while everyone wanted to take photographs and pat him. That perhaps was the moment I really knew what it was to win the Derby, and realised just how much it meant not only to everyone directly involved with the stable but even to the people of Kingsclere.

Early the next morning Emma and I flew off to America to attend the marriage of my little sister Gail to David King, so we barely had time even to read the newspaper accounts of the race. I cannot pretend, however, that the long transatlantic flight passed without more than average feelings of gratitude and satisfaction.

Mill Reef's main midsummer target was to be the King George VI and Queen Elizabeth Stakes at the end of July. For this I felt that the Eclipse Stakes at Sandown was the most suitable preparation; it would also mean he would have an easy local journey rather than having to travel to the Curragh for the Irish Derby the previous weekend. The Eclipse is a great race in its own right, of course; and it is also the first contest of any consequence between the three-year-olds and the older horses.

Irish Ball, who was third at Epsom, won the Irish Derby, so our form was looking pretty good as the Sandown race approached. However, there was a four-year-old colt in France called Caro who had won their Two Thousand Guineas the previous year and had carried all before him this season – and he was coming over for the Eclipse. The duel between him and Mill Reef was eagerly awaited, and the race had the added interest of Welsh Pageant, the top English older horse, also taking part. Trained by Noel Murless, he was to be partnered by Lester Piggott. Then there was our pacemaker, Bright Beam, ridden by Geoff's great friend and leading lightweight jockey, Tommy Carter. Making up the small field of six were Caro's pacemaker, Quebracho, and a top-class handicapper called Quayside.

In the race Lester went so fast early on that it took Tommy Carter some time to get by him on Bright Beam. The hectic early pace had set up a wonderful contest and as Caro came to join

Mill Reef with just two furlongs to run the pair quickened dramatically clear of the rest of the field. One could feel the tension and excitement in the packed stands. Then, with a furlong to run, Geoff asked for a bit more. My throat choked up as I watched our little champion come bounding away from his rival to win by four lengths in a new course record. It was a hugely impressive performance, considering that three years before the brilliant Derby winner, Sir Ivor, had failed to beat his older rivals Royal Palace and Taj Dewan in the same race. The crowd reacted to this great triumph with a virtual stampede down to the winner's enclosure, and the reception they gave Mill Reef was as loud and sincere as any I can remember after a horse race.

Our golden summer continued to glow: three weeks later our champion won the King George VI and Queen Elizabeth Stakes at Ascot by a then record margin of six lengths. Perhaps he beat nothing of any great merit; but Ortis, who was second, had won the Italian Derby as a three-year-old and at four had taken the Hardwicke Stakes over course and distance the previous month by eight lengths. There was also enough concurrent form to suggest that Mill Reef's performance was almost certainly better than Nijinsky's in the same race the previous year. Lester Piggott, who had ridden the Triple Crown winner then and finished almost twenty lengths behind on Politico now, was heard to say afterwards that he thought Mill Reef on that day was as good a horse as he ever saw. Geoff too always felt that this was our horse's finest hour, and was often quoted as saying, 'Daylight was second at Ascot.'

There was one great target left for our superstar that season – or just possibly two. I had said to P.M., who was very much a man of international thought and ambition, that it would be wonderful if his horse could become the first English-trained winner for twenty-three years of the great French autumn race the Prix de l'Arc de Triomphe. In order to have our best chance of winning it, I felt we should resist the temptation to run in the St Leger at Doncaster beforehand. In 1970 Nijinsky had become the first Triple Crown winner in England for thirty-five years. He was narrowly beaten in the Arc, however, and I felt that in winning the St Leger he may well have forfeited his chance at Longchamp. I explained to P.M. that if we forgot about the St Leger I could give the horse a proper break of six weeks and still have four weeks in which to get him fully fit for the first Sunday in October.

In those days there were no end-of-season distractions such as the Breeders Cup or the Japan Cup, and the Arc was arguably the most valuable and prestigious race in the world. So the decision sounds sensible now; but it was not easy then just to abandon the idea of winning the oldest English Classic. I had no doubt that Mill Reef could have won it, because it appeared that the further he went the faster he went. A mile and three-quarters would not, in my opinion, have been any problem at all, and Athens Wood, who won it in his absence was not in the same class. P.M., however, agreed that we should dismiss any thoughts of Doncaster and concentrate entirely on trying to win the Arc.

So for a couple of weeks we gave Mill Reef a nice easy time wandering around the many different tracks, avenues and winter gallops that Kingsclere offers, mainly with Aldie as companion. He was turned out in a small paddock for an hour or so at evening stables, again with his sensible grey friend next door to stop him from galloping around. At this stage he didn't go out of a trot and he looked to put on quite a bit of weight. After two or three weeks he was getting so fresh we had to start cantering. Even so, we did not start serious work until a month before the big race.

There was no suitable Arc trial race in England at that time, so I decided we would have a public gallop at Newbury racecourse on the Sunday morning exactly two weeks before Longchamp. We used Aldie, ridden by Tommy Carter, and National Park, a good five-year-old gelding ridden by our senior work rider Jimmy Miller, as galloping companions for Mill Reef, who was naturally ridden by Geoff. Although Mill Reef finished a couple of lengths clear of the other two in a very good time the workout was far from impressive. We gave him three more shorter pieces of work on the downs before he left for France and in none of those gallops did he show any real sparkle.

It was no easy task to get a three-year-old colt spot-on for the Arc when he had been fit to win the Greenham in mid-April and had run in four major races since then. This was perhaps my greatest test as a trainer. No one remembers if you happen to win a small race with a bad horse who has no right to win anything. What they do remember, though, is how you handled the very good horses; and I had this awful feeling that I had done too much with Mill Reef and he was what we call 'over the top'.

Remembering the difficult journey to France the previous year, I had taken every conceivable precaution to ensure a quick and easy crossing this time. With P.M.'s agreement we hired the same Boeing jet that Nijinsky had used in 1970 and, with a great many strings pulled for us in high places, we got permission to fly out from Greenham Common – the American air base only ten minutes down the road from Kingsclere.

Early on the Friday morning the team set off: Mill Reef himself, with Aldie, his faithful companion and galloping partner, and the usual human contingent of John Hallum, Bill Jennings, blacksmith Tom Reilly and, just to be on the safe side, our vet Peter Scott Dunn. On this occasion Emma and I made up the group. When we got to Greenham Common I recall meeting the big American commander in charge of flight operations. His name was Sergeant Hinz, and although not exactly unfriendly he made it quite clear how much of a nuisance the whole procedure had become. He said that it had taken ten pounds of paper work and a final clearance from the Pentagon in Washington to secure permission for a civilian aircraft to leave from their military air base. Finally he said, 'What is all the fuss about for this one wretched horse anyway?' I replied quietly that this one wretched horse was quite valuable property and that in fact we had just insured him for two million pounds for this one journey. I enjoyed watching the colour drain from his face. 'Christ,' he said, 'I better get out there and check there are no pot-holes in the runway!' He was no doubt almost as relieved as we were that the trip went smoothly.

We had arranged for our two horses to be stabled at La Camargo. This beautiful little isolated yard for just four horses, with grooms' accommodation above the stables, is owned by the French Jockey Club and is kept especially for foreign trainers to use. It has its own little training ground near to the main gallops at Lamorlaye, the next village to Chantilly. Emma and I stayed in a pretty little country *pension* almost within walking distance of the stable on a hill overlooking the gallops. On our own on this little paradise island, the next couple of days were a wonderful break for us – for me, reminiscent of my month with Caduval in Mesnil-le-Roi eight years before.

I asked the groundsman to prepare a special four-furlong strip of turf for our two horses to use on the Saturday morning, the day before the big race. Here Bill Jennings on Aldie and John on Mill Reef had a little spin on the marked-out gallop. I had asked John as usual to sit behind Aldie and join him about a furlong and a half from where I was standing at the top. I said to John, 'Let him enjoy himself and put his toe out the last furlong if he wants to.' For the first time for weeks it looked like the old Mill Reef as he skipped four lengths clear with ease. At this point I felt happy at last that our horse was somewhere near his best.

There was an interesting sequel to this gallop. I had walked the specially watered strip beforehand and had noticed one or two patches of ground which appeared to be a shade softer than the rest. Afterwards, with not much else to do, Emma and I strolled down and walked it again, and I did some 'treading in' for their groundsman. Aldie was a firm-ground specialist, what we call a real 'daisy clipper' with a fluent low-to-the-ground action; he had always been hopeless when the ground became soft. Mill Reef had the most beautiful action I have ever seen on any racehorse, and at speed his stride lengthened as well as quickened. The ground was almost perfect and there were hardly any marks to repair at all, until we came to the slightly softer patches. On the left where Aldie had travelled there were some divots three or four inches deep which I repaired. On the right, to my amazement, one could hardly see where Mill Reef had been – it was as if a ghost horse had galloped there. Obviously there was some strange quality in Mill Reef's action which enabled him to float where others were apt to flounder. It explains to some extent the total superiority he showed on the heavy ground at York for the Gimcrack – and he was still to race one more time on a similar surface.

Longchamp on Arc day has an atmosphere similar to that of a major rugby football international. The Brits invade this beautiful area of Paris as at no other time. This particular year my brother-in-law, William Hastings-Bass, had organised for two or three hundred pin-on badges in P.M.'s colours to be made. On a black circular background they had the two words MILL REEF emblazoned in gold across the middle. These were rapidly distributed to the English visitors, and he could easily have found takers for double the number if he had had them. And yet, although Mill Reef was a hot favourite and the French racing public were keen to see this little marvel from England, everyone was aware of the recent painful defeats that such superstars as Sir Ivor, Park Top and Nijinsky had suffered in this race. We all knew it would be no easy task.

Mill Reef's superb temperament withstood the noisy and demanding preliminaries much better than Nijinsky had the previous year. As he and Geoff cantered smoothly round to the start in front of Le Moulin, my confidence was seeping back. Having given Geoff a leg-up and therefore being one of the last to leave the paddock, I had considerable difficulty finding somewhere to watch from. I finally settled for the rear of the Tribune des étrangers and as I was at the back I could hardly see the race at all, especially as there were no big screens at the time.

As there is always a strong pace in the Arc we had dispensed with the idea of a pacemaker and Mill Reef, who was well drawn, settled on the inside in fifth or sixth place. As they turned for home Geoff was in a good position but behind three horses who were not quickening and Pistol Packer, the great French filly who was his main danger, was beginning her run on the outside. At this point, through the maze of heads, arms and binoculars, I could not see our hero at all, and for one ghastly moment even wondered if somehow he might have fallen. Then suddenly, as Geoff dived for a narrow gap to the right of these three beaten horses near the rail, I could see our familiar white sheepskin noseband. Our little horse was through the gap in a flash and quickened again to win by three lengths in a new course record.

Our whole team, including head lad Bill Palmer, who had somehow got himself there, gathered in triumph in the winner's area of that big paddock at Longchamp. Mr and Mrs Mellon, Emma, her mother, her brother William and I were there to greet our hero along with thousands of other ecstatic enthusiasts, both French and English. It was a memorable reception of the kind reserved for those few truly great horses, and for me it was of course a very emotional moment. I had time to give Emma a kiss and a longer than usual hug. Here was an occasion that was very special, one which we could share and recollect together fondly for many years.

Even now I would have to say that this was my most exciting and satisfying moment as a trainer. To win this great international race with a three-year-old colt who had started his season in April was something that many much better trainers than me had failed to do. Even though, almost certainly, I had got him past his best, Mill Reef was still good enough to win.

In those last four races of 1971 Geoff had never been anywhere but in the right place at all times on our champion, and at Longchamp in a big field he was nothing less than brilliant. I was so happy for him and his wife Noelene and also for our whole team, not just the ones out there with Mill Reef but all those back at Kingsclere whose consistent hard work had helped to make this moment possible. From vet to secretary, from head lad to gallop man, from horsebox driver to blacksmith to youngest apprentice, there should in a well-run establishment be a happy sense of satisfaction and achievement at a time like this. I would like to think it existed then and still does to this day.

Paul and Bunny Mellon knew how to celebrate. They hosted a wonderful dinner that evening at the Crillon Hotel for all those of our family, including Charles and Ruth Halifax who were in Paris. P.M., with typical thoughtfulness, had also organised for a small team of seven from Rokeby to come over to Europe for this week. Emma's brother William was put in charge of looking after them in Paris, after which they came on to England and paid their first visit to Kingsclere.

The plan had always been to hold a Derby party in England on the Wednesday evening after the Arc. This was a brave idea; if the Arc had not gone according to plan it would certainly not have been quite the same. In the event it was fantastic. The Mellons took over Annabel's, the famous nightclub in Berkeley Square, for the evening. Where artistic good taste is concerned no one has ever had more than Paul and Bunny Mellon: the décor was superb, all in black and gold, and every person had a small but significant gift at their table place – a thick bamboo ballpoint pen from Garrard's with 'Mill Reef 1971' inscribed on it for the men, and a lovely Hermès scarf similarly inscribed in the right colours for the ladies. Emma and I were encouraged to invite up to twenty of our best friends, and Geoff and Noelene likewise. There were probably a hundred people there, and the dancing and partying went on well into the early hours. P.M.'s daughter Cathy, was there; at that time she was married to Senator John Warner (who later married Liz Taylor), President Nixon's secretary for the navy. Seeing my brother-in-law William dancing very closely with Cathy, my great chum Rogie Dalzell came rushing over in great concern and with his usual sense of humour said, 'You had better warn that brother-in-law of yours to keep his hands to himself – her husband has only got his finger on the bloody button!'

At the end of that season we had our own party for all the stable staff and their wives or girlfriends, as well as all the other people who had contributed to Mill Reef's success – including, of course, Sergeant Hinz and a small team from Greenham Common air base.

Quite apart from Mill Reef, we had enjoyed a wonderful season. There were forty-eight eight winners from only forty-nine horses who actually ran – about ten did not make it to the racecourse. Philip Waldron, now making an impact as a senior jockey and only a year out of his apprenticeship, rode twenty-five of those winners and half of the sixty-four placed horses. Our total prize money won in England was just under £300,000, with quite a lot won abroad as well. It was easily enough in any case to ensure that for the only time in my career I was leading trainer in England.

Nor was all the excitement on the racetrack. Earlier that year Emma and I celebrated the arrival of our first child, a daughter named Clare Victoria after Aunt Clare, a first cousin of my mother and my godmother. The following year, a photograph was taken of Clare sitting on Mill Reef's back whilst he was recuperating at Kingsclere. Two or three years after that, she had her photo taken sitting on the life-size bronze of Brigadier Gerard at the Hislops' home in Berkshire. Even now she likes to think that she was the only person who ever sat on both horses!

The 1972 Flat season began with a buzz of excitement that I

have rarely known since. Mill Reef, in spite of being beaten by Brigadier Gerard on the only occasion they had met, had been rated equal to his rival both in the official ratings and by Timeform. This, of course, was as a result of his four unprecedented wins after that defeat in the Two Thousand Guineas. The whole racing world was holding its breath until these two could meet again. It would certainly not be over a mile, which was the Brigadier's specialist distance, and more than likely it would not be over a mile and a half, which was Mill Reef's best trip. The obvious race looked to be the Eclipse Stakes at Sandown over a mile and a quarter in early July, and both camps seemed keen for the encounter.

With a horse as good as our fellow the races plan themselves, and we were hoping to run first in the Prix Ganay, a Group I race over a mile and a quarter at Longchamp at the very end of April. This was to be followed by the Coronation Cup at Epsom a month later over a mile and a half. Then we hoped to meet Brigadier Gerard in the Eclipse back at a mile and a quarter in early July, after which we would go to the King George VI at Ascot three weeks later – and finally, of course, take a second crack at the Arc.

Early that year P.M. had been approached by a film company who asked if they could do a documentary-length film about Mill Reef, focused on the rematch with Brigadier Gerard. P.M. had agreed – to my surprise, because up until then he had never even had a horse painted, let alone filmed, until it had retired, because he felt it was unlucky. Emma and I were pretty lukewarm about the whole project at first, but the producer was to be Brough Scott, who was a good friend and a knowledgeable horseman, so we knew the camera crew at least would be kept out of harm's way.

Mill Reef had been, to my eye, the most perfect shape for a two-year-old, as described by John Oaksey on the day of the Coventry Stakes at Royal Ascot. Although he stood only fifteen hands two inches he looked so rounded and mature that many people (and I have to admit to being one of them) thought that he would be an out-and-out miler and unlikely to stay further. It was noticeable, however, that as a three-year-old he had lengthened markedly. He had also grown half an inch to fifteen two and a half, and at the time of his victories at Sandown and Ascot, even though still small, he looked much more the shape of a middle-distance horse. Through the following winter he appeared to put on quite a lot of condition, so that one would say physically he had done very well, and he looked a bigger stronger horse in the spring of 1972. Unfortunately we had no weighing machine at that time, so I did not have an accurate way of confirming what my eye was telling me. There are plenty of horses who do not improve from three to four, but to my eye Mill Reef did not look to be one of them.

His first serious gallop that year was yet another public workout at Newbury racecourse after racing on Greenham Stakes day, just over two weeks before the Ganay. Tommy Carter led the gallop over a mile and a quarter on Aldie, and Philip Waldron on old Morris Dancer joined him at the entrance to the straight. Geoff on Mill Reef sat about three lengths behind them until about two furlongs out, then joined them and with just over a furlong to go let his partner quicken impressively to go ten or twelve lengths clear. It was good enough to confirm my feelings that our champion had indeed improved, if that were possible, from three to four. Earlier that afternoon Martinmas ridden by Philip Waldron had won the Greenham Stakes decisively, so it had been a rewarding day.

We took one of our other lead horses, called Merry Slipper, to Longchamp – not just to keep Mill Reef company on the journey, but also to ensure a strong gallop in the race itself. Tommy rode him and went a decent pace on very soft ground. Geoff settled comfortably back in fifth or sixth place but then went by his pacemaker earlier than expected, just before the final right-hand turn into the straight. With two furlongs to run he gave Mill Reef a nudge and away they went. I cannot recall a Group I race being won by such a wide margin. Our boy just skipped over the rain-sodden ground, and was going so easily and fast at the end that the official distance of ten lengths still annoys our jockey now. It really did look nearer twenty! M. Jean Romanet, the long-time director of French racing, was heard to remark, 'That is the best horse I have seen at Longchamp' – and he had, of course, also seen Sea Bird!

The Brigadier had won the Lockinge Stakes over a mile at Newbury comfortably, but when given a trial over the Eclipse course and distance nine days later in the Westbury Stakes he had struggled a bit to beat a horse called Ballyhot by half a length. The betting at this stage for their expected clash in the Eclipse would have been somewhat one-sided – but there were still several weeks and another race for each horse to go.

Mill Reef had had the normal ten-day break after his successful trip to France, and I geared his preparation for the Coronation Cup towards one serious gallop over a mile and a quarter, ten days before the Epsom race. All seemed well right up to 24 May, when my old work sheets show that he and Martinmas covered six furlongs together on the left-hand side and my notes in red said, 'Both finished very strongly together.' Then on Monday the 29th we had the main gallop as planned on exactly the same piece of ground we had used for the Derby work the previous year. Conditions were windy and the ground was soft – and the gallop was a major disappointment. Martinmas, ridden by Philip Waldron and getting a stone from Mill Reef ridden by Paul Cook, had won the gallop but finished tired, according to my notes. Aldie ridden by John Matthias worked well and Mill Reef, giving him twenty-four pounds, struggled even to get to him.

It was not a fast time and I sensed that something might be wrong with our champion. I thought at first that perhaps I had given him too many days off after the French trip and that he was just taking a lot of work to get back to full fitness. We worked him twice more on the downs before Epsom, on our usual work days, and I was so worried that I even got Geoff down to gallop him over six furlongs on the Monday just three days before the race. I had also asked Peter Scott Dunn to come that morning to check the horse's heart and respiratory rates. To be on the safe side, we also took a nasal swab and blood test. The blood test result a day later showed nothing of any significance, and the nasal swab would not yield any definite conclusion for at least a couple of weeks. Peter had said that the horse was blowing rather harder than a fit horse should and his recovery rate was on the slow side.

I should have known we had a problem when on Derby Day Martinmas, who had finished a very close second in the Irish Two

Thousand Guineas after his Greenham win and started favourite for the mile Diomed Stakes, finished last. Just after that, however, Aldie made all the running to win the valuable Daily Mirror Handicap; so my worries receded once again.

Mill Reef was already declared for the Coronation Cup the next day and as there were only four runners, with Homeric the only rival of any note, I still felt we should run. I have to admit that I was not happy with our little superstar and if I had had a cautious nature we would have pulled out. In hindsight, of course, it was possibly the biggest mistake of my training life to let him run.

In the race Bright Beam and Tommy Carter set a decent gallop. Turning into the straight, Joe Mercer on Homeric kicked for home; Geoff seemed to cruise up to him with two furlongs to run, and we all thought Mill Reef would then come easily away. When Geoff pushed the button, however, nothing happened, and although he was by now half a length up he had to ride as vigorously as he could to hold off Homeric's renewed challenge. Mill Reef just hung on to win by a neck.

I was mortified, and although Mill Reef was now unbeaten in six consecutive Group I races, I had not enjoyed this victory one little bit. In my defence I will say that we could not 'scope' horses in those days. All vets and trainers nowadays know just how much we have come to depend on the endoscope – a long, flexible fibre-optic tube which can be put up a horse's nostril so that the vet can see the larynx and any mucus or blood that may be present in the windpipe. Back in 1972 we could only wait for the result of Mill Reef's nasal swab to come back from the Equine Research Centre at Newmarket – too late to help us make our decision about Epsom. When it did arrive, it showed that at the time it was taken he was harbouring the dreaded respiratory virus rhinopneumonitis. This was in fact the first time any of us in the training community had come across this virus in racehorses, though it had been known to cause abortion in broodmares. For the next couple of decades it was to prove the scourge of most racing stables throughout Europe. Its main symptom is sudden premature exhaustion under stress, so that a racehorse tends to weaken noticeably towards the end of a race when asked for a final effort. As most people know, horses can breathe only through their noses, not like us through their mouths as well. Consequently, any form of obstruction to the airways is a significant handicap. Nearly always nowadays we scope horses up to a week before they run just to be sure they are healthy.

When some months later I first saw the shots of Mill Reef in the Coronation Cup in the film *Something to Brighten the Morning* I was horrified. Mill Reef looked so light behind the saddle I could scarcely believe it. Seeing him all day, every day as I did, I suppose I just had not noticed how much weight he was losing. All through his sick period for the two weeks before the race I had been giving him more and more work, foolishly thinking that he was not fit. To have survived all that work and then run his heart out when suffering from this awful virus was as brave a performance as when he bounded up the horsebox ramp on three legs a few months later.

Tragically, that episode was to spell the premature end to his racing career. We had no option but to cancel any plans to meet the Brigadier in the Eclipse. This was a heavy blow, not just for the whole racing public but especially for Brough Scott, his director Kit Owens and the rest of the crew making the film. Ironically the ground came up soft for the Eclipse, and although Brigadier Gerard won it gamely by a length from Gold Rod, I suspect he might have been pulled out under those conditions had he faced a fit Mill Reef.

It often happens after a horse has suffered badly from this wretched viral infection that resistance is lowered and other problems occur. With yearlings these usually take the form of ringworm and then sore shins. Mill Reef came back after a suitable rest in midsummer and even worked well once or twice in a hopeful preparation for the new Benson and Hedges Gold Cup at York. The luck had turned sour, however: a bang on the back of his near fore held him up for a week or so, and then an unaccountable pulled muscle in his quarters finally put paid to any lingering hopes we had of running in that race. Once again it seemed ironic that in the race itself – which was the only other opportunity the two great horses would have had for a rematch – the Brigadier was beaten for the only time in his career by Roberto.

All these years later, it is probably of little value for this obviously biased writer to argue the relative merits of these two great racehorses. However, including even Sea Bird II, I would say that Mill Reef, Brigadier Gerard and Nijinsky were, in that order the three best middle-distance horses I have ever seen on this continent. All three proved it time and time again over all distances. The fact that Mill Reef was equally brilliant over any distance on any ground is why I would put him top, even though the only time they met the Brigadier beat him decisively. That these three great horses were all foaled within a calendar year of one another is quite remarkable.

Following our two setbacks P.M. had asked for his own vet from Belmont Park, Chuck Allen, to come over and give Mill Reef a thorough assessment. He arrived in mid-August and his opinion, expressed to P.M., was that Mill Reef was by then fit to go back into full work. Consequently both P.M. and I were reassured that we could and should prepare Mill Reef for a second tilt at the Arc. There had been, as I mentioned earlier, just a hint of a whistle in his breathing ever since the Coronation Cup. However, I felt that if all went well we just had time enough to get him back to his best. Thus we came to that fateful morning of 30 August which I have described earlier.

My first task after the accident was to try to assemble the best veterinary brains to ascertain if and how Mill Reef could be saved. I had asked Peter Scott Dunn and Chuck Allen for advice on who was the best surgeon to attempt an operation, and they both agreed on Edwin James Roberts. Ironically, Jim Roberts had recently resigned from the Equine Research Station at Newmarket, but was well known for his pioneering surgery. Strangely enough I had come across him already, for he had operated on Magna Carta, a good colt of the Queen who had broken his jaw. It was probably no fault of his that Magna Carta died as a result of too much anaesthetic during the operation, but it did give me a touch of concern.

I set up a meeting at Heathrow Airport at which these three eminent veterinary experts and I looked at and discussed the X-rays that had been taken of the broken leg. A triangular piece of bone nearly three inches long had broken off from the cannon bone. It had not pierced the skin, but unless it was suitably repaired the horse would never walk again. The two main sesamoid bones either side of the fetlock had also shattered, but all three men felt that these would mend, or at least fuse together well enough to enable the joint to become stable. There was no need, therefore, to touch them. Jim Roberts was confident that he could operate successfully.

I was aware that Jim Roberts no longer had access to the fabulous operating facilities at Newmarket, and I felt strongly in any case that there would be far less trauma for our patient if he did not have to be moved to a strange place in a horsebox. Fortunately, we had the perfect spot for the operation – and Mill Reef would only have to walk about forty yards in his plaster cast to get there. John Porter's old mess room had been a Catholic chapel when I first came to Kingsclere, and on Sunday mornings the whole courtyard outside the stables was full of cars. We had nowhere for a gymnasium for our many apprentices, so I managed to persuade the Catholics to move to a far more suitable building in the village. We had had our building deconsecrated and I had just had a new floor put down and a decent lighting and heating system installed. As a temporary hospital it seemed almost a gift from heaven. Here it was that the operation would take place; and the top half of this big room was made perfect for the patient's recovery area.

My brother-in-law William liaised between Jim Roberts and our maintenance man and we quickly constructed an operating table to the surgeon's specific design, made of straw bales covered in polythene and supported by moveable wooden frames.

Exactly a week after his accident, Mill Reef was given a sedative and then led slowly and gently to the edge of the operating table in the middle of our new 'hospital'. Then came the terrifying moment: in the absence of a tilting operating table, the horse had to be pulled over on to his side at the exact second the surgeon decreed. I held a rope which went round the horse's girth, John Hallum had one attached to his head and my head lad Bill held one around his tail. I recall Jim Roberts telling us that a short time after he injected the initial dose of thiopentone into the horse's jugular vein the horse would collapse. We were to pull together on our ropes exactly when he said 'NOW'. If we were a second too early the horse would struggle and consequently subside to the ground. If we were a second late he would also collapse on the ground. 'In either case, end of operation, lads, so please get it right and pull together when I tell you!' We were more than a shade nervous.

In the event, pulling him over went so well I was amazed – and mightily impressed, too, by our surgeon's sangfroid. Jim was assisted throughout by Peter Scott Dunn's partner Tony Ward, who was a fine surgeon himself. The anaesthetist was Jim's wife. After the disaster with Magna Carta he had found the best female student around at the time, trained her himself, and then married her just to make certain she was available for his operations alone. That was the story I was told, anyway! The operation basically entailed putting the fragmented piece of cannon bone back in place and securing it with a plate through which three screws were drilled to hold it in place. They had to go in at certain special angles, and I remember many X-rays being taken and developed at once in Bill's bathroom the other side of the communicating door between the 'hospital' and the head lad's house.

The surgeon was painstaking, to say the least – in fact the whole operation lasted seven hours. I was totally fascinated and never left the horse's side during that time. For almost the first time I can remember I really wished that I had passed those wretched A-levels and got qualified myself, I was so envious of his skill and wondered at the precision of it all. John, Bill and I took turns to stretch Mill Reef's other legs every half an hour or so in order to maintain his circulation. Mrs Roberts was showing me how he needed less than half the normal dose of anaesthetic (oxygen mixed with fluothane in this case) for a four-year-old colt to keep him unconscious. Finally Jim applied a full-length plaster cast around the leg, reinforced by iron splints specially made by our farrier, Tom Reilly.

Not long after the surgeon had completed his marathon task the patient came round. This was potentially a dangerous time because colts in particular may struggle; but Mill Reef as usual was as sensible as he could be, and with a little help from us got up at the first attempt with the minimum of fuss.

There were all sorts of minor problems still to cope with, but the invalid was as helpful and amenable as one could hope for. Gradually we gave him the whole area of the old mess room and it was to be Mill Reef's home until he moved to the National Stud at Newmarket a few months later. Public interest in our invalid was huge: there were more than five hundred get-well cards sticky-taped around the walls of his 'box', and his progress just before and after the operation was a major item on all the news bulletins. Jim Roberts came back to check him regularly and seemed very confident that his leg would be well enough healed for him to be able to cover some mares the following spring.

There was an interesting sequel to this operation. I had not fixed a price with Jim Roberts beforehand, either for the surgery or for his later visits. For several months he did not send a bill and finally P.M. asked me about it. I said that I was quite sure the surgeon had not forgotten the matter, but for some reason he seemed unwilling to send his account. It was not until a year after this amazing surgery that Jim Roberts finally sent the bill. By then we all knew that Mill Reef had got his first mares in foal.

The invoice on A4 paper just had one line on it:

To saving Mill Reef's life   £25,000

I rang P.M. and said I felt the surgeon had taken an extortionate liberty; I had expected his charge to be a tenth of that figure. He listened to what I had to say and simply said, 'Pay it.'

Teaching Mill Reef to walk again after the plaster was removed was the hardest part; at times the horse was obviously in some discomfort and understandably became unusually bad-tempered. Trying to make him walk properly and to use his bad leg was very difficult. We also had to build up his near fore shoulder muscle, which had wasted quite badly during his inactivity. In addition there were so many letters and gifts and even cash coming in from well-wishers that one way or another dealing with Mill Reef Inc. after his injury took more time than when he was fit! Eventually we took a risk and turned him loose in a small paddock – and were mightily relieved when he survived the inevitable gallop around.

We had fixed a date in early January for him to leave us, and decided to hold a kind of open day one Sunday morning when the locals and other fans could come along and say their farewells. On the day, John led his friend through the large crowd gathered in the area in the middle of our covered ride. As always Mill Reef seemed to enjoy the attention and it was a happy occasion. Finally the day of departure arrived, and on the morning of 9 January 1973 our whole team assembled to watch him walk up into the horsebox for the last time. It was the end of an amazing era, and I was not the only one to shed a tear or two.

The training of a horse as good as Mill Reef over those three years was a privileged experience that very few people can have had, and it was obviously something I will never forget. His injury, operation and subsequent recuperation left me feeling a little bit older and certainly a lot wiser. As a result of that episode, however, I cannot now imagine any situation where horses are involved in which I could not, with God's help, somehow cope.

John of course travelled to Newmarket with Mill Reef and he led him proudly into his new box at the National Stud with his own name on the door. Although there was still a limp in his step it would have been hard to guess how near to death he had been only three months before.

It was entirely typical of P.M. that he had ignored considerably higher offers for the horse to stand as a stallion in his own country and insisted that he should go to the National Stud. Colonel Douglas Gray was the director at that time and Mill Reef was to be looked after by their senior stallion man, the Romanian-born George Roth, an outstanding horseman. Once again Mill Reef was under the care of an absolutely top-class groom. George in fact was to look after him until the horse's somewhat premature death at the age of seventeen. I used to go and see Mill Reef at Newmarket at least once a year. I had a feeling that he recognised me on the first occasion, but after that he was just as keen to bite me as the next person. In fact he became, as some stallions do, quite savage in later years and towards the end of his life only George could handle him.

In his first season he was limited to twenty mares and only after Jim Roberts had examined him and pronounced him fit to cover a full book of mares the next season was he finally syndicated. Forty-one shares were distributed at £50,000 each, and of these P.M. kept eight from which he gave me one nomination each year. The National Stud, with the help of the Levy Board, retained nine shares for the use of British breeders. These were allotted by ballot each year at a fee of £15,000. The remaining twenty-four were sold to breeders all over the world – nine in France, five in the UK, five in America, four in Ireland and one in Italy. P.M. had always regarded his horse as an international figure and wanted that to be reflected in his syndication.

Mill Reef was to become the leading stallion in the UK on two separate occasions, and the vast number of pattern races all over the world won by his progeny were a testament to his success as a stallion. The Aga Khan, who is probably acknowledged as the most successful owner/breeder in Europe, was one of the original shareholders and was not slow to appreciate the value of Mill Reef in his pedigrees. Many of his great horses of the 1990s have his blood directly or that of his best son, Shirley Heights.

The National Stud was to prosper both financially and as a tourist attraction during Mill Reef's lifetime. The beautiful Skeaping statue which P.M. gave them still stands proudly as a centrepiece near the stallion boxes. Of the other two bronzes that were cast, one was a gift to me and stands in the Mill Reef yard at Kingsclere; the other adorns the middle of the broodmare barn at Rokeby. John Skeaping's widow recently told my mother-in-law, Priscilla, that John considered this particular half-life-size bronze the best piece of art he produced in his whole life. P.M. would have liked that.

Paul Mellon had come into my life in 1964 with my move to Kingsclere, and I first met him that autumn when he came over to see Silly Season win the Dewhurst Stakes at Newmarket. He reminded me very much of Jock Whitney, another American anglophile with a great love for both horses and art. Both men came from two of the most famous and wealthy families in

America, but both were quiet and modest – P.M. especially so. I happen to know that at one stage he was offered the post of American ambassador to Britain, but he would have been too unassuming to have accepted – or, indeed, to have told anyone but his wife Bunny about the offer.

His love of England stemmed from the fact that his mother was English and for the first seven years of his life their family spent every summer over here; and it was when he went to Cambridge University in 1929 that horses became a part of his life. An Irish-bred hunter called Dublin carried him boldly on the hunting field and even in the occasional point-to-point. In England he hunted with the Vale of the White Horse, the Heythrop and the Beaufort and later on with the Middleton as well; in America he became master of his local Piedmont hounds in Virginia for a few years and always encouraged the hunt to cross his land. His first racehorse was called Drinmore Lad, who after some successes over timber in the USA came over here to be trained by Ivor Anthony and Mrs Aubrey Hastings, to whom he was introduced by Ambrose Clarke; thus began an enduring friendship between P.M. and the Hastings family. He would have enjoyed living long enough to be an owner of Andrew Balding and thus have horses with the fourth generation.

P.M. always took great trouble with the naming of his horses and his sense of humour was often apparent. One colt by his own stallion Crackpot out of a mare called Night Sound was rather mischievously named Trickle. Then almost in his last crop of yearlings at the age of ninety-two he called a colt by Seeking The Gold out of the mare You'd Be Surprised – Wait For The Will!

As a person he was humble, charming, amusing and invariably thoughtful in everything he did, said or wrote. He was always extremely generous without ever being ostentatious. I am sure that one of the reasons he loved racing in England so much was the beauty of our grass tracks. I can recall days at Newbury, Ascot, Goodwood and Bath when he seemed sublimely happy even if we did not have a winner. I will always think of him as not just the best owner that any trainer could wish for, but as a great lover of horses, both in reality and in art form.

When P.M. died in 1999, my brother-in-law William, who was

his godson, and I flew out to his funeral at his local church in Upperville. His widow Bunny insisted that we all went back afterwards to the Brick House for refreshments. This was where he lived with his first wife until she died; later it became his personal museum, housing all his favourite paintings and sculptures. It is a hugely evocative place.

Paul Mellon remains the only person to have bred and owned the winners of the world's three greatest Flat races: the Derby, the Arc and the Kentucky Derby. But of the many wonderful achievements in his life, it will always give me particular pleasure that most of all he just wanted to be remembered for one thing more than any other – as the person who had bred and owned Mill Reef.

9

Training for the Royal Family

The royal colours had hung in the trainer's tack room at Kingsclere as far back as the 1880s, when Prince Edward, later King Edward VII, had had horses with John Porter; but it was in October 1963 that the yard welcomed the first yearlings sent by the present Queen.

Her own first visit to the place, as far as I can recall, was in the spring of 1965, when she came to see the young horses out on the gallops. I could tell at once that she was very knowledgeable not only about horses' pedigrees (much more so than I was) but also about racing in general. I was to learn over the years what a superb natural horsewoman she was as well.

Things had gone well for us in my first season with ten winners in the royal colours, one of them, a sweet little filly called Garter Lady, at the Ascot autumn meeting. During the early summer of 1965 we learned that the Queen would like to go around evening stables, and that on this occasion Prince Philip would be coming with her. We looked at her ten horses plus a selection of ten others belonging to different owners. Almost at once Prince Philip was asking me questions in his usual inquisitive manner about any little defect he noticed. 'What is that spot on its neck?' he would say, and I would reply that the horse had had ringworm a few weeks before and this had left a bare spot on its coat. More than once he commented that the Queen's horses seemed to look rather smaller than those of our other owners. Because I was patiently answering all his questions as best I could, we seemed to be taking a shade longer than usual to get round. Finally, towards the end of the tour, we came to Garter Lady, now a three-year-old. She was ready to run and I must admit she looked a shade on the light side. This time Prince Philip said to the Queen, who was just ahead of him, 'Why are your animals all so *thin*?' The Queen turned to him and with a touch of impatience said, 'If you did but know it, that is how a fit racehorse should look!' She then moved fairly quickly on to the next horse. Prince Philip did not ask any more questions that evening and sadly has never been to Kingsclere since then!

Until Lord Porchester took on the role in 1970 the Queen had no official racing manager. Richard Shelley was her stud manager, and occasionally we would phone him, but generally Priscilla or I would ring Buckingham Palace and speak directly to the Queen to give her all the necessary information on her horses.

At that early stage of my career her yearlings were being divided fairly evenly between Sir Cecil Boyd-Rochfort, who had trained very successfully for the royal family for years at Newmarket, and us at Kingsclere. She also leased some horses belonging to the National Stud, and these were trained by Noel Murless, also at Newmarket. On one visit to us she told the story, with some amusement, of how 'the old Captain' – as Cecil Boyd-Rochfort was known – had asked her rather directly, 'Ma'am, *who* decides which yearlings go where?' The Queen, somewhat taken aback at this rather abrupt approach, said that she replied after some thought, 'God!' She meant, of course, that she herself made the decision – but perhaps looked for some divine guidance in reaching it. The old Captain, totally perplexed by this answer, just said, 'Who? Who?'

One autumn in the late 1960s the Queen did not have many colts among her crop of yearlings and asked her trainers to buy one colt each at the autumn yearling sales. We bought a lovely brown youngster by the stallion Kings Troop, with whom Peter Hastings-Bass had won the Royal Hunt Cup at Ascot. He was not expensive but straight away looked classy, and all of us at Park House liked him enormously. The Queen named him Musical Drive, and the following spring he looked as if he might be one of our first two-year-olds to run.

On a chilly Monday morning in March, our first string of about twenty horses was having its warm-up trot out in our 'starting gate' field. The horses were all very fresh and before I knew it three of them were loose, which was unusual. Two of the lads had tried so hard to hold on once thrown off that their mounts were now galloping around with no bridles on. Then a fourth horse got loose and there was total chaos. Musical Drive, who was being ridden by his lad Peter Williams, suddenly went berserk and threw in two of the biggest bucks I have ever seen; Peter was thrown off and the colt galloped flat out straight at the metal gate in the corner of the field. He had no chance of jumping it cleanly at that pace, and took one of the most horrendous falls I have ever seen. Somehow he bravely managed to get up, and instinct told him to stagger back in my direction. To my horror he collapsed and died at my feet.

It was as nasty an incident as I can remember, and I left it until about midday, by which time I felt more composed, before I rang the Queen. Her reaction was wonderful – so similar to Paul Mellon's after the Mill Reef injury a few years later. 'Oh, Ian – How horrid! How is the poor lad who was riding him?' She went on, 'I know how much trouble you had taken in buying him, and I really am so sorry for you all.' Sadly, over the next thirty-odd years there were other disasters involving the Queen's horses, and I have to say the bad news was always received with the utmost understanding and consideration on her part.

In 1970 Magna Carta, a big, handsome home-bred bay colt by Charlottesville, won at Royal Ascot as a four-year-old and went on later that season to win two more valuable handicaps before capturing the Doncaster Cup in September as well. At that stage he looked an outstanding prospect for the next season's Ascot Gold Cup. I was mortified when one morning that winter Bill Palmer found him at dawn lying on his back in his box with a hind leg entangled in his empty hay net. X-rays soon showed that he had broken his jaw in the struggle to get his leg free, and in the subsequent operation at Newmarket he later died. This was another terrible loss, for both his owner and us.

Before this occasion the Queen had told me how Doutelle, a promising young stallion of hers at Sandringham, had died as a result of an accident with a rack chain. She indicated that a silly mistake had been made, and I gathered then that she did not take kindly to unnecessary errors. While she did not imply that this unfortunate accident with Magna Carta had been our fault in any way, the Queen nevertheless requested that her horses from then on did not have haynets – and in fact, ever since then none of our horses have had hay nets in their boxes.

In the early 1970s we had a beautiful chestnut filly by the great French stallion Exbury called Example, bred at Sandringham. An outstanding race mare, she won the Park Hill Stakes at Doncaster and then a similar prestigious race at Longchamp at three, ridden by Lester, and in the spring of the following season won a Group II race at Saint-Cloud. Almost unbelievably, this lovely mare died when having her first foal – a filly by Nijinsky called Pas De Deux. This was a savage blow for the Royal Studs and an intense disappointment for the Queen in particular.

Every year without fail, one morning in the spring the Queen would come with Lord Porchester to see all the horses out on the gallops. This evidently gave her great pleasure, and I imagine it was fascinating for her to go to her various trainers over the years and to see the different training grounds and systems used.

She would always come on a separate occasion for a tour around evening stables, when she liked to see as many horses as possible rather than just her own. On these occasions she would come into the box itself to see each particular horse more clearly, and if it was one of her own I would pass her a carrot or a handful of clover to give the horse as a treat. She would give the horse its titbit and a pat, chat to its groom, and spend a couple of minutes at least with each one. Every once in a while we had the odd horse who might be likely to bite or kick. With most owners I would warn them not to come into that particular box, but in the Queen's case this wasn't necessary; she seemed to have an uncanny sixth sense about horses' temperaments and would be staying outside the door before I turned to warn her not to come in.

One year the Queen paid her visit when our stable had been going through a rough time, with most of the string suffering from respiratory problems and a distinct shortage of winners. It was autumn, and we had kept all the outside doors closed to try to keep the horses warm. We had returned to the house for a drink, having been round stables, and after a while she said thoughtfully, 'Ian, I noticed while we were going round how stuffy and dusty it seemed to be. I really think you might have a problem with the ventilation in those old boxes.'

Almost at once I organised for a specialist firm to come in and test the ventilation. The Queen had been absolutely right; the number of air changes per hour was totally inadequate, and straight away we took all sorts of steps to improve the conditions.

There was one other occasion when I was made particularly aware of the Queen's natural horsemanship. During one of her many visits to our area, when she always stayed with the Porchesters at Milford Lake House, Emma and I were invited to go up with her and Lord Porchester to her stud called Polhampton, which is only a mile from us, to look at the yearlings. All the fillies – about eight of them – were in one field, and the five of us, including her stud groom Sean Norris, wandered across and looked at each one individually. Then we went across the lane to another paddock where the six colts were. Again all five of us walked towards the middle of the field, where the colts were milling around, and tried to have a look at them individually. It was just before these young horses were due to come in to be broken in, and they were in a very cheeky and playful mood. They had no wish to be inspected and suddenly they all took off at a gallop, went round in a small circle and came back at us and started rearing up just as they got near. They then began what might be described as 'dive-bombing' us and it became a little frightening. Three of our party took off and ran for the safety of the gate. The other two stood quite still where they were, realising that was in fact the safer thing to do and that the colts would not actually attack them. One of those two was of course the Queen.

In 1974 we had a genuine Oaks candidate among the royal

horses. She was a chestnut filly and, like all the Queen's horses, beautifully named: Escorial, by Royal Palace out of Asturia. She had won the big fillies' mile race at Ascot the previous autumn and came to the premier Oaks trial, the Musidora Stakes at York in May, as the favourite. Lester was to ride her and the Queen had come to see her run. At York there is a long walk from the racecourse stables across the open spaces of the Knavesmire to the paddock and saddling boxes. Escorial was a temperamental lady, and as I stood beside the Queen in the Royal Box with my binoculars, watching her start the long walk, I explained that I was taking no chances of her misbehaving and getting loose: she had one lad riding her as well as her own lad leading her and my travelling head lad walking with her on the other side. About halfway across, Escorial suddenly reared up, lost her balance and fell over; the next moment she was loose and galloping off to the bottom end of the racecourse. The Queen laughed and said, 'I thought you were taking every precaution to avoid just that happening!' I quickly mumbled my apologies and was very happy to dash out and assist somehow in catching the runaway. Fortunately for me a local trainer, Joe Mulhall, happened to be down by the one-mile start and managed to catch the filly before any damage was done. To my great relief Lester rode her beautifully and won that race in some style – which was just as well, for she was a disappointment in the Oaks and in fact failed to win another race.

This particular year was an excellent one for the Queen's horses. Her home-bred filly Highclere, trained by Dick Hern, had won the One Thousand Guineas at Newmarket in a photo and then memorably had gone on to win the French Oaks (Prix de Diane) at Chantilly. The Queen was there in person and I am sure it must have been one of her happiest days on a racecourse. Towards Christmas she gave a party at Buckingham Palace for not just her trainers and her jockeys, but all the senior members of our staff with their wives as well. Films of the main races her horses had won were shown, and all in all it was one of those especially memorable occasions. It demonstrated the Queen's thoughtfulness, and her awareness of just how much a trainer depends on his or her key helpers for any success they might have.

I have often thought that the Queen would probably have relished being a trainer herself, had she not been born into the royal family. She not only loves horses, but genuinely loves Flat racing as well. In the many evening conversations I have had with her over the years, I have always detected a real pleasure in talking over not just the ups and downs of her own horses but anything else of interest in the racing world as well. These discussions would often stretch into ten or fifteen minutes – especially if we happened to have had a winner!

Peter Williams (affectionately known as 'Cazzy' because he was apprenticed to the Queen Mother's former trainer Peter Cazalet) is one of our longest-serving stable lads and certainly one of the best I have ever had, and he is still with us now. If, annoyingly, he is always the last one to pull out in the mornings, his horses still look better than anyone else's, with artistic quarter marks and greased feet. After the disasters with Musical Drive and Magna Carta, both of whom were 'his' colts, 'Cazzy' became just about the Queen's personal groom at Kingsclere, and certainly always had first choice of her yearlings when they arrived. In 1977 he looked after English Harbour, a handsome bay colt by Mill Reef out of Albany, one of the Queen's best race mares. The Queen had very much admired Mill Reef as a racehorse, and when Paul Mellon made a nomination to him available each stud season she took great trouble selecting her mare to visit him. With a pedigree like this, English Harbour naturally aroused great hopes. This was the Queen's silver jubilee year and it produced providentially probably her best ever year as an owner, and almost certainly her best ever racehorse: the bay filly Dunfermline, trained by Dick Hern and ridden by Willie Carson to win both the Oaks and the St Leger. Kingsclere had not contributed much to her great year, but when English Harbour won the Yattendon Maiden Stakes for two-year-olds at Newbury in mid-August we thought we might just have a top-class colt for her.

The following season Willie and English Harbour won both the Somerset Stakes at Bath and then the Predominate Stakes at Goodwood, where he beat a high-class horse called Ile De Bourbon. Although he was lazy, we thought he was my only serious chance up to then of winning the Derby for Her Majesty; but at Epsom, ridden by Joe Mercer, he never threatened to win and finished well behind Shirley Heights. He was third in the Gordon Stakes at Goodwood, after which we sold him as a stallion to New Zealand.

The year after English Harbour came to us the Queen had a bay colt by Mill Reef out of her brilliant race mare Highclere, in training with Dick at West Ilsley. The colt was named Milford after Henry Porchester's own house in the grounds of Highclere Castle. In this particular year the Major was at the height of his success, and they had at Ilsley an even better colt called Troy, whom Willie chose to ride in the Derby. Milford had a pretty useful deputy on board in Lester and had won the Lingfield Derby Trial in a hack canter, so coming up to the two-hundredth running of the Derby he was third favourite. But Milford turned out to be a bit of a playboy, and although he won good races later he didn't come up with the goods when it mattered most, finishing in mid-division at Epsom.

A few years later, in 1982, 'Cazzy' took into his care another two-year-old Mill Reef colt. This one was out of Light Duty and was named Special Leave. He was a tall dark bay colt with great quality and in his first race he was third in the same maiden at Newbury that English Harbour had won. After that he was third again in a good race at York in September, and then at the October meeting at Ascot with Joe Mercer riding he won the Listed Hyperion Stakes. Joe was very impressed and said that this could well develop into a proper Derby horse for the Queen the following year.

In the middle of March 1983 Henry Porchester came one day to watch work up on the downs. The grass was very soft, so we decided to use our one-mile ash gallop. Special Leave, ridden by our best work rider Steve Woolley, went with Diamond Shoal ridden by John Matthias. Diamond Shoal, another Mill Reef colt of Paul Mellon, was later to prove himself the best four-year-old colt in the country that season, and on this damp morning, at level weights, the three-year-old Special Leave worked better than him. The Queen's racing manager and her trainer both thought we had just seen the horse that might at last win the Derby for her. I knew that for sure he was the best horse I had ever trained for the Queen.

It was not to be. Special Leave only ran once that season – on unsuitably soft ground in a Derby trial at Sandown – and disappointed. After that we had various setbacks that kept him from running and finally there was yet another disaster. I was away in America at the Saratoga sales in the first week of August when Emma rang me with the sad news that Special Leave, with 'Cazzy' riding, had broken a hind leg when working on the downs and had had to be put down. There were terrible echoes of Mill Reef himself, of course; but this poor horse had never had the chance to fulfil his potential.

A decade later, in 1993, we had a three-year-old half brother to Special Leave by Shareef Dancer called Spring To Action. He won an important listed race at the July meeting at Newmarket, but again failed to go on and become a really good horse. In fact, after such a promising start at Kingsclere, the Queen's horses here seemed to experience the sort of bad luck that was hardly credible. I was gradually seeing all the nicer yearlings going to other trainers and it was no great surprise when towards the end of the 1999 season Henry Carnarvon (formerly Porchester) told me that we would not be receiving any of Her Majesty's yearlings that autumn.

However, when Queen Elizabeth The Queen Mother died, the Queen took over her horses and one of them here, Captain Ginger, won twice in the Queen's colours in 2002. His half-brother Royal Warrant – yet another thoughtfully named horse, being by Royal Applause out of Brand – won as a two-year-old in 2003 and thus became Andrew's first winner for the Queen. It is satisfying to think that Her Majesty has now had horses in training at Park House with three generations of the same family. Her yearling colt by Zafonic out of Brand named Banknote is the latest from the Queen Mother's old family to arrive here, and we all hope that he may be the one to change our luck for the Queen.

In 2003 Emma and I had the honour of being invited for lunch at Windsor Castle before driving up the course at Royal Ascot in the coaches. It was a great experience. The whole operation is timed with intense precision, and so it was no surprise to see the Queen leave the luncheon table very punctually at the appointed hour. What did surprise me, however, was to see a mixture of ten little corgis and 'dorgies' get up from under the dining table and follow their mistress as if in convoy out into the next room. It was a wonderful sight, and proved to me that her great affinity with animals did not merely extend to horses.

Nothing would give me greater pleasure than to see the Queen breed and own that elusive Derby winner, wherever it may be trained. Her participation and enthusiasm have added so much prestige and glamour to our great sport for well over half a century. It would certainly be a well-deserved and extremely popular outcome if one day the famous colours could be first past the post in the race that matters most.

Early in 1980 the Prince of Wales was invited to ride in a charity Flat race at Plumpton. He was keen to do it, and I imagine the Queen had advised him that we might be able to produce a suitable mount for him. There was nothing of Her Majesty's that fitted the bill, but Paul Mellon had a four-year-old gelding called Long Wharf who was due to go jumping that season, and he appeared to be ideal. His owner was delighted to lend him and I advised Prince Charles, who at that stage had never ridden in a race, that he should come down and ride him, preferably more than once if he had the time.

We decided to have one decent gallop up on the downs over a mile and three-quarters so that the Prince could get the flavour of a race and get a good feel of his horse over that distance. So about ten days before the race we had a proper old-fashioned trial gallop. Two other horses took part; the leading amateur at the time, Ray Hutchinson, led, with Prince Charles lying second and our head lad Bill on a very useful dual-purpose horse called Cheka bringing up the rear. Three furlongs out they were to join up with Long Wharf in the middle and then kick on and finish as fast as they could. I had advised Prince Charles that Long Wharf was lazy and to give him a real good kick in the belly and a slap down the shoulder with his whip at the three-furlong marker. They duly joined up as intended, and watching through my binoculars, I was amazed to see Bill pick up his whip in his left hand and apparently give Cheka a good wallop with about two furlongs to go. All three horses finished together and I was slightly surprised and pleased that Long Wharf had stayed with the other two. Prince Charles had looked very tidy and acquitted himself well. We were riding home and when I got Bill on his own I said I was surprised to see him hitting Cheka as I didn't expect he would have needed to. 'Oh, no, Guvnor, I didn't hit Cheka at all; that wretched Long Wharf was doing nothing so I gave *him* a whack!'

There was another amusing incident on the way back. I was at the rear of the string on my hack, chatting to the heir to the throne. About a quarter of a mile from home the lad in front turned around and shouted back, 'Which way, Guvnor?' At that point we had the choice of going through the farm or left down a track and through a beautiful avenue, which had originally been planted in honour of Prince Edward when he had horses here. It had been known ever since then as the Prince of Wales Avenue.

Without thinking, I hollered back, 'Up Prince of Wales!' I saw Prince Charles giving me a rather old-fashioned look and realised suddenly that it must have sounded somewhat rude. Hastily I explained the history of the avenue.

The Prince rode out at least once more before the race and took the whole experience quite seriously. Long Wharf ran very well; sadly, Prince Charles did not get after him quite early or vigorously enough, or else he might well have won. He was an honourable second, however, and it was a good effort on the rider's part considering it was his first ever ride. To everyone's eternal regret, because he has never let anyone forget about it, the race was won by Derek ('Tommo') Thompson!

Prince Charles went on to have several rides over fences and it was sad that he never quite managed to ride that elusive winner. He appeared to enjoy his morning riding out very much, and although polo has always been his greatest love where equestrian sports are concerned, it would not surprise me altogether if one day he came back to racing and being more involved in it again.

Queen Elizabeth The Queen Mother, of course, had always been involved with National Hunt racing. She always took a keen interest in the Queen's Flat horses, however, and I expect she kept an eye open for one that might go on to make her a nice jumper.

In 1983 we had a three-year-old gelding called Insular, out of Pas De Deux and thus a grandson of Example, who won four races in succession in the autumn and gave promise of making up into a good stayer for his owner. Insular was never top-class on the Flat but continued to win races, and at the end of his five-year-old season the Queen decided to lease him to the Queen Mother for the National Hunt season.

I was thrilled when the Queen Mother agreed to leave him at Kingsclere. He had proved to be a useful but not outstanding stayer on the Flat and was perfect to go jumping. He had been gelded as a yearling because his front legs turned out so badly, but surprisingly had been very sound up to this point. He was also a tall, strong horse and very genuine.

Amid much rejoicing he won his first race over jumps – a novice hurdle at Newbury in November 1985. Fortunately, as it turned out, he was only fourth in his maiden at closing at Ascot a few weeks later. This meant that he was very nicely handicapped as a novice in the Imperial Cup at Sandown in March the following year. Eamon Murphy rode him and Insular made virtually every yard of the running to hang on bravely and win this prestigious race. He was the middle leg of a glorious treble that day for the Queen Mother at what was almost certainly her favourite racecourse. Special Cargo had won the Military Gold Cup for the third time and The Argonaut finished the day in style by winning the Dick McCreery Chase.

Queen Elizabeth the Queen Mother celebrated this historic treble with a party at Clarence House about a month later. Most of her own family were there, all her racing friends, and of course the jockeys and trainers involved together with their senior members of staff and wives. At the time she was blessed with a wonderful and hugely popular private secretary, Sir Martin Gilliat, who knew just how to ensure that a party of this nature was tremendous fun for everyone, including the hostess herself. Indeed, the many helpers who surrounded the Queen Mother were all ideally suited to their roles. Michael Oswald had been the Queen's stud manager at Sandringham for many years, and it was he who took over the role as the Queen Mother's racing manager. His wife Angela just happened to be one of the Queen Mother's ladies-in-waiting as well, so to a large degree this couple devoted their lives to her service and always accompanied her when she went racing or visited her trainers.

At the age of seven Insular suffered an injury and as a consequence had a totally barren year. In the early part of 1988 (now aged eight) he ran three times in the Queen's colours on the Flat without any great distinction – and then, to my surprise, I was suddenly offered him as a gift for my apprentices to ride. I accepted readily, and towards the end of May Reg Griffin of *Timeform* contacted me and asked if we would consider running the old boy on their charity race day at York in the Queen Mother's Cup. This was a valuable conditions race over a mile and a half. Reg then went on to say it would be wonderful if we could persuade Princess Anne to ride him. I said I would try. When I rang the Princess to ask if she liked the idea of riding Insular in this race she was full of enthusiasm, and in fact said she had been a little miffed not to have been asked before as he seemed such a perfect ride for amateurs as well as apprentices.

So the Princess came down and rode Insular in a little spin on the gallops and got on with him beautifully. It was what I would assume was a typical morning for HRH. She said she would have to leave straight after first lot because she had to be in London to present awards and make a speech at the 'Women of the Year' luncheon ceremony. At that stage she had not prepared her speech and would have to change and get her hair done when she got to London – and, just with her detective for company, she was driving herself! It was a work morning, so a couple of our jockeys were there and came in for breakfast afterwards – as also was the well-known National Hunt trainer David Nicholson, who had ridden out as well. I encouraged her to come in and grab a quick cup of coffee with us. 'Oh, all right then,' she said. 'I should be going now really, but I will come in for a moment if I may.' Almost an hour later she said, 'Oh goodness, time flies – I must go.' How she managed to do all she had to that day I can't imagine, but I'm sure she did it in style.

At York a week later she and old Insular excelled themselves and in my colours they stormed home to win the Queen Mother's Cup by a good ten lengths. (Ken Cox, who led him up that day, was later our travelling head lad for many years, and is still with us.) Three weeks later, ridden by our own good apprentice, Micky Marshall, Insular won another valuable race at Sandown. At this stage of the season I had the unusual experience, entirely thanks to Insular, of being the leading owner in the yard!

Shortly after this Emma and I happened to be invited to lunch at Windsor Castle and I was placed next to the Queen. I explained how very embarrassed I was about the old boy's sudden success in his new colours. As always she was very easy and in fact quite amused about it, and said how much she had enjoyed seeing Princess Anne win on him.

The following spring Insular, back in the Queen Mother's colours, ran just once over fences in a novice chase at Exeter. He won in a canter and looked even more natural than he had over hurdles. For a few moments I even had visions of the Cheltenham Festival for him; but by the time he returned to the winner's enclosure he was in some distress, as he had somehow managed to pull the tendon off his hock. It finished his racing career, but I'm glad to say he enjoyed a long and happy retirement turned out and acting as a nanny for our youngstock on the stud.

Every year at the Christmas National Hunt meeting at Ascot the Queen Mother took over the Royal Box and used it to entertain all her friends' young children. The Queen and Princess Margaret were nearly always there also. There was always a real Christmas party atmosphere. Andrew and Clare were asked several times as children and then later as teenagers to help entertain the youngsters.

It was at one of these parties that what I imagine was not an altogether unusual incident occurred and I still smile when I think about it. The Queen Mother was asking me about my own horse, Ross Poldark, who had won a hunter chase or two the previous season and whom I was going to ride again the next spring. She seemed interested in what I was saying, but after a little while I realised her attention was wandering. She appeared to be looking over my right shoulder, and as I was standing with my back to the mantelpiece I knew there was no one behind me. Almost in the middle of our conversation she suddenly said, 'Ian, would you like a drink?' Luckily as it turned out (and normally I would not be thinking of having a drink in the middle of the afternoon), I said, 'Oh, yes please, Ma'am, what a good idea.' She smiled broadly and said, 'I'm so pleased – so would I – and there just happens to be a decanter right behind you.' I've never been happier to pour out two glasses of port!

I recall another occasion at Kingsclere as equally typical. She had come down in the spring to see her two jumpers and was also keen to see some Flat horses of the Queen. She was excited about going up on the downs to see them, even though it was a cold windy morning. As usual she was dressed in a smart blue overcoat with a matching hat, and of course no scarf or anything to protect her neck and throat from the cold wind. When we got out of the car and were about to walk across the grass, which was very wet, I noticed that she was wearing high-heeled shoes. Emma had thoughtfully put her own boots in my car for the Queen Mother to use if she wanted, and I said, 'Ma'am, the grass is very wet, wouldn't you like to borrow Emma's boots which are right here?' 'Oh, no,' she said. 'Thank you very much but these are my walking shoes!' – and on she strode purposefully through the soaking grass.

In 1993 and 1994 we had some more success with two of the Queen's horses who had both won on the Flat from Kingsclere and had been passed on to the Queen Mother to go jumping. Bass Rock won twice over hurdles and so did Moat Garden, who looked quite classy. As an additional prize for one of the latter's winning races at Exeter the owner of the winner was entitled to a weekend for two at the local Thurlestone Hotel, which had sponsored the race. I rang the Queen Mother that evening to tell her all about the race and told her also about the extra prize she had won. She laughed and asked who looked after the horse. I told her it was one of our senior lads called Melvin, who had been with us for years. She enquired if there was a Mrs Melvin, and when I said 'Yes' she replied, 'Well, tell Melvin I am thrilled about Moat Garden, and I hope that he and his lady will enjoy a very good weekend at the Thurlestone Hotel.'

In late July 2000 Michael Oswald phoned me to say that the Queen Mother would like to come down and see her horses on the last day of that month. She had bred a Flat horse called

Double Brandy, who had won twice and thus in 1998 had become her first winner on the Flat for over forty years. Moreover, when the horse won a competitive handicap at Newbury he had beaten a horse of Sheikh Hamdan's. This victory had rather tickled the Queen Mother's fancy, and it amused her enormously to think that her one Flat horse had beaten one of the hundreds belonging to the Sheikh.

The day she had chosen to visit us was only four days before her hundredth birthday, and I was told that we must be absolutely certain not to take any chances, as it would obviously be disastrous if she had a fall at that particular time. I asked Michael Oswald if he thought Queen Elizabeth would like to go up to the paddocks on the hill behind The Lynches where old Insular and a couple of her other jumpers were turned out. I explained that although it was not the easiest drive to get up there, from the top you had one of the best views in England. Michael said, 'Yes, I would think she would love to.' As a result I organised for us to go up and look at the jumpers first, and then to come back down to the main yard to see Double Brandy.

The day before the visit the Queen Mother's driver rang and said, 'Oh, Mr Balding, I gather you intend to take us up a steep hill to see some horses. I'm afraid that won't be possible because we will be coming in one of the saloon cars which will not be able to get up there.' When I said we could go up in my car he replied, 'No, I'm afraid the Queen Mother can't get in and out of your car very easily – the only chance would be to come in her Range Rover which has a special swivel seat that makes it easier for her Majesty to get in and out – but we would not bring that car all the way from Windsor to Kingsclere.'

I said, 'OK, don't worry, we will bring the old horses down to the main yard for her to see them here.' The next morning the horses were on their way down when, about an hour before the Queen Mother was due to arrive, her driver rang again and said, 'Mr Balding, I'm so sorry, but the Queen Mother somehow heard that her old horses live up on the hill, and we *are* coming in the Range Rover as she would like to see them up there.'

Although the lads who had just arrived down at Park House with her three old horses had to turn around and walk back up the hill again, I was delighted by the change of plan. As soon as the Queen Mother arrived, I got into the front of the Range Rover to direct the driver; Michael and Angela Oswald followed us in their car. Happily it was a beautiful day, and when we got up to the top the view, as always, was stunning. It looks south over the stud paddocks and all the winter gallops and up to Cottington Hill beyond us. Westward it stretches over William's farm and on to Beacon Hill at Highclere. Finally, one can look north down over the village and in particular the lovely old Norman church.

I had been advised that the fewer times the Queen Mother got in and out of the Range Rover, the better. Needless to say she got out in each of the three paddocks we drove into to see the three different groups of horses. She spent at least ten minutes with old Insular, giving him lots of polo mints, chatting to our girl who was holding him and reliving the Imperial Cup with us all. Then we went on to Whitechapel, who in the Queen's colours had won the Moët and Chandon Amateurs' Derby at Epsom with Andrew riding. Emma's brother William had trained him then, but we had him later when he ran over hurdles in the Queen Mother's colours; he too was now retired. Finally we got to Cherry Brandy, a young jumper of hers who had won a bumper for us at Worcester the previous season and was now resting before going back into full training.

By this point we had been up there for at least half an hour, and I had told my head lad we would be down to see Double Brandy a quarter of an hour after we left. I said to her Majesty, 'Ma'am, I think we had better be going as they will be expecting us back at the main yard.'

I will always remember her reply: 'Ian,' she said, 'please don't hurry me. I never want to forget this beautiful view or this special time I have spent up here with some of my old friends.'

With her failing eyesight she may not have been able to take in all the detail of the view, but I began to understand why her memory was always so brilliant. I was also able to comprehend why old friends, whether equine or human, always meant so much to her.

We drove slowly back to the yard to see Double Brandy and then she, Michael and Angela all came in to Park House for lunch. Emma had invited her mother and Dick Hern, who were both old chums of the Queen Mother, and Clare and Andrew made up a very happy party. It was, of course, the Queen Mother's last visit to Kingsclere.

I was only to see her once more. For many years she had hosted a drinks party at Royal Lodge for her racing friends after the Grand Military Gold Cup at Sandown. In 2001 she was obviously quite determined to do it one more time in spite of being very frail. The Queen herself was there, as usual, but this time keeping an especially attentive eye on her mother. Alistair Aird, who had taken over from Martin Gilliat as the Queen Mother's private secretary, together with Michael and Angela, made sure that her trainers and a few of her other friends had a chance to speak to the Queen Mother. I was talking to her myself when my big brother came up. Worrying that she might not see his face well enough to recognise him, I said, 'Ma'am, you remember my brother Toby?' She turned towards him and said, 'Of course I do – Toby, I remember you once rode a point-to-pointer for me. It was called Gypsy Love and I know he was not a very good ride. I always thought you were very brave to ride him for me.'

That had happened just about fifty years before this memorable evening at Royal Lodge.

Emma and I had the huge privilege of attending the Queen Mother's funeral service at Westminster Abbey. It was a beautiful service that did full justice to this amazing lady. Like everyone else who ever met her, we will all have at least one treasured memory. Mine will always be her remark to me up on the hill behind The Lynches, just four days before her hundredth birthday.

10

Success at Home and Abroad

The whole of 1972 seemed to be taken up with Mill Reef and his injury. Even the film that was being made about him suddenly had to switch focus to his actual survival rather than a rematch with Brigadier Gerard.

From his departure until 1980 we went through what seemed to me to be a drought of high-class horses. We had plenty of handicappers that did well, though, and one of them was my first home-bred animal, a filly who turned out to be Emma's foundation mare for her Kingsclere Stud. She had bought the lovely old Victorian yard, with twenty boxes and about ten paddocks, from her mother, who had run it up until then. It borders straight on to the stables, with just the crescent of six staff cottages which her father had built between the stud yard and the lower stable block which we now call the Flying Fox yard.

Arthur Owen, the lovely man who had bought Caduval from Laurie Morgan and owned him while Toby trained him and I rode him, had wanted to support me when I first started training and had sent me a little bay filly by Agressor called Anippe. We won a couple of races with her as a two-year-old, and when Arthur Owen died his widow kindly agreed to sell Anippe quite cheaply as I was looking for a mare to use for my nomination to Silly Season in 1968.

The outcome of this mating was an attractive bay filly we named Siliciana. We leased her in a four-way partnership with my old friends David Back, David and Liz Pettifer and Jeremy and Penny Willder. Running in David's easily recognisable colours (purple with black and white striped sleeves), she won a little race as a two-year-old and then improved considerably to win the valuable Ebbisham Fillies' Handicap at the Derby meeting at Epsom the following year. At the end of that eventful season of 1972 we took a bit of a gamble by running in the Prix de Flore, a Group III fillies' race at Saint-Cloud. Not only did she win, but the two Davids are still enjoying the proceeds of their bet on her as she paid 60–1 on the pari-mutuel!

Emma had gone on the journey when quite heavily pregnant but the excitement of the occasion did her no harm, and just after Christmas our son was born. He was named Andrew (I always told Andrew Wates he was named after him just to keep 'in' with my favourite family). His middle name, Matthews, was my grandmother's maiden name and also my father's middle name. His godparents were Tony Lewis, my old chum from Cambridge, Peter Scott Dunn's wife Anne, who had become a close friend, plus his uncles, Robin and Simon.

With Clare just two years old we decided to employ a temporary nurse/nanny to give Emma some much-needed help. This turned out to be a well-known young lady in the eventing world called Jane Bullen. Jane rapidly became a great family friend – although I can remember enquiring from Emma after a week or two how much we were paying her and, feeling that the figure was outrageously high, immediately saying she had better ride out two lots as well just to be sure that her time was fully occupied!

Jane in fact rather enjoyed riding racehorses – she thought it was good for her event riding – and we ended up giving her quite a few rides in ladies' amateur races. She eventually rode a winner for us on an old gelding called Mailman in 1988. Long before that, at the end of July 1973, she rode a nice horse of Paul Mellon called Kafka in the major ladies' race at Ascot on Diamond Day, the event sponsored by De Beers. She was a narrowly beaten and fast-finishing third, and was, shall we say, unlucky! Jane, who later married Tim Holderness-Roddam, had already won Badminton and an Olympic gold medal on Our Nobby; and she went on to win the premier three-day event again with another marvellous little horse called Warrior. She and Warrior used to come occasionally to have a gallop with my point-to-pointers just to ensure he was fully fit before Badminton. Jane later became a lady-in-waiting to Princess Anne and chairman of British Eventing.

It was at about this time that we had a tiny Shetland pony called Valkyrie, kindly given to us by the Queen. Valkyrie was a great character and both Prince Charles and Princess Anne had ridden her as small children. She was one of those ponies that believed she should really be living in the house rather than in a stable, and needless to say our children very much encouraged that thought!

I took Clare riding on her own one day when she was only about two and a half years old. When we reached the stables down at Park House, for some reason I handed the two of them over to an apprentice to take them back up to The Lynches. Valkyrie 'dumped' Clare on the way home and it was discovered that she had broken her collarbone. Emma was furious about it and I had to console them both by telling them that according to Dave Dick, the famous jump jockey, 'no bloody jockey is any bloody good until he/she has broken their bloody collarbone!'

As children, both Clare and Andrew believed most of the stuff I told them. So a few years later Emma had been somewhat alarmed to find them both throwing themselves off their ponies in the field one day, and asked them why they were being so stupid. Dad got the blame of course: I had said they couldn't possibly make the grade as jockeys until they had had at least a hundred falls, and they had thought it made sense to get most of those falls over with in one session!

When the Queen came to see her racehorses, Valkyrie was usually presented at some stage and always demanded attention and polo mints from her previous owner. We bred her twice to a smart Shetland stallion of Hec Knight (Henrietta's mother) and had a lot of fun with the two offspring. The first one, called Parsival (Percy for short), soon went to Pat and Carolyn Eddery and their children. He was a great success there and lived to an enormous age – as did his mother.

In 1973 Siliciana, with Geoff Lewis riding, went on to win the Cambridgeshire as well as the valuable fillies' Virginia Stakes at Newcastle. She had given immense pleasure to all her owners and later at stud bred us a host of winners.

Silly Season was doing well as a stallion and that year, quite apart from Siliciana, we had several good horses by him in training, including Pantomime, a very useful filly of the Queen who won on the Saturday following the Royal Meeting at Ascot. There was also Martinmas – one of the top milers, belonging to Colonel Berry – and a decent horse of Bud McDougald called Idiot's Delight. I had bought the latter as a yearling and although he won at Royal Ascot as a two-year-old and went on to win good handicaps at three and four, I was amazed when his owner said he was going to send him to stud as a stallion. How wrong one can so often be in these opinions! Idiot's Delight went to Bud McDougald's great friends Frank and Cynthia Haydon, well known in the world of Hackneys, who ran the Cotswold Stud near Moreton-in-Marsh; and from there Idiot's Delight became in due course one of the most influential National Hunt stallions of his time. On several occasions he won the prestigious Horse and Hound award for the National Hunt stallion who had sired most winners in England. Occasionally when Frank did not go to collect the award at the Thoroughbred Breeders' Association annual dinner he would ask me to, and I always felt rather guilty about it because I knew that if I had had my way Idiot's Delight would have been gelded long ago!

In 1974 my mother-in-law named a two-year-old brown filly of hers Adriana. Luckily she was not useless and won a little race at Chepstow, because she was named after one of our very best long-time family friends, Adriana Zaefferer, a beautiful Argentinian who was also an extremely talented artist. At that stage she worked in pastels and had done lovely matching portraits for Emma and me of both Mill Reef and Siliciana. Nearly every year since she first came to England aged about twenty, Adriana has spent almost a month in England, usually staying across the road from us at Wells Head House with Priscilla, who has always been known as her English mother. Adriana later did a beautiful study of Mrs Penny's head and an even better drawing of three of our favourite dogs. These pictures are still favourites around the walls of Park House.

That same year Lady Beaverbrook all of a sudden decided to send some horses to us. She had experienced considerable success with her horses at Dick Hern's, and I suppose she wanted to expand. To say she proved to be a difficult owner would be a considerable understatement. I could not handle her at all – in fact, I found her impossible. The one big advantage to having her as an owner was that her manager was the legendary former champion jockey Sir Gordon Richards. Gordon used to enjoy coming to ride out on work days. He had his own hack at West Ilsley, but with us I would put him on any of our old geldings which we often used as hacks anyway. Gordon was one of nature's gentlemen, and I respected him as much as – perhaps more than – anyone else I knew in racing.

One day I put him on an old horse of ours called Royal Rebel who had been yet another gift horse from Herbert Blagrave. Royal Rebel had won on the Flat and over hurdles for us and even then, aged about twelve, he pulled very hard. We had watched the horses have their first canter and I said to Gordon, 'Why don't you track me and we'll go first and just have a strongish canter up to the top.' I set off on my point-to-pointer and realised after a couple of furlongs that Gordon had closed up and was right on my tail. I could hear the click-click of his hooves just touching my horse's, so I quickened up a shade to help him out. There was no way that Gordon's pride was going to allow old Royal Rebel to go past me but as we pulled up he himself was having a good blow. He smiled and said, 'Ian, you're testing me!'

On one occasion Lady Beaverbrook had asked if she and her sister could stay for lunch after seeing her horses down at the yard. Emma had the good sense to ask what they would like to eat. The answer was abrupt and to the point: 'Scrambled eggs, perfectly done and not too runny with no toast underneath and piping hot coffee.' There was no please or thank you. Well, Emma was always a superb cook, and has catered for some important guests over the years, but I have never known her as nervous as she was on this occasion. Lunch was a nightmare.

Lady Beaverbrook's horses were with us for precisely two years. How Dick and Clive Brittain managed to deal with her so successfully for all those years I just cannot imagine! I have to say she was a terrific character however and very good for the sport of racing generally.

In 1975 we won the Coventry Stakes at Royal Ascot for the fourth time in eleven years with a strong little bay colt called Galway Bay. He was owned by Jim and Meg Mullion, who had had enormous success with Paddy Prendergast in Ireland. We also had a very good filly of the Queen called Joking Apart, who finished a very close third in the One Thousand Guineas and later won two good races.

That year, however, was memorable for one thing in particular: the purchase of Park House and the stables complex from my brother-in-law by one of our main owners, the Canadian, Bud McDougald. On his father's death, my brother-in-law William had been left the whole property in trust until he was twenty-five years old. Unhappily for him, our punitive tax laws decreed that he then became liable for capital gains tax on the increase in value of the whole property since the time he had inherited it ten years previously. The consequence was that he had little option but to sell either the house and stables on one side of the road or the one-thousand-acre farm on the other side in order to pay the tax.

As I was a sitting tenant anyway, it was simpler for him to sell the Park House complex to me, and the farm in any case was far more valuable to him at that time. As I had no money to speak of I had to depend on one of my wealthy owners to help. Naturally I tried Paul Mellon first, but he was always firmly guided by his advisers and they told him that it was disadvantageous from a tax point of view for him to own property in this country. Sadly, therefore, he had to decline.

Emma and I had got to know Bud and his wife 'Jim' McDougald very well in a relatively short time. We used to make a point of going to Florida for our annual winter holiday almost every year. Not only did my mother and stepfather live there, and my sister Gail nearby, but we were always kindly invited to stay with the McDougalds in their spacious and beautiful house in Palm Beach. To give an idea of how esteemed Bud was as a businessman I will quote a tiny passage from an enormous book published at that time called *The Canadian Establishment*, written by Peter Newman. The very first chapter was entitled 'The World of Bud McDougald', and it starts as follows: 'If the Canadian Establishment has a grand master, that all-powerful figure has to be a nearly invisible Toronto capitalist named John Angus "Bud" McDougald. He is the archetype of the tycoons the radicals love to fantasise about.' It goes on: 'His lifestyle, his sense of personal imperative, his manners, his use of metaphor, his looks, his view of public power and private prerogative – everything about him is perfect.'

I was fortunate in that Bud had liked and admired Peter Hastings-Bass very much, and on Peter's death he had made up his mind to support the young man who had taken over the reins in every way he could. He liked encouraging young men in business, and I know that he became genuinely fond of both Emma and myself. He and his wife had never had children and in a funny way that in itself may have helped us.

So now I went to Bud and explained that I had the opportunity of purchasing the property but had no money, and asked if there was any way he could help me. He said that he needed an English racing stable at that time like a hole in the head – but that he would help, and that it was probably easier for him to deal with my brother-in-law and his trustees rather than for me to do so.

A neighbour called Charles Clifford-Kingsmill owned the top twenty acres of our gallops up on Watership Down, a section of the property which was crucial to the whole operation, and I was allowed to try to deal with him; but Bud personally was handling the rest of it. I did my part, and he negotiated a deal with William's trustees that he thought was fair.

I will never forget him writing out his arrangement with me in longhand on a loose sheet of paper in a coffee-house in Palm Beach. He was to own the Park House complex and lease it to me at a peppercorn rent for a five-year period. At the end of that time I could buy it from him at the same price he had paid for it. It was the most amazing bargain for me, and by setting it up in that way he knew it would give me something to aim for.

I was pleased I kept that loose sheet of paper with his signature on it because when, tragically, Bud died three years later I certainly needed it. His wife 'Jim' loved her horses and much enjoyed coming to visit us. Through her solicitor, who knew all about my arrangement with Bud, she indicated that she would like to go on owning the place herself at the end of the five-year lease. Emma and I felt that the very least we owed them both was to agree to her request. As long as we could complete the purchase without fail at an agreed future date, which was to be a further five years on, and still at the same price, then I was happy enough.

Then Jim changed her solicitor. The new one was far from pleasant and obviously thought I was being allowed to 'steal' this property from his client. Luckily for me, at the start of our dealings Bud had organised for a good friend of his called Tim Powell to look after Kingsclere on his behalf. Tim had been on the board of Massey-Ferguson (one of Bud's companies) and was in fact an old acquaintance of mine in that as a teenager I had briefly gone out with his daughter Libby. With Tim Powell's enormous help and my sheet of paper with Bud McDougald's signature scribbled across the bottom, I was able to complete the most important 'deal' of my life. A lot of successful trainers have never actually owned their own establishment, and if there is one thing in my life that I can be proud of it is that with Bud McDougald's invaluable assistance I am now the owner of our lovely property at Kingsclere. Our whole family will never forget the debt we owe to that fine gentleman.

Although he was extremely wealthy, Bud preferred racing to be his hobby and never wanted to pay big money for the yearlings we bought him. He was E. P. Taylor's business partner, but did not wish in any way to emulate E.P.'s style or the magnitude of his participation in the sport of kings. Nothing gave Bud more pleasure than when one day an eight-thousand-guinea purchase of his beat a three-hundred-thousand-guinea purchase of Lady Beaverbrook's (Bud had known of her as Lord B's secretary 'Christopher' before they were married) in a major handicap at Epsom. This was Turnpike, who won the City and Suburban Handicap – and he too followed Idiot's Delight off to stud at Frank Haydon's!

In 1976 we won three of the One Thousand Guineas trials. A grey filly of the Queen called Gilding won the Ascot trial, Rowantree a full sister to Martinmas won the Fred Darling at

Newbury and Memory Lane, Mill Reef's full sister, won the Princess Elizabeth Stakes at Epsom. We duly had three runners in the fillies' Classic – but none of them was placed. It was rather typical of my record over the years in the two Newmarket Classics!

Although I personally was buying a yearling or two each year for the McDougalds, I was depending very much on our owner/ breeders for the new intake of yearlings each year. Fortunately, as well as our longstanding relationships, at that time we had interesting new owners, including John Galbreath, owner of the renowned Darby Dan Farm and the Derby winner Roberto, and Bert Firestone, who was an acquaintance of Paul Mellon and a big name in American and Irish racing. My godfather, Joe Roebling, a wealthy American who had played polo with my father before the war, now wanted some horses with us too, and Bud Willmot, a Canadian friend of the McDougalds and a big owner/breeder, also sent us some. So we had no problem in filling the yard, which now ran to eighty-five boxes: for after Mill Reef's success I had built a new set of thirty boxes around an attractive courtyard with the lovely Skeaping statue of our champion in the middle.

One of my very favourite owners was Colonel the Hon. Julian Berry – another whom I had inherited from Peter. He was a lovely man, very quiet and unassuming; one would never have guessed that he had commanded the English army contingent that policed Cyprus during their problems. He lived locally at Tunworth and had his stud farm on the family property, Hackwood Park, just outside Basingstoke. His family were the proprietors of the *Daily Telegraph*. When I first took over at Kingsclere, his home-breds were of little account, although I was always grateful to him that my very first winner, Atholl, was one of his. Julian Berry's fortunes seemed to change for the better when he started to use Silly Season as a stallion. First of all he got Martinmas, who was for two seasons one of the best seven-furlong/one-mile horses in the country. Soon after that his full sister Rowantree was a Group-class filly. Then a couple of years later another Hackwood-bred colt by Silly Season, called Fair Season, won a mass of good races over a career of four years including the Horris Hill Stakes at Newbury and the Lincoln Handicap. He ended up being a useful stallion in South Africa.

It was in 1978, however, that Julian Berry produced probably his favourite horse – an enormous chestnut called Centurion, whom we had gelded at the end of his two-year-old season when he had not run. He was still very backward at three and did not see a racecourse until mid-June. He looked very slow and idle at home, and I almost begged the Colonel not to come to Newbury for his first run as I felt sure it was going to embarrass us all. To my surprise he finished fourth and did not embarrass anyone, and the Colonel was thrilled with him.

Centurion won a mile-and-three-quarter maiden at Sandown three weeks later, and in the next three months improved as much as any horse I have ever trained – including Lochsong. He won three more races, including a valuable two-mile handicap at Ayr, and started favourite for the Cesarewitch over two and a quarter miles at Newmarket in mid-October. Ridden as usual by John Matthias, he came from behind to win this great old race impressively, carrying more weight than any three-year-old had previously done.

Sadly and perhaps predictably, he did not stand training as a four-year-old – he just got too heavy for his legs. For many years afterwards he lived up in Yorkshire, turned out at Ken Thompson's farm where Colonel Berry wintered most of his youngstock.

Early in 1977 a young American lawyer from New York City who had been very successful in the music business arrived one day at Kingsclere and said he would like to have horses with us. His name was Eric Kronfeld. He explained that he had no background in racing and no knowledge of horses, but was very keen to get involved – possibly one day in a big way. His first horse was a two-year-old half-sister to Siliciana called Split Personality; she was not very fast, but did win a little race at Lingfield as a three-year-old. Eric was keen for me to come out to Saratoga and buy a yearling there, as well as a couple at Newmarket. At that stage I hardly knew anyone over there, and not having been to the sales in America before, I was rather nervous about it all; so I asked Eric if he would mind if I got my old Uncle Ivor to come up and help us. He would be invaluable because he knew most of the breeders and the other players, as well as the people at Fasig Tipton, the company who run the sales. The filly we ended up buying with Uncle Ivor's help that year never actually won a race – but I had greatly enjoyed the atmosphere of the whole place, and was determined to go again.

Saratoga is a lovely old town in upstate New York. It is full of Victorian houses, most of them built in red brick and with tall pillars and columns. For a century and a half it has been the late summer resort for most of the American racing fraternity. The racetrack itself has a charm about it that is – dare I say it? – almost English. Here racing goes on every day except Tuesday all through the month of August; there is another, training track very close at hand, and enough stabling there for about 250 trainers and 2,500 racehorses. Unlike some of the other big New York tracks, Saratoga still very much encourages jump racing: there is one hurdle race or steeplechase on every other race day, and they are still popular with the public, albeit more as a spectacle than as a betting medium.

All the big owner/breeders – the Phippses, the Bradys, the Farishes and the Whitneys – have houses in Saratoga, and for the month of August the town really comes alive. Thanks to those wealthy families, and even more so, perhaps, to Paul Mellon, the National Racing Museum was built there and has been superbly developed over the years. Every year it hosts their 'Thoroughbred Hall of Fame' ceremony. Just across the road one way is the famous old Reading Room, the perfect place to eat before the sales and within easy walking distance of the racetrack. In the other direction, and also only a stone's throw away, is the relatively modern Humphrey Finney sales pavilion. It is named after the greatly respected president of Fasig Tipton and is as well designed an arena for a horse sale as I can imagine. Even the stables behind the sales ring are beautifully laid out among the trees, with square grass areas bordered by soft gravel tracks which are perfect for showing young horses.

For the first few years I went over, Eric would take a house and I would stay there with him. After that I sometimes stayed with Marshall and Bettina Jenney: Marshall was one of the great characters of racing, both in Europe and in his own country. He ran a very successful operation at Derry Meeting, but was probably better known as a bon viveur and an exceptional raconteur. More recently I have stayed with our good friends Annie and Richie Jones. I have come to love the place, and that sales week has become for me a short mid-season holiday.

In our second year there I saw a chestnut filly in Marshall's Derry Meeting Farm draft – and could not take my eyes off her. She was by a relatively unfashionable English stallion, Great Nephew, and although there was some black type on the dam's side it was not enough to inspire interest from the American purchasers. We managed to buy her for only $40,000 which was relatively cheap at the time. Eric also loved the look of her and named her Mrs Penny, after his wife.

Mrs Penny, apart from Mill Reef, was almost certainly the best racehorse I ever had through my hands. She was sound and genuine, she had terrific speed and, like all the great horses, she was probably at her best over a mile and a half.

She showed enormous ability at home straight away, and we could not believe it when she was beaten in her first two races. I stuck with my belief in her, though, and in her third start as a maiden she won the Cherry Hinton Stakes at Newmarket in July 1979. She went on to win the Lowther Stakes at York and ended the season by winning the Cheveley Park Stakes at Newmarket in the autumn. Her breeder Marshall Jenney couldn't have been prouder of her if he had still owned her, and in fact became good friends with Eric. They always seemed to be there together at her races.

All that winter Mrs Penny was ante-post favourite for the One Thousand Guineas, and once again – as with Mill Reef – I felt sure that if she was going to win a Classic it would be that first one at Newmarket. Mistakenly again, most probably, I thought that to have her at her best for her first major test at the beginning of May she should have a pipe-opener in the Fred Darling Stakes at Newbury. John Matthias, our stable jockey, had ridden her in all her races at two, and he was to be her jockey again in 1980. In the Fred Darling John felt he let her go to the front too soon and she was just beaten on the line by an inspired ride from Lester on a filly called

Millingdale Lillie. Just two weeks later she did not run quite up to her best, but still finished a respectable third in the first Classic at Newmarket. Three weeks after that we went to the Curragh for the Irish One Thousand Guineas, but here Mrs Penny finished only third, behind the very impressive winner Cairn Rouge.

Although the filly had now been placed in two Classics, at this stage my owner was not too happy with our jockey. I felt I should shoulder some of the blame, because I knew we had not managed to have Mrs Penny at her best for either of those big days. She was entered in the Oaks, of course, but I thought that the distance of the Prix de Diane (the French Oaks) at just over a mile and a quarter would suit her better than the Epsom Classic – and for that race we all made the agonising decision to replace John as her jockey. It just happened that Lester Piggott was available and keen to ride her at Chantilly, which helped our decision somewhat.

Eric, Marshall and I watched the race from the top of the small old stand, and we shouted ourselves hoarse as Lester, in one of his typical power-packed finishes, just got up to win in a photo. I thought Eric was going to have a heart attack on the way down the old staircase afterwards. Without a doubt this was one of the great days in my career.

We had some training problems with Mrs Penny leading up to the King George VI and Queen Elizabeth Stakes and, considering that, she probably ran the race of her life. With Lester in the saddle again she went down bravely by half a length to the very good four-year-old colt Ela-Mana-Mou, trained by Dick Hern. At York she was fourth in the Benson and Hedges Gold Cup, and then we decided to run her over one and a half miles again in the Prix Vermeille at Longchamp – the historic autumn Group I test for three-year-old fillies. Lester was suspended, so quite rightly, albeit not unanimously, we decided to put John back on her. My favourite protégé of all our young Kingsclere jockeys rode the race of his life and Mrs Penny triumphed in her second Group I race in France that season – and this time Cairn Rouge was well behind her. She ran in the Arc de Triomphe three weeks later, but by then had probably had too many hard races and was obviously past her best when finishing in mid-division.

For some reason we could never get her quite right as a four-year-old. She only ran twice, finishing fourth in the Coronation Cup at Epsom and unplaced in the Hardwicke Stakes at Royal Ascot. Towards the end of July Eric decided to take her back to America, which was understandable. Over there she won the Queen Charlotte Handicap at Meadowlands and was second in the Manhattan at Belmont Park, but never quite rekindled the sparkle of her brilliant three-year-old season.

All her time at Kingsclere Mrs Penny had the benefit of being looked after by Geoff Rigby, who is a star – except that he is a fervent Manchester United supporter! Geoff rode her almost every day, except for work days when John took over, and he cared for her in the stable with more devotion than most men give their spouses. Geoff is still with us now and is just as good as ever with all his horses. In those days I liked to ride our best horses myself just once if and when it suited their programme. I never had the chance to sit on Mill Reef, but I remember having a strong canter one day on Mrs Penny up our one-mile gallop on Watership Down – and I have to admit I have never had a feel quite like it. She just floated along, and we seemed to be at the top before I even had time really to savour the experience! She was a sweet-natured filly, just as kind and genuine an animal as one could ever find, and I loved her.

As a broodmare she bred six winners, including two stakes-class horses, but nothing anywhere as good as herself. Sadly, I never had the opportunity to train any of them.

In 1980, the year of Mrs Penny's two great wins in France, we also had in the yard three top-class two-year-olds. In a fine autumn Robellino, a Roberto colt I had bought quite cheaply as a yearling for Mrs McDougald, won the Royal Lodge Stakes at Ascot; Leap Lively, a big chestnut filly of Paul Mellon, won the Group I fillies' race at the same meeting; and just a couple of weeks later Mill Reef's son Glint Of Gold won the Group I Gran Criterium in Milan. All three gave promise of greater things to come.

An incident occurred in 1979 which taught me vividly just how much having a winner can mean to an owner. We had a full sister to the Queen's good filly Joking Apart, who had finished a close third in the One Thousand Guineas a few years before.

This filly was named Strathspey and she had done pretty well in the royal colours as a two-year-old. At three, however, she ran poorly in the Guineas trial at Salisbury and the Queen's racing manager made up his mind that Strathspey did not try and that she should be sold at once. In fairness to him he found a buyer, negotiated the deal and made sure that for our sake the filly stayed in the yard.

Our new owners were Nigel Pilkington and Sue Chaplin in a fifty–fifty partnership. Sue was quite a bit older than Nigel and had broken her back badly in a hunting accident some years before. She could walk a few steps slowly with help, but generally needed to be taken everywhere in a wheelchair. Nigel was very good with her and, when with us, pushed Sue everywhere. Strathspey had one run in her new colours in a fillies' conditions race at Sandown at the end of May and I told Nigel and Sue that as she would be well handicapped we would aim for the good fillies' handicap (the Fern Hill Stakes) on the Saturday following the Royal Meeting at Ascot. Before the race Nigel, Sue and I made our way up to the fifth floor and took Sue to a good vantage point some thirty yards away from the lift and virtually opposite the winning post. Under a fine ride by Greville Starkey, Strathspey came from behind and got up to win decisively well inside the final furlong. It was an extremely exciting race and a lovely surprise for us all, so we had a good shout in the closing stages. Then Nigel and I turned to each other and shook hands, and after no more than a few moments we turned to push Sue in her wheelchair back to the lift.

The wheelchair was there, but it was empty. We looked towards the lift and there was Sue, in a slow, ungainly trot, just getting there. Nigel and I could not believe our eyes – the sudden enormous joy must have produced the necessary adrenalin to make this virtual miracle happen. I have never forgotten it, and since then have never underestimated the power of unadulterated happiness that such a winner can produce.

Strathspey went on improving enough to win two more valuable fillies' handicaps first at the July meeting at Newmarket and then again at the big Goodwood meeting three weeks later. I do not know if that amazing moment at Ascot prolonged Sue's life or shortened it – maybe her son Mervyn, who was usually present for her runners, is the only person who might know.

In the following year, 1980, a new young American owner arrived at Park House: Marshall Jenney's great friend and next-door neighbour in Pennsylvania, George Strawbridge. George was a well-known owner/breeder in the States and kept all his mares and youngstock at Derry Meeting under Marshall's care. He had a few horses over here at Newmarket, but felt he wanted a change of venue and fortunately chose us.

We had sent our mare Siliciana to Brigadier Gerard one year mainly in order to try to remain friendly with *Emma*'s relations the Hislops! The resultant offspring was a colt named Junta, and we sold him privately to George. Junta won as a two-year-old and then the next year gave George and his wife Nina a very happy day out in Belgium when he won the Grand Prix de Bruxelles. This was the prelude to a happy arrangement whereby George sent us many excellent home-breds over the next twenty-odd years. It was also the beginning of a firm and lasting friendship between our two families.

Of the three high-class two-year-olds of 1980 only one in fact went on to achieve really great things as a racehorse. Robellino fractured a bone the next season and won only one more race. Marshall Jenney had always loved him and was determined to buy him to stand as a stallion at Derry Meeting. I organised the sale on behalf of old Mrs McDougald and Robellino stood in Pennsylvania for a few seasons. Sadly, he did not get enough mares over there and Marshall had to sell him. With James Wigan organising the deal, Robellino moved back to England to stand at Jeff Smith's Littleton Stud near Winchester. There, ironically, Marshall was proved right: this wonderful old horse has been an enormous success as a stallion and is still going strong now, aged twenty-five. He has bred a mass of good horses, including our own best broodmare Spurned.

Leap Lively was actually a very good three-year-old. After winning the Lingfield Oaks trial in May she went on to finish third in the Epsom Oaks and second in the Yorkshire Oaks, but failed to win another race thereafter. She made her mark, however, as a broodmare for Paul Mellon: her very first foal was none other than Forest Flower, who will figure prominently later in these pages.

But it was the third of that trio, Glint Of Gold, who turned out to be the real star. He proved to be one of Mill Reef's very best sons and ended up with the amazing record of winning five Group I races and being second in three more, including the Derby and St Leger. Paul Mellon had sent several mares over to England in order to use his nominations to Mill Reef, and they boarded with Emma at her Kingsclere Stud. One of them was a lovely Graustark mare called Crown Treasure, from one of Paul Mellon's most successful families. Glint Of Gold was her first foal and, although a couple of sizes bigger, he had very much the look of his sire. He was such an honest and sound horse as well as a top-class performer, and I came to like and admire him enormously.

He won the Italian Derby at Rome in style and came to the 1981 Epsom Derby as about third favourite. He was unlucky perhaps to bump into one of the best ever Derby winners in Shergar. John Matthias, who rode Glint Of Gold, had been very unfortunate in that he was badly bumped and nearly brought down early on in the race. He subsequently came from a long way back to finish strongly in second place, but still ten lengths behind Shergar. When asked afterwards on TV how it had gone, John replied, 'Fantastic – in fact I thought I had won, because I never saw Shergar!'

Glint Of Gold went on to become the first English-trained winner for many years of the celebrated French race the Grand Prix de Paris. That race was over a mile and seven furlongs then, and after it I felt we must target the St Leger. Consequently we rested our colt for several weeks in midsummer and waited for the Great Voltigeur Stakes at York: our main prep race for the oldest Classic of them all, three weeks later at Doncaster.

Glint Of Gold won the Great Voltigeur impressively and came to the St Leger as second favourite to the odds-on Shergar. I was unusually confident that over the extra two and a half furlongs we would have a good chance of reversing the form with the brilliant Derby winner. Dick Hern had two runners – the Gordon Stakes winner Bustomi, ridden by Lester, and a relative outsider of Jakie Astor's called Cut Above, ridden by Joe Mercer. Paul Mellon came over for the race and I watched with him in the directors' box. Lester took the lead over half a mile out and from a quarter of a mile out it was evident that Shergar had come to the end of his tether. At that point Glint Of Gold took up the running with some purpose, and I recall some of the directors and their fellow Jockey Club members turning to Paul Mellon and starting to congratulate him. His colt did look all over a winner – but suddenly from out of the pack came this bay horse ridden by Joe. Jakie Astor's home-bred quickened well to beat us by a couple of lengths in the end. If I didn't know it already, I certainly learned that day never to be sure you have won until the judge has actually announced the result!

Glint Of Gold was a tough colt, and instead of getting a well-deserved rest after such a gruelling race he was off to Cologne a month later for the most valuable race of the whole year in Germany: the Preis von Europa. John Matthias, who had done nothing wrong in the St Leger, rode him again and beat a field of useful older horses comfortably. This completed a superb season for our good horse.

We kept Glint Of Gold in training as a four-year-old, in the care of one of our best young lads, who looked after both him and his younger brother Diamond Shoal. This was Micky Weedy, a fabulous young athlete who could ride anything we put him on; if he had had more ambition and certainly more self-discipline he could easily have made the grade as a jockey. He was a fine footballer also and without question the best stable-lad boxer that we ever had at Kingsclere.

Glint Of Gold's four-year-old season began with a narrow victory locally in the John Porter Stakes at Newbury. He was then beaten in a photo-finish in the Jockey Club Stakes a couple of weeks later by the great Gold Cup winner Ardross. Some people felt that John was outmanoeuvred here by Lester on the winner, but to my mind Lester just had the better horse that day.

Then in the Coronation Cup at Epsom about a month later came one of my major disappointments. Paul Mellon had come over to watch and Glint Of Gold was quite a warm favourite for the big race. We had a couple of other runners for P.M. that day, and one of them, Fairy Tern, was odds-on with only four opponents in the race before the big one. John managed somehow to get shut in on the rails, and hardly came off a tight rein in finishing close up fourth. I tried to defend him to my owner, saying how difficult the camber was at Epsom, but in fairness John must have come out for the Coronation Cup with his confidence at a pretty low ebb. To help ensure a good gallop for our slightly one-paced favourite I ran Show A Leg, ridden by Paul Cook, who was deputed to make the running at a decent pace. Unfortunately for John, Show A Leg was in rather an unhelpful mood and Paul had to scrub him along like a dervish just to get him to lead at all. Glint Of Gold was 'pulling a cart' in second place and dying to go faster; but John, who had been told to wait till at least the three-furlong marker before making his move, did just that, instead of taking up the running at least a mile out – as, with hindsight, he should have done. Glint Of Gold still led and with a furlong to go looked the winner, just as he had in the St Leger the previous season. Suddenly Bruce Raymond on the 20–1 outsider Easter Sun – trained by Michael Jarvis for my recent patron Lady Beaverbrook – came wide and fast to get up and beat us by half a length. There was not too much time to discuss John's ride and luckily for us both, John went straight out on Diamond Shoal in a good handicap and made partial amends by getting up in the last stride to win a short head.

It is always galling to be beaten by a 20–1 shot when you are a hot favourite, and especially in a Group I race. Even I felt that John should have won. When he realised our pacemaker would not go fast enough, he should have had the confidence to take matters into his own hands and to go on himself and make the race into a true test of stamina. Glint Of Gold was at his best that day and ready to break a track record if allowed to go a real good gallop all the way. There was one other interesting thing that none of us knew at that time and which could well have been a factor in the result of that race. When we sold Glint Of Gold as a stallion a few months later, he had his first full veterinary examination. As he had been home-bred and was always remarkably sound there had never been any good reason for a vet to look at him closely before. Now the vet discovered, to our dismay, that he was almost totally blind in his right (off-side) eye. At Epsom I suspect that he never even saw Easter Sun, who was well wide of him. Knowing how game he was, he might well have found a bit more had he been able to see the other horse.

Anyway, that Epsom meeting suddenly plunged me into a major confrontation about our stable jockey John Matthias. All my friends in racing and most of my owners were telling me that he had to go. Even Paul Mellon, who was normally so easy, and agreed with virtually any suggestion I made, was adamant. I argued that John should have one more chance on Glint Of Gold, but when he was beaten again two weeks later in the Hardwicke Stakes at Royal Ascot, I knew that his time was up. Up to that point my natural loyalty to my own protégé had probably blinded me to reality.

John had just bought a large new property on the strength of his substantial retainer with us, and to tell him he had lost his job was one of the most difficult things I can remember having to do as a trainer. Most of our apprentices in those days came straight from school, having never sat on a horse, and we taught them from scratch. The system worked well: we had already had two champion apprentice jockeys in Ernie Johnson and Philip Waldron. John, however, had come even earlier and had done his last two years at school while living in the hostel at Park House; and though he had not officially been the leading apprentice, he was the first of three of our boys to win the Crown Decorators Apprentice title (the others being Shaun Payne and Joey Brown). On top of this, I knew his parents well and we had employed his younger sister Annie as a nanny for Andrew and Clare.

John was a superb horseman and a very good jockey, especially at the smaller courses, and of course I was very fond of him as well. But, forcing myself to take a dispassionate view, I could not argue that he was as good as the top jockeys on the big occasions at the big meetings. Even the Queen, who was as shrewd as anybody could be about most racing matters, was inclined to feel that he was not as experienced or as strong in a finish as the very best. I learned then that it is always better in the long term to let owners choose their own jockeys, and as a trainer not to be too dogmatic about it.

Glint Of Gold next ran in the Grand Prix de St Cloud, and ridden by Pat Eddery he won this valuable prize narrowly, beating a very good French-trained horse of Lord Weinstock's called Lancastrian. Three weeks later, again ridden by Pat, he finished third in the King George VI and Queen Elizabeth, beaten by Kalaglow and the Irish Derby winner Assert. Interestingly, his Coronation Cup victor Easter Sun finished ten lengths behind him that day. Glint Of Gold was then aimed for the Arc de Triomphe, and we chose the Grosser Preis von Baden at Baden Baden as his prep race. With Pat on board he made every yard of the running and won that race comfortably.

Sadly, the Arc was not to be: Glint Of Gold somehow managed to get a bit of a tendon strain and could not be prepared for the race. He was sold to Souren Vanian as a stallion and did not run again. It was a great shame, because the ground for the Arc that year was heavy, which our fellow loved, and his old rival Ardross was only beaten a head. Our horse must have gone very close.

Even more sadly, his career as a stallion at Newmarket was very short: after only a couple of seasons he was found dead in the paddock one day from some sort of obscure grass sickness.

Apart from the emergence of Glint Of Gold's younger brother Diamond Shoal into what my friend and fellow trainer Jeremy Tree would refer to as a 'serious' horse, there was one other interesting happening in 1982.

Marshall Jenney, who by now was a very good friend and tended to treat Park House like his English home, had a very good home-bred two-year-old filly of his own with us. She was called Flamenco and by the end of August she was unbeaten in three races, which included the Sweet Solera Stakes at Newmarket and, most importantly, the Group III Waterford Candelabra Stakes over seven furlongs at Goodwood. At this stage she was already being quoted at quite a short price for the next year's One Thousand Guineas and Marshall, being no fool, realised that she was at that point worth enough money to pay off at least part of his mortgage on Derry Meeting Farm. He really had no option but to sell, and, as he always mixed in the best company, he managed to sell her to his friend Robert Sangster. He had insisted that the filly should stay with us at Kingsclere, and naturally I was delighted to have this celebrated new owner. I had even got as far as asking if he would send us a set of colours, as I told him the filly might run again quite soon. But barely a week later Robert rang me to say sorry, but he had sold the filly on to Sheikh Mohammed and that he would be a much better owner for us in any case! I expect that Marshall was a shade upset when he learned just what sort of a profit Robert had taken, but in the event Flamenco was somewhat disappointing afterwards, so it turned out that he had made a very good commercial decision at the time.

The next year, 1983, proved to be the year of Diamond Shoal as far as we were concerned. As a three-year-old he had won just that one handicap at Epsom on Coronation Cup day, but had gone on to be third in the St Leger and placed in a Group I race in Germany, and finally came home fourth in the Washington International at Laurel Park.

This year, however, with the great American jockey Steve Cauthen riding him, he started by winning the John Porter Stakes at Newbury and then went on to win three of the most valuable Group I events in Europe – the Grand Prix de St Cloud in France, the Gran Premio di Milano in Italy and finally the Grosser Preis von Baden in Germany. Like his elder brother, he was not quite good enough to win a Group I race in England, though in the King George VI and Queen Elizabeth Stakes at Ascot, ridden this time by Lester, he was only just beaten by the brilliant filly Time Charter, trained by my good friend Henry Candy. Diamond Shoal had been a tricky character to train, but had turned out to be a brilliant racehorse as a four-year-old and ended up with the very high rating in *Timeform* of 130.

Henry and I often visited each other to inspect each other's gallops as they were very similar, both beautiful old downland turf. I remember on one occasion having tea with his elderly father and mother, Derrick and Cerise. Derrick had been a good old-fashioned trainer but rather lacked his son's natural sense of humour. Quite apart from Time Charter, Henry had had several other good horses and plenty of winners, so to get the conversation going I said to Mr Candy, 'I am so pleased – isn't it marvellous how well Henry is doing?'

Father Candy replied rather gruffly, 'I'm afraid he's got an awful lot of slow horses!' It was quite difficult to know what to say after that!

Emma and I saw quite a lot of Steve Cauthen that year. By now we had sold The Lynches and moved down into Park House. (A couple of years previously Priscilla had built her own very smart house across the road. She called Wells Head House her bungalow, but all the rest of her family have always called it 'The Pink Palace'.) Often, after a long journey back from racing abroad, Steve would come with me to Park House and stay the night. He had a permanent struggle with his weight and was at the time an awful fridge thief, prone to raiding the kitchen when the rest of us had gone to bed. He was a delightful person, and Clare and Andrew both thought he was wonderful. Paul Mellon loved him riding his horses and that season he also won important Group races for us in England on the promising two-year-olds Elegant Air and Gold And Ivory.

This had turned out to be a very special year, in fact, because not only had we had a really good season in England, with sixty winners, but we had managed to win fourteen races abroad – in France, Germany, Italy, Belgium and Ireland.

I suppose for a few years in the early eighties I became rather besotted with racing abroad. Emma could have been forgiven for thinking I had an Italian girlfriend, so many times did I seem to be flying off to Milan or Rome at the weekend. Finally I agreed to take her with me and spend a weekend in Rome, and on one eventful Saturday at one in the morning Paolo Benedetti drove us around the capital city at about eighty miles an hour to see all the famous sights. By now I had been renamed 'Baldini' by my American friends Marshall Jenney and George Strawbridge. One of the plus sides of these overseas forays was that the International Racing Bureau by then was giving an annual award for the leading international trainer of the year. We won it in 1981 and 1984 and must have gone very close in 1983 too, when we earned just short of £400,000 in prize money won abroad. It might perhaps be said that, as far as English trainers taking advantage of the slightly easier but very rewarding opportunities in Europe was concerned, I was making the running at that time.

One downside to all this international racing on Sundays was

Colorlabs International

Mrs Penny, nearside, winning the Cherry
Hinton Stakes at Newmarket in 1979

Fred Spencer

HRH Princess Anne on Insular, with Ken Cox and me after winning the Queen
Mother's Cup at York in 1988

HM Queen Elizabeth
The Queen Mother up in
the Lynches paddocks
on her last visit to
Kingsclere just before
her 100th birthday

An aerial photo of
Park House, the
stables and the
stud farm

My sister, Gail, up
on the Cannon
Heath Down
gallops

Paul Mellon's wonderful little filly, Forest Flower (left), ridden by Tony Ives, just beating Milligram in the Goffs Irish One Thousand Guineas in 1987

Our 1981 Italian Derby winner Glint Of Gold, with John Matthias riding

Fiona Vigors

One of my familiar poses when skiing at Aspen, Colorado

R. H. Wright

The two trainers – me and Toby

With my most famous 'scalp' as a
bowler – Barry Richards at Highclere

Me on Ross Poldark (left) with John Oaksey on Paintbox and Dick Hern on Badger
at a drag hunt meet at Highclere

Emma on her
favourite
home-bred
hunter, Stuart,
on the winning
team at our
Team Chase

The four of us at
Buckingham Palace after I
had received the L.V.O.
from HM The Queen

Herald Photography

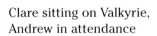

Clare sitting on Valkyrie,
Andrew in attendance

Emma travelling up the
course in one of the
carriages at Royal
Ascot

The beautiful form of Selkirk as a stallion at Lanwades Stud

The young trainer and the retired one with old favourite, Grey Shot

Champion jockey
A. P. McCoy on Duchamp
'schooling', with me on
Diviner up on the downs

Quirk and me 'ponying'
Lochsong (ridden by
F. Arrowsmith) away from
the rest of the string

Lochsong and Frankie Dettori winning the Nunthorpe Stakes at
York in 1993

that I hardly got a moment to spend with Clare and Andrew during the racing season. In fact, Emma became entirely responsible for their upbringing, aided by a succession of young girls. Two in particular – Jackie Knee from Trowbridge and Annie Matthias, John's younger sister – took the children riding from an early age; both Clare and Andrew adored them. Emma ensured, of course, that our offspring did not miss out on all the fun that the local Craven Pony Club provided.

I did take some part in at least the fun side of the children's life, though, and recall in particular organising some riding picnics for them and their friends late on summer evenings. These were based on one memorable occasion in Long Island, New York, when Uncle Barney and I, then aged about nineteen, along with six of his teenage girl pupils, had ridden the three or four miles cross-country to Uncle Ivor's house, jumping various fences as we went. There we turned the horses out while we swam and had a barbecue with Uncle Ivor's family before saddling up at midnight and riding back in the dark. It had been enormous fun.

In the Kingsclere version about ten of us, which included Charlie and Sarah Vigors, Alexander and Daisy Dick, and Werner Aeberhard and his daughter Lai, would take a long route up to the downs, jumping a few optional fences on the way up. At the top ring we would meet up with their parents and a couple of other friends. Emma would provide the picnic when all the horses were tied up to a rail, and after plenty of food and wine we would head home on our horses and ponies virtually in the dark. Knowing the way as well as I did, I would always take the lead, and it would be unusual if we didn't find a small obstacle or two to jump on the way back however dark it may have been.

After a couple of years at our local school in Kingsclere, Clare was educated at Downe House, where Emma herself had been a pupil, and after a few hiccups on the way she ended up as senior prefect. I remember going to visit for one play she was in – and that evening was the only time I ever met the headmistress, Miss Farr, and all I remember of it is that we had a slight disagreement as to where I should park my car!

Andrew, who like Clare began his education in the village, then went to a very good boarding school near Slough called Caldicott. It had been recommended by my old friend Dennis Silk who was now the Warden at Radley College. At Caldicott the headmaster Peter Wright discovered straight away that Andrew was quite badly dyslexic, and after plenty of special tuition he passed his Common Entrance rather against the odds to get into Radley.

Caldicott was a fine rugger school and Andrew ended up on an unbeaten first XV. He became very fond of the lovely school matron Pam, and Emma made a point of taking Pam with Clare and Andrew to Epsom on Derby day and having a picnic down near the Derby start. This was for quite a few years a regular pilgrimage, and was an easy and enjoyable way to get the children enthused about one of the great sporting occasions in the calendar.

It was said (mostly by Emma, I suspect) that life at Park House always stopped for one of these historic sporting occasions. It didn't matter if it was racing, rugby, cricket, soccer or boxing – we all had to stop what we were doing and watch the vital moment on television. I expect this may have helped Clare in her later role as a sports presenter. I'm afraid, though, that I did not extend my sporting enthusiasm to darts or snooker, which have never been favourites of mine!

In 1984 we had six horses of Paul Mellon that were good enough to win or get placed in pattern races around Europe. These were the high-class colts, Gold And Ivory, King Of Clubs, Elegant Air and Spicy Story, and two very good fillies, Clare Bridge and English Spring. Half of these had been bred at our Kingsclere Stud from his English-based mares and half came from Rokeby, and it was at this time that our success for P.M. was at its height.

At the end of sales week in Saratoga Paul Mellon, who had a summer house at Cape Cod, would usually pick up Mack Miller, his American trainer, and me in his private plane and fly us both down to Virginia to see the yearlings at Rokeby. He had a landing strip right in the middle of the farm, and we always marvelled how the broodmares in the neighbouring paddock hardly even raised their heads as we came in to land. His plane was a Gulf Stream II and could carry eight or ten passengers in some comfort. As one would expect it was beautifully designed internally, with small paintings here and there and a very nice bar which P.M. always proudly tended himself. That one day at Rokeby was something that Mack and I would look forward to all year. We always looked at the twenty-odd yearlings with Bernie his stud groom, making notes as we went, and then came in to join P.M., and sometimes Bunny too, for a superb and very spoiling lunch at Oak Spring. Before lunch our host would make us one of his special cocktails and we would sit and discuss the yearlings. Although P.M. tried to be as fair as he could about the division, I sensed that Mack, who was a better judge of a yearling than I was in any case, kept most of the ones he wanted in America. After lunch P.M. would give us a tour around the Brick House, and then, after visiting my old friend Martha Tross, his long-time racing secretary, for a cup of tea, I would be driven to Dulles International airport to catch the night flight back to London.

P.M. occasionally flew to England in his own plane; sometimes he would fly over in Concorde himself and have the plane come later so that it was on hand for him to use to go to Ireland or France. This particular year I persuaded him that he should come across just once to Italy for one of these many Group I races we were trying to win. So with Steve Cauthen, Emma, and Paul's great friend John Baskett, plus a lady friend of his, Pam Grundy, we flew in his plane to Milan, where Steve and Gold And Ivory did their stuff and P.M. went home with two very attractive gold cups to add to his winning trophies.

In 1984, too, I had a new American-style wooden barn for twelve horses built out beside the tennis court. This was mainly to make room for some yearlings for Sheikh Mohammed, who ever since Flamenco had – somewhat surprisingly, because she had not distinguished herself in his colours – wanted us to have half a dozen yearlings each year. One of the early ones, a speedy little filly called Welsh Note, won a stakes race in Ireland, but we had very little success for him and once he started to concentrate his horses in Newmarket a few years later they stopped coming to Park House. Nevertheless he was always extremely friendly and especially generous to the lads and to me. The one time Sheikh Mohammed came to visit us he was on his way from Newmarket to Goodwood and landed in his large maroon helicopter in the paddock we call Wroughton House field just south of the main house. He looked quickly at his horses and one of his managers John Leat followed just behind him, giving all the lads a nice present. He then asked if I would like a lift to Goodwood. I thought it was too good an opportunity to miss so I ran in to get my binoculars and then flew off with them. It took us exactly a quarter of an hour to do the journey that usually takes me just over an hour in my car. I had not planned my return journey, so I came back rather more sedately in the horsebox with our runners.

I was fortunate to be included in the Sheikh's large team of trainers to be taken to Keeneland sales one year. About six of us, plus his managers Anthony Stroud and John Leat, flew on Concorde to New York, where we went through immigration so quickly I could hardly believe it – no customs – and straight on to a Lear Jet which flew us directly into Keeneland airstrip. We had left London at 8 a.m. and arrived at our final destination at 8 a.m. exactly five hours later – ready to do a full day looking at yearlings! I spent the week staying with our good friends and owners Ron and Lori Kirk at their lovely Woods Edge Farm and then flew back on what we called the 'Magic Carpet'. This was Sheikh Mohammed's enormous jumbo jet, which took all his family and helpers, plus about twenty of us trainers and agents. This was luxury itself, and the flight was an experience to remember.

I went to the Keeneland sales for two or three years but rarely had an order to buy a yearling. It was good for business, however, and I was delighted to look around some of the fabulous stud farms in the Lexington area and to see all the famous Claiborne and Three Chimneys stallions at their best. A new owner for me at the time was Mr Bill Young's daughter Lucy, who was then married to an Italian prince called Mario Ruspoli. Mr Young himself and his wife were charming, and their stud farm Overbrook was even prettier than the much older farms. Two of the fillies I trained for Lucy and Mario, Northern Eternity and Storm Star (who actually ran in Bill Young's colours), were top class as two-year-olds and, as they were both superbly bred, went home as valuable broodmares.

I had one stroke of bad luck in 1984. The family were very keen to send over a colt by Storm Bird called Storm Cat to be trained here; we had done well with the Storm Bird filly, Storm Star, and they all felt at that time that his offspring might be better suited by the English grass tracks. Sadly for me, Storm Cat failed an EVA blood test in Kentucky, which all the yearlings had to have then. This meant that he had to stay in the USA – which may have affected the course of racing history, because this colt later became one of the most influential stallions of all time.

At about the same time Sir Michael Sobell and his son-in-law Arnold Weinstock became owners of ours. Sir Michael was very old and never came racing, but I much enjoyed talking to him on the phone, when he was always extremely courteous. We had some very well-bred yearlings for the few years I trained for them but we didn't seem to get much luck, and to be honest I never got on as well with Simon Weinstock, who virtually ran the family's racing interests, as Dick Hern obviously did. However, Sir Gordon Richards managed for them, and it was lovely to have him coming over again on work days. Peter Reynolds, their very astute stud manager, was also delightful to deal with.

In 1985 we had quite a good Royal Ascot: Insular came fourth in the Queen's Vase, and one of the best fillies I ever trained for the Queen, Soprano, was just beaten two heads in a very exciting race for the Coronation Stakes. Pat Eddery had ridden her – in fact, he was riding most of our horses now when he was available, and on the first day he had ridden a useful stayer for us called Meadowbrook in the Ascot Stakes. This was a Mill Reef colt whom I had bought for Mrs McDougald as a yearling, and the elderly owner and her sister Cecil were there to see him run. Up to now he had won a maiden and a couple of small handicaps, but this was his biggest test thus far. The Queen and Prince Philip, who had stayed in the McDougalds' house in Toronto once a few years before, had kindly invited the two old ladies up to the Royal Box, where I was watching the Ascot Stakes with them. That race, over two and a half miles, starts well down the straight, comes up past the winning post and then goes a full circuit of the track.

I had told Pat to make the running if he could as this horse was a natural front-runner and somewhat one-paced. As the field approached us for the first time, I was glad to see him in the McDougald colours in a clear three-length lead. I suddenly noticed the old ladies getting very excited as he got within a hundred yards or so of the winning post. As we were all in the Royal Box they were suppressing their cheers somewhat, but I realised to my horror that they thought the race was finishing on this circuit! They were both mortified when I explained that the horses still had a full circuit of the track to go before they finished. Mercifully Pat and Meadowbrook were still in the lead when they came round the next time, and now I did encourage them to get excited. The horse held on to win well and I suspect this might have been one of old Mrs McDougald's very happiest moments. To watch your own horse win at Royal Ascot from within the Royal Box, and to have the added excitement of getting two wins for the price of one, as it were, must have been very special!

Things generally were going well in the eighties and life was as busy as it could possibly be; but I never treated myself to the luxury of a driver. Emma drove me occasionally and John Matthias was as good an unpaid chauffeur as I could have had; but generally I still enjoyed driving myself and taking the odd risk. We seemed to be spending too many hours in a car, however, and very often doing two meetings in a day once the evening racing started. It was with considerable interest, therefore, that I said I would talk to a local man called John Cull who had phoned and said he wanted to sell me a half share in his aeroplane.

I had never met John before but he seemed very pleasant, although even at that first meeting I had a suspicion that he was very much an easy come/easy go character. The deal he suggested was that I should buy half his aircraft, which was a single-engined Cessna 177 with seating for a maximum of three. He, a qualified pilot, would fly me wherever I wanted to go for nothing, but as far as I remember I paid for the fuel. I thought this might present a problem, but no; our little aircraft could fly on the same cheap petrol which we kept in the tank for our cars and horseboxes to use. Also, the plane itself cost no more than a small secondhand car to buy or to run. Better still, 'Snoopy' (as we named the plane) could live on the downs right by our top ring, virtually out of sight, and we could take off and land straight down our left-hand-side gallop! It all seemed too good to be true, and I was quite excited by this new venture.

Our first flight was a trip to York. I am awfully apt to go straight to sleep as soon as I take off in a plane, and now I did it again. Suddenly John was waking me up and saying, 'Hey! You're my navigator. How soon will we be at York?' I looked at his maps to find that they didn't go any further north than Nottingham! When I complained about this John just said, 'Come on, Ian, you must have been to York dozens of times.' I said, 'True, but it all looks a bit different up here.' We were flying at a height of only about fifteen hundred feet, which I suspect was below the legal level anyway, but at least it meant I had no trouble following the A1 as far as Doncaster. We didn't seem to be going an awful lot faster than the traffic down below, but it was all great fun. I nearly got us in trouble when I thought Selby Abbey was York Minster, but eventually, more by accident than anything else, we found our landing strip at Acaster. By the time we got to the racecourse the journey had taken us about three hours – which was no more than half an hour less than it would have been by road!

We had better journeys thereafter to Newmarket and to Haydock – the only two courses other than Newbury which actually have their own landing strips. John had by now acquired the nickname of 'Biggles', and Snoopy I am sure was the envy of all my trainer friends! There were odd occasions, particularly when the grass was wet, when we had trouble actually leaving the ground. More than once I can remember pedestrians on our footpath that goes up beside the gallops diving to the ground as we cleared them by a few feet. We occasionally took a jockey in our back seat but the extra weight slowed us down even more.

Eventually, however, an incident occurred which convinced me that dear Snoopy would have to go. John had rung and asked if I wanted to accompany him to the Isle of Wight for a famous old air race called the Schneider Cup. It was a weekend event and we would have to take off early on the Saturday morning in Snoopy and return on the Sunday evening. I was tempted, but we had quite a few runners on the Saturday and I had to make my apologies to John.

I heard him taking off at the crack of dawn and thought no more of it until about midday, when I had a call from the Hampshire police. 'Mr Balding, I believe you are the part owner of a Cessna aircraft number Gulf, Bravo, Alpha, Romeo, etc. etc.,' came the voice. 'I am sorry to tell you, sir, but your aircraft is down in a farmer's field of wheat near Southampton. The plane is locked up and there is no sign of the pilot. I am afraid the farmer is not very happy about it.' I had no explanation for him at all except that I knew my partner was flying himself down to the Schneider Cup.

Eventually on the Monday morning 'Biggles' appeared and told me the whole story. When he had filled up with petrol early on the Saturday morning he had somehow neglected to screw the petrol cap on at all! Not surprisingly Snoopy ran out of gas quite quickly and John had to make a very rapid emergency landing. The only place he could see for any sort of landing in a hurry was this field of wheat beside the motorway. It was very early in the morning and rather than try to explain his predicament to the farmer, John just hitched a lift to the Schneider Cup!

The farmer had the last laugh, though, because he would not let 'Biggles' collect our plane until several weeks later, when the corn had been harvested! I gathered that had the petrol lasted for two more minutes John would have been over the Solent with nowhere to land in a hurry but in the sea . . . I was rather grateful that we had had runners that Saturday!

In the autumn of 1985, I heard that P.M. was sending over to us a chestnut filly by Green Forest, the first foal out of Leap Lively. When she arrived, I thought they must have put the wrong animal on the plane. Presumably I had seen her in August during my annual visit to Rokeby, but this tiny filly, measuring just 14.2 hands, was ewe-necked and looked half-starved. So small and unimpressive was she, in fact, that none of our senior lads wanted to look after her. I can remember telling one of our youngest apprentices, Chris Avery, that he was doing her, and no argument please! Little did anyone know at the time of her arrival that this diminutive filly would turn out to be one of the best two-year-olds of her sex to run in this country for many years.

Forest Flower was ready for her debut by mid-May and, ridden by Steve Cauthen, she won a fillies' race over five furlongs at Newbury comfortably. This set her up for what turned out to be an even easier victory in the Queen Mary Stakes at Royal Ascot – this time ridden by Pat Eddery. She looked to be an out and out two-year-old so we went straight on to the Cherry Hinton Stakes at the Newmarket July meeting. Here she carried her three-pound penalty for winning at Ascot and beat Minstrella by three-quarters of a length in the first of three somewhat controversial clashes that season. On this occasion she was ridden for the first time by Tony Ives, who was notoriously good on sprinters.

We then decided to have a crack at the Heinz Phoenix Stakes at Phoenix Park, which was not only a Group I race but the most valuable two-year-old race in Europe that year. Pat Eddery took the ride again and from a bad draw on the wide outside she was beaten a short head by Minstrella. She was flying at the finish and looked a shade unlucky, but showed the courage that was to be her trademark later on.

We then gave her a short mid-season break before running her in the Group II Mill Reef Stakes at Newbury over six furlongs. Naturally I had been anxious to win this race, named in honour of our great champion, but so far success had eluded us. This year, amid much rejoicing and reunited with Tony Ives, our little filly comfortably beat the colts again.

Her final race of the 1986 season was the Group I Cheveley Park Stakes at Newmarket – which this year was run on the July course. It proved to be the most controversial race of the season. There were only six runners and our filly, partnered by Tony Ives, was the hot favourite. Her old rival Minstrella, ridden by John Reid, was the obvious danger. Two furlongs from home our little lady was pulling double but was boxed in, with John Reid legitimately trying to keep her there. Instead of waiting a shade longer, Tony in his anxiety to get out bumped Minstrella. It made not the slightest difference to the result of the race as Forest Flower won comfortably by two and a half lengths. The objection by Minstrella's connections was quickly overruled by the experienced panel of Newmarket stewards and P.M. who was there to see his filly, was able to receive his trophy. Winning punters were also happy. Then, somewhat to my surprise, an appeal was lodged by John Reid.

Obviously I attended the appeal hearing at Portman Square – and I could just not believe the ruling. Tony Ives was found guilty of 'intentional foul riding' and suspended for twelve days. Forest Flower was not only disqualified but placed last. (Fortunately, the Jockey Club has now amended this rule so that it is much fairer; nowadays the jockey would get a three- or four-day suspension and the result of the race would not be altered.)

To have lost a Group I race on an unfair disqualification rankles to this day – and one of our owners, Jeff Smith, will remember just how much, because it happened again a few years later when Blue Siren won the Nunthorpe Stakes at York decisively, only to be relegated to second place. But Forest Flower still finished the season as champion two-year-old filly and was rated second in the Free Handicap, just a pound behind Reference Point. *Timeform* rated her at 127 and wrote about her as follows: 'Seldom does one see a racehorse show more gusto than Forest Flower. She is indomitable of spirit and wonderfully game and genuine, qualities which have endeared her to the racing public. Let's hope she sets the seal on a notable career with success in a Classic.' Her speed and courage were exceptional and Tony Ives, in spite of his very expensive mistake at Newmarket, was retained as our first jockey for the following season – mainly so that we would have a regular partner for this filly in her three-year-old campaign.

She was, of course, ante-post favourite for the 1987 One Thousand Guineas, but it was one of those miserable springs when our horses were struggling under some wretched respiratory problem. Forest Flower was not sparkling at home, and after a very disappointing gallop at Bath racecourse with Tony on board we had to abandon any hopes of running at Newmarket. I was very keen to get her right for the Goffs Irish One Thousand Guineas three weeks later, which meant treading a tightrope of trying to maintain her fitness while not doing too much with her. I had kept P.M. informed of her progress and at the last moment he decided not to fly over for the Irish Classic.

It was a great shame, because he missed one of the bravest performances that any of his horses have ever produced. Forest

Flower challenged the leaders with about two furlongs to run under strong driving from Tony and, without ever really looking as if she would win, she managed to get up in the very last stride to beat Milligram a short head. The latter had been second in the English One Thousand Guineas and went on to win the Coronation Stakes at Royal Ascot and also the Queen Elizabeth II Stakes there in the autumn. Forest Flower's performance at The Curragh therefore was not just brave but also of the highest quality.

Tragically, that very hard race so soon after the virus had finished her, and I should never have run her again. But I talked myself into thinking she was somewhere back near to her best in July and we ran her in the Group II fillies' race at the Newmarket July meeting. The little filly – still only 15 hands – was never going well and sensibly Tony Ives virtually pulled her up. It was a sad end to a brilliant career; but I will never forget the smiles on both Tony Ives and Chris Avery's faces when the result of the photo at The Curragh was announced.

She then retired to stud, and stayed with Emma for four seasons before P.M. started to wind down his breeding operation. She was then sold as part of his dispersal sale at Tattersalls and bought by Betty Moran. Her English-bred progeny certainly did not reach dizzy heights on the racecourse – but her first foal by Shirley Heights, called Hill Of Dreams, managed to win two amateur races with a certain Mr Andrew Balding as the rider!

P.M. had a small gilt bronze made of her by Tessa Pullan, who had been a pupil of John Skeaping and is now a marvellous artist in her own right. I was given a copy from the cast, and I would happily say that it is my favourite possession. It is absolutely brilliant of the filly and totally recognisable; every time I look at it I recall with pride and pleasure her exhilarating speed and the courage which she possessed in abundance.

In the autumn of 1986 George Strawbridge sent over to us a beautifully bred dark brown filly who looked easily the nicest yearling that he had so far sent. She was called Silver Fling and was a full sister to Silverdip, who had been good enough to win three Listed races and finish second in the Group II Diadem Stakes at Ascot three years before. This younger sister had more quality altogether. She did not excel as a two-year-old, winning only a humble maiden race at Bath in the last of her three runs; but she was entered in the One Thousand Guineas and I felt that we should at least see if she was that sort of class. So after winning a little six-furlong conditions race at Brighton she took her chance in the Fred Darling Stakes over seven furlongs at Newbury in the spring of 1988. She pulled much too hard and proved there that sprinting was her game.

After three second places, her first win of that season came in the Trafalgar House Sprint at Sandown – a Listed race over five furlongs. She followed up three weeks later by winning her first Group race, the King George V Stakes at Goodwood, where she was ridden by Pat Eddery. In the William Hill Sprint Championship at York in August (now the Nunthorpe), Silver Fling finished a somewhat unlucky second, and towards the end of her three-year-old season was beaten only a head by Dowsing in the Vernons Sprint Cup at Haydock over six furlongs. In her final start she was third in the Prix de l'Abbaye at Longchamp on Arc de Triomphe day. She was obviously in the very top class as a sprinter, and thankfully George decided to keep her on in training as a four-year-old.

She had been ridden by Walter Swinburn on her last two outings but now John Matthias took over for all her races at four. She ran in all the top sprint races that season, winning two early on and being placed in four others, including another second in the Group I William Hill Sprint Championship at York. Her final race was to be a second tilt at the Prix de l'Abbaye, which proved to be one of the most exciting and dramatic races I have watched.

Silver Fling as so often seemed to be outpaced in the early stages, and with only a furlong to run looked to have an impossible task. John then produced one of his most determined and inspired rides to get our filly up to win in the very last stride. Even then, George and I had to survive the drama of first the photo-finish result and then an objection by the second before we knew that Silver Fling had won. This was what she so deserved – a Group I victory in her very last race. To win any race on Arc de Triomphe day is a great thrill, and to witness his beautiful home-bred filly do it in such courageous style gave George, I feel sure, one of his happiest days on a racecourse.

In twenty races over three seasons, nearly all of them in the highest class, Silver Fling had only been out of the money twice. My own feeling was that if any of the sprint championship races were over five and a half furlongs she would have been virtually unbeatable.

There was an interesting and painfully expensive incident that happened at about this time which is worth recording. Paul Mellon had always insisted with typical generosity that I charge him 10 per cent of the many private sales that I was arranging for all his good colts – the fillies of course went back to stud; the less good horses went through the public sale ring where, as with most of our owners, we charged 5 per cent commission. Obviously, with so many good colts coming through the yard, I was earning a lot of money; and, rather stupidly, I had asked P.M. if some of it could be paid in dollars into a bank account which I had in New York. With the help of Lester Piggott's notoriously good advice on these matters, I even had some put into a new bank account in Geneva! I had not discussed any of this with my accountant, I hasten to add, because I was vaguely aware that I was not conforming strictly to UK tax laws.

Suddenly our accountants said that we were to have an investigation, and that it was to do with money earned abroad. I hoped initially this might refer to some of the considerable prize money we had won in Europe, but as we got nearer to the day of the investigation it became clear that it was to do with money earned in the USA specifically. I felt the time had now come when I had to come clean with my own accountant, Jon Lisby. When I explained what I had done he informed me that the Inland Revenue has a reciprocal arrangement with the US tax authorities, and if the money I had in my bank account in New York had been earning interest this was most probably where the problem lay. In spite of my having told my American bank manager that I just wanted it to remain in a current account, he had been unable to resist the temptation to put it on deposit, and had allowed it to 'grow' considerably. When I then admitted to Jon that I had a Swiss account too, he said this was now getting beyond his remit and could we please take on an expert to help us at the inquiry.

I agreed and organised for the three of us to meet about an hour before the tax inspectors arrived. Emma understandably did not wish to be involved in any way, and could not believe I had been so incredibly stupid. I think I even had trouble persuading her to bring in some coffee at the main meeting!

At our get-together before the serious meeting Jon introduced me to our expert; I forget his name, but he looked quite young and wore glasses. We agreed to admitting all about my bank account in New York and pleading ignorant innocence. Then I asked if I really had to own up about my precious Geneva account, which surely no one could possibly know about. Although he did not approve, he felt we might just hold fire with it, and suggested a slight compromise. He asked me to watch him carefully: if at any stage of the meeting he removed his spectacles, then I should admit to having my Geneva account.

One of the senior tax inspectors for Her Majesty's Government, together with his assistant, arrived sharp at the appointed hour and I politely ushered them into our drawing room. After the introductions had been made and we were all seated, the senior tax inspector said to me: 'Mr Balding, you will see that I have on my lap this large book which is the current edition of *Hansard*. It contains all our English tax laws and I wish to quote to you a paragraph that appears in the very first chapter.' The passage he read went something like this: 'If any person conceals a bank account which he possesses outside the UK and fails to declare that account for tax purposes, that person will be liable to considerable penalties and even to a prison sentence.'

Well – hearing this, our tax expert was so anxious to remove his spectacles immediately that in his haste he knocked over his cup of coffee! I have laughed about it many times since, but at the time it was far too serious for mirth, and I couldn't wait to tell the inspectors all about both bank accounts. Needless to say, the episode cost me all the dollars I had saved in New York, plus the Swiss francs and more. I learned my lesson – as sadly, of course, Lester did not.

In the early 1980s when we had all those good Mellon horses, I hoped and expected nearly always to finish the Flat season in the top ten of the trainers' table. Not every year was a good one, though, and with P.M.'s stud going through an unusually poor run after Forest Flower retired, I felt under quite a lot of pressure to keep up there among the top trainers. Emma and I were always incredibly busy and we found it very difficult to find the time to relax and enjoy life.

So with the advent of my fiftieth birthday we all decided we should let our hair down and throw a big party. Emma and I invited all our best friends and Clare and Andrew did likewise, so that it was very much a party of mixed age groups. We arranged for a marquee to go up in the garden with a covered walkway to the drawing room. There was a band and catering for about one hundred and fifty people. As always Emma organised everything – including, with her usual sense of humour, a seating plan which placed all my favourite ladies at my table!

I remember Tony Lewis making a very amusing speech. My reply, in an effort to recall some humorous reminiscences and to mention too many friends, was much too long. I was never informed who was responsible, but in the middle of this lengthy dialogue there suddenly appeared an extremely well-built black lady who headed straight for me. When she got to where I was standing with the microphone, she gave me a big kiss and then removed her big fur coat – underneath which she was wearing nothing at all. I am told that, much to everyone's surprise, even the voluptuous naked figure so close to me failed to shorten my address to the assembled company!

11

Selkirk and Lochsong

The 1990s started with one top-class horse in the yard already, went on with lots of old favourites and produced two champions to rank with the very best I have trained.

In 1988 Ron Sheather retired from training, having for several years been Jeff Smith's private trainer at his Palace House yard in Newmarket. Before that Ron had been assistant trainer to Barry Hills, and before that he had been one of my brother Toby's old faithfuls at Fyfield. In fact, Ron had been my father's jockey at one stage; so his relationship with the Balding family went back a long way. He had enjoyed some breathtaking success as Jeff's trainer, especially when he won the Coventry Stakes at Royal Ascot with a first time out 20–1 shot that was very well supported by owner and trainer. The horse in question, Chief Singer, went on to be the best miler in the country the next season. However, Ron found it more and more difficult to cope with the pressures of training, and when he gave up Jeff gave him a lifetime job as his racing manager. It was perhaps not surprising that Ron recommended that most of Jeff's home-breds should be trained at Kingsclere, as not only did Ron know me well, but we are only a twenty-minute drive from Jeff's Littleton Stud near Winchester.

It was a happy decision for us, as Jeff Smith is an ambitious and successful owner/breeder in the Mellon/Strawbridge mould and as nice a person to train for as one could ever wish to have. In the very first crop of yearlings to come from Littleton, there was a tall leggy colt by the Mellon-bred stallion Elegant Air. Dashing Blade straight away looked useful, but was a nervous and difficult horse to ride. One day before he even ran he got loose on our winter gallops and jumped a gate on to the main road. Luckily he turned left up the hill towards Overton rather than towards the village and went a decent pace in the fog until our old downsman Jona Holley, having heard a horse coming, managed to shepherd him off the main road and up a hard track to the Lloyd Webbers' farmyard about three miles away. When I eventually caught up with the colt on my hack there was not a scratch on him – so I immediately thought he must be useless!

Fortunately that was far from the case, and Dashing Blade turned out to be one of the best two-year-old colts in Great Britain that season, winning four of his five starts including the Group I National Stakes at The Curragh and the Dewhurst Stakes at Newmarket. John Matthias, who rode him in all these races, was interviewed on TV after winning the Dewhurst and was asked at what stage we first thought Dashing Blade was a good horse. John, who was a master of the one-liners, replied, 'When he overtook a Porsche on the road one foggy day before he even ran!'

In his three-year-old season injury hampered his preparation for the Two Thousand Guineas, where he was unplaced; and I recall we were all a shade disappointed with his fourth place in the St James's Palace Stakes at Royal Ascot. After that we went travelling to Europe, with better results: our colt won the Group II Prix Eugene Adam at Saint-Cloud over one and a quarter miles and ended the season in style at Milan by winning the Group I Gran Premio d'Italia over one and a half miles very easily. After this impressive victory his owner was keen to run in the Arc de Triomphe, and he would certainly not have been out of place in that race; but sadly a tendon injury ended his racing career prematurely. Dashing Blade has had a very successful career as a stallion in Germany.

That same year of 1990 we had a big, gawky, chestnut home-bred two-year-old colt of George Strawbridge, by Sharpen Up out of the good race mare Annie Edge, called Selkirk. He was one of those loveable goons who for months didn't seem to know how to put one foot in front of the other. Most of our top two-year-old races close so early that a backward colt like this one is not usually entered in these contests – at least, not by a mercenary trainer like myself.

It was not until the middle of August that our colt had got his act together at all. In the first week of September I faxed George's secretary Joyce to say that I intended to run Selkirk in a one-mile Listed race at Goodwood first time out. George himself was in hospital at the time but had his wits about him enough to realise that I must think quite a lot of this horse if he was going to run in a Listed race where there was no maiden allowance nor even a weight allowance for a horse who had never run before.

He was right – and so was I: with John Reid aboard, Selkirk won his first race impressively and in a very fast time. There was now no obvious target as I didn't have any smart entries for him, and the only option was to supplement him for the Group I Grand Criterum at Longchamp the day before the Arc de Triomphe. It was aiming high, but our horse looked to have improved again after Goodwood and we went to France full of hope. Selkirk never looked like beating the very mature and experienced colt Hector Protector but with a furlong to run he did look as if he was sure to be second. Then – in sharp contrast to Goodwood, where he had finished very strongly, Selkirk dropped out tamely at the end to lose second place and then even third in the last few yards. Fourth in a Group I in only your second race sounds pretty good, but in truth I was very disappointed.

George was fighting a horrible battle with the dreaded cancer and I knew that any good news about the horses would give him a lot of pleasure and some encouragement; and yet at the beginning of Selkirk's three-year-old season there was no good news to give, because the colt was not winning. He ran four times and each time he was placed, mostly in Classic trials, but each time the same thing happened: he looked all over a winner until the last furlong, when he faded badly – no matter what distance we ran him over. The horse was beginning to look ungenuine, but knowing his character well I could not believe that.

Then suddenly one day out at exercise I noticed he was not trotting quite sound behind, and when I took a closer look I could see that he was actually sweating between his hind legs. We were well aware that he was a rig, but up until this point I had never imagined that it bothered him. The next day when our vet Simon Knapp came, I discussed it with him, and asked if the one testicle that had not dropped could possibly be hurting him. Simon said yes, definitely; and if it were in the inguinal canal rather than right up in the abdomen he could be pinching it when he moved. When asked if we could do anything about it, he said, 'Most certainly – I can take it out very easily under a local anaesthetic, and it will heal very quickly.'

After Simon had assured me that having only one ball would in no way affect Selkirk's chances of being a successful stallion, I decided (probably without even consulting George) that we would proceed with this minor operation at once. Simon did it the next morning, and interestingly said that the testicle when extracted showed distinct signs of bruising. We gave Selkirk a few easy days and the moment I saw him trotting again he was quite obviously a totally different horse.

He had not run for six weeks now, and this was the middle of the August of his three-year-old season. Mercifully I had taken a chance and at the end of July had entered him in the Queen Elizabeth II Stakes at Ascot in late September. His early-season form certainly did not warrant the entry in this, the most important all-aged one-mile race all year, but with George desperately ill I felt we had to take every opportunity of trying to win a big race anywhere.

Luckily there was a suitable prep race at Kempton in a Listed race, also over one mile, three weeks before Ascot, and we had about two weeks to get him ready for that. Almost at once he was working like a truly good horse and I recall being really excited about him running again. John Reid and Ray Cochrane were riding most of our horses that year and John had ridden Selkirk in his first three races. Ray had ridden him in his fourth race, however, and had told me afterwards that there must be something wrong with the horse, so quickly had he stopped. I kept Ray on him for the Kempton race, and it was a thrilling moment to see

Selkirk stretch six or eight lengths clear of the others in record time. I asked Ray afterwards if he thought that was good enough to have a crack at the Queen Elizabeth II Stakes three weeks later and the answer was very positive.

The ground had been firm at Kempton but at Ascot it came up very soft. Selkirk started at odds of 10–1, but handled the soft ground well to get up and win decisively by one and a half lengths from the Classic-winning fillies Kooyonga and Shadayid. Ray had ridden our horse with great confidence, and these last two performances were impressive enough to make Selkirk the champion miler of 1991.

George, thank God, had made a dramatic recovery after a brilliant operation at the Sloane Kettering hospital in New York but was still having chemotherapy and was not fit enough to come over for the race. Nevertheless, he was able to watch it on his own television thanks to SIS coverage, and what he witnessed must have given him a tremendous boost.

Selkirk's four-year-old season was awaited with great anticipation by his owner and all of us at Park House. If he improved even a little bit, he might just become one of the outstanding milers of recent times. His first target was the Lockinge Stakes over the straight mile at Newbury. It was still a Group II race at that stage (it is now a Group I), but very valuable and also conveniently local. This time George did come over for the race, and witnessed one of his colt's very best performances. He came from off the pace to win in breathtaking style by two and a half lengths from Lahib, a good colt trained by John Dunlop. Interestingly, the previous year's Two Thousand Guineas winner, Mystiko, was about ten lengths behind us. I then made the decision to run Selkirk back at Longchamp two weeks later in the Group I Prix d'Ispahan over nine furlongs – but something was amiss and for the only time in his life Selkirk finished out of the money.

I decided to give him a good break and prepare for the big mid-season all-aged mile race – the Sussex Stakes at Goodwood. Unfortunately an insignificant leg injury slightly hampered our preparation and I remember wishing that we had had another week to get him ready. The race produced almost certainly the most exciting contest of the year and one of the best ever Sussex Stakes finishes. It was run at a very strong gallop, and Ray on Selkirk took up the lead with just over a furlong to run. It looked as if he had timed it perfectly, but in a prolonged duel the high-class three-year-old filly Marling, trained by Geoff Wragg and ridden by Pat Eddery, just pipped us in a photo-finish. It was galling to miss out on another Group I so narrowly, but strangely I found myself admiring the persistence of the brave filly who had just beaten us. It was the sort of race where the trainers and connections tend to shake hands and commiserate with the loser afterwards, and where the sport of horse racing itself is the ultimate winner.

A month later Selkirk returned to Goodwood for the Group II Celebration Mile. With Ray riding as usual, our colt won in majestic style and looked like the champion he was. We then waited for the Queen Elizabeth II Stakes at Ascot a month later in hopes of setting the seal on a great season and seeing our good colt become the first horse since the great Brigadier Gerard to win back-to-back runnings of this important race.

Things in racing very rarely go smoothly for long, and I was livid when Ray managed to get himself suspended (for a minor whip offence) on the big day at Ascot (again, sensibly, this rule has been amended so that nowadays a jockey would not miss a Group I race). John Reid, who had ridden Selkirk several times as a three-year-old, took his place – and, sadly for everyone, rode possibly the most ill-judged race of his career. Here in the Group I race that mattered most poor Selkirk got shut in and was denied a gap everywhere John tried to go. Lahib, who had finished behind us in the Lockinge Stakes, won this race, but our team left Ascot feeling incredibly frustrated.

There was fairly quick compensation next for Selkirk in the Group II Challenge Stakes at Newmarket over seven furlongs two and a half weeks later. I recall Kirsten Rausing, who had recently negotiated for Selkirk to stand at her Lanwades Stud as a stallion, being extremely nervous about this drop back in distance. She need not have worried: Ray, riding him with the utmost confidence, brought our horse through late to win in a canter.

George had been keen all along to round off Selkirk's career with a shot at the valuable and prestigious Breeders Cup Mile. Had the race been in New York or Toronto, where not only are the turf courses superb and very like English tracks, but the climate in late autumn is similar to ours, I would have been more optimistic; but that year the venue was Gulfstream Park in Florida, and neither the track, which was barely a mile once around, nor the climate, which was baking hot, was going to suit us.

Selkirk was impressive in his early morning workouts and was quite a warm favourite for the race until such time as all the local population realised that he was *not* going to run on Lasix (the diuretic drug which is very helpful to horses who break blood vessels in particular). As Selkirk had never 'bled' (broken a blood vessel so that blood trickled down his nostril) and was very sound generally, there seemed no point to me in running on either 'bute' or Lasix, both of which were legal in Florida.

On the day of the race it was over 100 degrees by mid-afternoon and Selkirk, who left his barn cool and dry, was in a white lather of sweat by the time he arrived across at the track for me to saddle him up. Needless to say he did not handle the tight turns well and ran way below expectations. Even so he finished fifth, about five lengths behind the winner Lure, and earned quite reasonable prize money. I had not much enjoyed my first experience of the Breeders Cup, and was ruing my stubborn ignorance in not using the drugs that everyone else was.

Selkirk went to stud at Lanwades as champion miler for the second year and has made a tremendous success of his career as a stallion. Even with only one testicle he is extremely fertile and nothing gives me more pleasure than to see one of his offspring walk into the yard as a yearling. Most of them look like him, with big, broad white blazes and white on their legs. Many of them are similar in temperament, too, delightfully laid back just like their sire.

For most of his time with us Selkirk was looked after by a girl, Louise Sheppard, which is unusual in our stable – I prefer the lads to look after colts. He was so lazy and lethargic, however, that it was certainly never a problem. He was a brilliant racehorse, and I often chide myself for not realising much earlier than I did that he was in pain. If we had done that simple operation six months earlier he could well have been a Classic winner.

At the same time that one champion was leaving us, another one was on her way to the pinnacle. In 1991 Jeff Smith had sent us a rather unsound but well-bred three-year-old filly called Lochsong with the instructions just to try and win a little race so that he could then retire her to stud. We managed to do just that when in mid-October, ridden by Ray Cochrane, she won a poor-class maiden race at Redcar over six furlongs. It was only her second start and she had been second in her first run in a similar race over seven furlongs at Salisbury in August.

I thought, 'Well done, Balding – mission accomplished,' and we started to rough her off ready to go home and become a broodmare. Jeff was in America on business, and a few days later I said to Ron Sheather, 'Look, would you mind if we gave that filly one more run at Newbury on the way home? She is roughed off and it is literally just to give the boy who rides her every day a ride.' Ron said he was sure Jeff wouldn't mind; so Francis Arrowsmith (known to all of us as 'Scully') rode her in the seven-furlong apprentice race at Newbury ten days after her win at Redcar. In a very close finish and having made all the running she hung on to win by a short head, but duly went straight on down to Littleton Stud after the race.

Midway through that winter of 1991–2 Jeff was talking to me about the new crop of yearlings when he suddenly said, 'By the way, you remember that filly Lochsong I was going to retire to stud? Well, I've been thinking about her, and you realise of course in only three races she has won twice and been second once – I really think we ought to try her again this next season.' To be totally honest I can recall a sinking feeling, but Jeff is such an enthusiast that I didn't dare say what I was thinking, which was: 'Oh God, please no, we did such a good job to win with her, and to keep her sound enough to do it, why can't he just be content to keep her there and let her have babies?' Luckily for all of us, I heard myself saying instead: 'Why, yes of course, Jeff, why not try her again this next season?'

This wonderful filly's racing career does not need to be retold here in every detail. I often wonder, though, at the little quirks of fate that happen in one's life, and I suppose that if I had been brutally frank with her owner, it is just possible that she might never have run again after her three-year-old season.

I will always be grateful to Willie Carson for the rides he gave

Lochsong in five of her seven races as a four-year-old. He did brilliantly on her and was the first to discover that she loved making the running. 'Scully' rode her in her first race that year and again when she won the Ayr Gold Cup towards the end of the season. She was already becoming somewhat difficult to train, from the point of view of both temperament and soundness, and he put up patiently with all her little moods and foibles when riding her daily. Chris Scudder, the young lad who looked after her all her time here, adored her and made sure her every need was attended to. I am indebted to both of them also.

By the end of 1992 Lochsong had won the unprecedented treble of Stewards Cup, Portland Handicap and Ayr Gold Cup, as well as finishing second in the Diadem Stakes in her only start in a Group race. This next winter it was the trainer asking the owner, 'Please can she come back to us again next season?'!

The following year, by the end of the first week in June she had run in four Group sprint races and, though placed in all four, had failed to win. So in the middle of the month, by common consent among trainer, manager and owner, she went back to Littleton Stud for a ten-day break – and it seemed to re-galvanise her. Now with Frankie Dettori as her permanent partner, she won a Listed race at Sandown in early July and then the Group III King George V Stakes at Goodwood at the end of that month. This race was run in dense fog (one of the sea mists that sometimes engulfs the Sussex course). The commentator, presumably looking at his monitor, shouted 'They're off!' – and then for about fifty seconds there was complete silence as he could not see anything. As the runners came into sight out of the fog with about a furlong to run, before he could say a word I spotted our sheepskin noseband and knew who was leading. Apart from Mill Reef's Arc it was the one time that I was truly grateful that we put these visible nosebands on our horses. Lochsong held on to win bravely, albeit narrowly, after which Jeff said: 'Roll on the Nunthorpe!' In my usual pessimistic fashion I told him that at level weights we had no chance of beating the horses who were giving us weight at Goodwood, let alone some even better ones who had not run there.

The Nunthorpe Stakes at York in 1993 was one of those days that so vividly illustrates the power of racing to stir the emotions.

It took Lochsong and Frankie just less than sixty seconds to have us all in tears. It was partly the unexpected ease of her victory, but mostly it was her style of doing it from the front. As a trainer for many years I had been fortunate enough to enjoy plenty of memorable winning occasions and survived many more disappointments, so that I have always tended not to get too over-excited in either case. This day was different – I knew it, and I believe that even the crowd and members of the press realised it. This was the day that the legend of Lochsong really began. If I had been Sue Chaplin that day at York, I too would have got out of my wheelchair and run to the winner's enclosure.

Later that season Lochsong won the Prix de l'Abbaye at Longchamp in similar breathtaking style by a long-looking six lengths. And there was one final event to savour. Harry Herbert and Arnaud Bamberger, with the early help of Tim Vigors, have built the evening of the Cartier Horse of the Year dinner into one of the most glittering and elite occasions of the racing social calendar. In December 1993 our family of four were invited, and Jeff and his wife Veronica were seated near the stage. We hoped and indeed expected that Lochsong would win the Sprinter of the Year award – but when she won the Racehorse of the Year award in addition, there was great rejoicing. It spoke volumes for her place in the hearts of the British racing public: no other sprinter of the 1990s won the top award.

Jeff Smith would be the first person to admit that he is not a horseman in the professional sense of the word. As an owner/breeder, however, he has an uncanny amount of good horse sense. Many times over the years he has persuaded me to run his horses in races where I thought they did not belong, and has been proved absolutely right. At the end of her five-year-old season I felt that Lochsong had probably had enough and should be retired after her glory day at Longchamp. She had become progressively more of a prima donna and I thought that in a fourth year in training at Park House she might become nearly impossible to deal with. Jeff convinced me otherwise, pointing out with great amusement that it had taken the trainer three years to discover Lochsong's best distance; now that we had found it, he said, why not take advantage of it all over again? It was another fine decision of his.

Explosive wins in the Palace House and Temple Stakes brought Lochsong to Royal Ascot a warm favourite for the King Stand Stakes. There again she delighted the huge crowd with a devastating front-running display and Frankie couldn't resist giving them his flying dismount. We all felt it was worth one more crack at a six-furlong Group I race, and where better than the July Stakes at Newmarket on fast ground? It was here that the parades for these Group I races began to cause trouble for her. With Willie back on her rather than Frankie, who was claimed by his boss to ride something else, she used up far too much energy in a scamper down to the start to run anywhere near her best.

A second win in the King George V Stakes at Goodwood, where there was no parade, put her back on target for the Nunthorpe at York. Here, because of the compulsory parade, I led her out on to the track myself in an attempt to see that she and Frankie at least set off at a trot which I hoped would progress to no more than a steady canter to the post. Lochsong had other ideas, however, and there was nothing that her jockey could do as she broke all previous records for the time taken getting down to the start. There was little point in her running after that, really, because all her energy and most of Frankie's had already been wasted. This was an occasion where Jeff had persuaded me to run another good filly of his in the same race – and to my utter amazement Blue Siren, ridden by Michael Hills, came through to win this Group I sprint fairly decisively. Still the drama had not ended, however, because we lost the race in the stewards' room and gallingly were demoted to second place behind Piccolo. Lochsong had trailed in last; and so we sent our temperamental star straight off to Littleton Stud to see if another ten-day break could revive her, as it had done the previous year, in order to have one final crack at the Prix de l'Abbaye.

I have already tried to describe the atmosphere at Longchamp on Arc day. It must be attributable mostly to the enormous influx of British racing enthusiasts, because sadly there is nothing like it on any other racing day at this great racecourse. The Prix de l'Abbaye is one of the early races and therefore really just an hors-d'oeuvre before the Arc itself. This year of 1994, however, there was no English middle-distance champion to support in the big race, and the greater part of the crowd must have been hoping to see our incredibly popular filly repeat her devastating win of the previous year. She had not, of course, run since the débâcle of the Nunthorpe, and even her trainer had considerable doubts about whether her volatile temperament would allow her to deliver one final coup de grâce. I should have had more faith. The French stewards had allowed Frankie to walk her down early to the start, and her mind and energy were once again focused only on the race.

Lochsong did not disappoint us. In the smallest field (ten) that I can remember for this race, she dominated from the start and passed the post five lengths clear with her ears pricked. Usually after a big win I cannot wait to leave the stands and get down to the winner's enclosure. Fortunately on this occasion I had a sixth sense that Frankie might do something unusual, and so I waited out on the steps of the Tribune des étrangers. For the first time I can remember (it is now commonplace after the biggest races), our jockey brought the heroine back up the track for an impromptu parade in front of those massive grandstands. It was yet another moment of great emotion as the crowd rose to her and I would hate to have missed it. She eventually returned through the tunnel to that unique tree-lined winner's enclosure, and I believe the feeling of the thousands of horse lovers present was as warm towards a racehorse as I have ever experienced.

Sadly, we all made the mistake of falling for the temptation to run Lochsong in the Breeders Cup Sprint over six furlongs at Churchill Downs. There seemed to be nothing to lose. Lochsong broke some watches in one amazing unscheduled gallop over three furlongs just two days before the race, but on raceday she hardly performed at all, and wisely Frankie virtually pulled her up.

Lochsong was probably not the best sprinter of her decade, but she was without question the most popular. She herself knew she was a superstar, and long before the end of her career had acquired the 'look of eagles' – as you can see from the cover photograph for this book! Jeff Smith puts a lot of time, money and thought into his racing and breeding operation, and he deserves to have very good horses to run in his colours. But even he knows how lucky he is to have had both Lochsong and Persian Punch in his lifetime as an owner.

Lochsong's first two foals never looked likely to emulate their mother – except that they were both unsound. Her third offspring, though, a filly by Indian Ridge called Lochridge, is sound in both limb and temperament, and can also run in a way that is more than a little reminiscent of her mother. Only time will tell if she can improve into the highest class in the same dramatic way. But whatever she does – now in Andrew's care – I doubt very much that I will ever have for her the same affection and admiration that I did for her dam.

If Lochsong's exploits on the Flat had lit up the mid-1990s, 1991 had produced one of my happiest days on a racecourse. It was at the headquarters of jump racing on the Wednesday of the National Hunt Festival at Cheltenham, and P.M.'s Crystal Spirit, ridden by Jimmy Frost, won the Sun Alliance Novice Hurdle. It happened to be the first race on the card, so there was no tension – just sheer joy for the rest of the day, with some wonderful races still to savour. The jumping crowd are superb – every winner seems to be popular, whoever it may be, and they certainly did not seem to mind that a Flat trainer had won this race with a four-year-old ex-Flat horse!

Early in the 1990s a lady called Audrey Hill approached us and asked if we could buy her a yearling. She had come on a visit with the Racegoers' Club and, having inherited a bit of money from an aunt, decided it would be spent on a racehorse. The first yearling we bought her was of no account and was sold halfway through his two-year-old career. The second one, however, a liver chestnut colt by Primo Dominie, turned out to be one of Kingsclere's favourite boys and is still an important hack: now aged sixteen, he teaches the youngsters to ride and leads the yearlings in their first canters.

Pay Homage gave Audrey some of the most exciting moments of her life, and one day in particular she will never forget. As a five-year-old he ran in the historic Jubilee Handicap at Kempton on the first bank holiday Monday in May. I had engaged Lester Piggott as jockey, and the owner was thrilled that the great man had agreed to ride her horse. As usual in the paddock beforehand Lester smiled a lot but didn't say much. I had already told him that the horse was at his best coming late off a very strong gallop and didn't mind getting into a bit of trouble. Lester rode a brilliant race, coming very late and just getting up on the inside rail to win by a neck. Audrey was deliriously happy and couldn't wait to hear all about the whole event from her jockey. Lester came in, slid off Pay Homage, took his saddle and, with a charming smile for Audrey, just said, 'Thanks very much' – and walked off to the weighing room!

Pay Homage went on to win many more races with lots of different jockeys and apprentices riding. Clare even won a charity race on him at Wincanton late in his life, and he still has at least one outing each year to Newbury racecourse, where the schoolchildren come to pat and admire him between races. He is always taken by Reg Corfield, who is also well past retirement age and used to look after 'Pommy' in his racing days. Reg is the only remaining employee at Kingsclere to have arrived before I did, and now, aged seventy-seven, he still has the responsible job of putting all the horses' haylage in their boxes every morning while they are out at exercise.

In the summer of 1992 I went to a sponsors' lunch at Ascot and quite by chance sat next to an older man called Robert Hitchins. I was aware that he owned some jumpers, but he told me he had had some Flat horses at one stage, and would quite like to get back into Flat racing again. Somewhat to my surprise he rang up a couple of weeks later and asked if Emma and I would go and buy him a couple of yearlings.

Emma has always had a wonderful eye for young horses and now suddenly she had the opportunity to go to all the sales to try and find a nice yearling or two for Mr H., as we called him. I have never enjoyed the hard work of looking at nearly all the yearlings in the catalogue; so Emma would do the 'spotting', as we call it, and I would swan in later and just look at the shortlist that she had prepared for me. For the next six or seven years we had great fun and no little success buying for the old boy. Luckily we agree with each other on most yearlings that we like – rightly or wrongly – and I would nearly always do the bidding.

Right from the start we liked old Mr H. and his wife Elizabeth enormously. I greatly admired the way he had made a fortune in building and property development starting from nothing – and his determination to spend a good deal of it and enjoy himself in his retirement. Emma and I enjoyed a fantastic weekend with them in Deauville in 1995, flying out with them in Mr H.'s own plane, when Tagula won the Prix Morny – the owner's first and, as it turned out, only Group I win. Tagula is an island in the Pacific, and after this major success all his horses were named after islands. Papua, Pantar, Halmahera and Nicobar were all good colts we bought for him in the next few years, and two of the very few fillies we bought both won Listed races: Putuna and Santa Isobel are two very well-bred broodmares now residing at Emma's stud. We hope that in due course they will breed good horses for Mr H.'s sons, who have taken up the reins of their father's racing interests.

The yearlings we bought for Mr H. at the Doncaster St Leger sale always used to go to Cliff and Jackie Percy's place, Snelsmore Farm, just the other side of Newbury, to be broken in. Mr H. liked to see the new ones we had bought for him as soon as possible, so more than once he met up with us there.

On one such occasion he and his wife arrived with their driver in their Rolls-Royce. They were coming on afterwards to have lunch with us at Kingsclere and to see their other horses, and Elizabeth as usual was dressed as if she were going to a wedding, in a long, very smart fur coat with high-heeled shoes and some very nice jewellery. Mr H. himself had a suit on.

We moved on to the lawn, where Cliff was leading a yearling colt up and back about ten or fifteen yards away from us. All of a sudden the colt stopped and reared up. We were not dangerously close to it, but the old boy was obviously a shade alarmed and moved sharply backwards. In so doing he might have just stepped on his wife's foot, but somehow he knocked her over on to the grass, then lost his own balance and fell right on top of her. Neither fall, thankfully, was a serious one and the ground was not very hard, so I was not overly concerned about them. Then, however, the fun started. Mr H. was short and quite round, and he now seemed to roll about on top of Mrs H. in his efforts to get off. I could not prevent myself from laughing as I saw her smart fur coat getting more and more grass stains on it as he rolled over on her once or twice more in his efforts to get up.

Much too slowly, I suspect, I moved in to help them back to their feet. Although a little out of breath, they were both laughing, realising how comical the incident must have looked. Once he had fully regained his breath, old Mr H. looked at me and said with his usual sense of humour, 'You know, it must be years since the Missus and I have had a good roll in the grass!'

After Paul Mellon died in 1999 Robert Hitchins rather assumed his mantle as our premier owner, and had more than thirty horses in training with us when sadly he died in 2001. His death was a real blow not just to us and his other trainers but to racing in general. He had always been wonderfully generous to many good causes both within racing and outside of it. He will always be remembered by our family with great affection.

A great friend of our own age group who became an important owner in the 1990s is Bob Michaelson – the younger brother of Roger, with whom I had played rugby at Cambridge. His family first had an interest with us in a very good horse called Twickenham who was syndicated among my rugby-playing friends in the early 1980s. Bob himself made a great success of his investment management business, and became particularly well known in racing when his firm Sagitta sponsored the Guineas meeting at Newmarket for several years.

Bob first tasted racing success with a very useful little stayer we bought called Brandon Prince. There followed several more Brandons (named after his parents' home in Porthcawl), and then in 1996 we bought him a Selkirk yearling colt which Bob named Border Arrow. This horse was owned in partnership with Wafic Said, Bob's boss at Sagitta, but always ran in Bob's name and colours. After winning his only race as a two-year-old at Newmarket at the back end of the 1997 season, the colt attracted a big offer from Godolphin – and Bob turned it down.

The following year Border Arrow finished third in both the Two Thousand Guineas and the Derby, and in later years went on to win or be placed in a mass of major races. If he had possessed four good sound legs this lovable horse could have won Group races all over Europe. He is now turned out down at the stud and enjoying a well-earned retirement. He certainly gave his owner enormous pleasure, as well as a few heartaches along the way.

In 1998 we managed to win the Group I Nunthorpe Stakes at York with Lochsong's full sister Lochangel. As a two-year-old she had been one of Frankie's 'magnificent seven' winners on that memorable afternoon at Ascot. Now, two years later and four years old, she enabled Frankie to win the big sprint at York for us again. If Blue Siren had not been disqualified, Jeff Smith would have had the enviable record of breeding and owning the winner of British racing's only Group I sprint over five furlongs three times within five years.

That same year Andrew told me he had seen a horse win a point-to-point in Yorkshire that had looked very impressive and that I ought to go up there and try to buy it. Bob Michaelson had said that he would like to have a chaser and when I saw this horse I liked him so much immediately that I decided to keep a quarter share myself and sell three-quarters to Bob.

Moor Lane won twice for us in 1999 but sadly over-reached, cutting right through his boot and halfway through his tendon, when finishing second in the Charisma Gold Cup at Kempton later that autumn. After a prolonged rest he came back really well to win two good chases in January 2002 and at that point was an early favourite for the Grand National, so impressive had he been in winning the Great Yorkshire Chase at Doncaster.

Winning that particular race meant a great deal to me sentimentally, because it was the same race my father had won with his good horse Arctic Gold, after which he too had become favourite for the Grand National exactly fifty years before. Neither horse won the great race, of course – but that is something that, as I write, Moor Lane still has an outside chance of doing!

That last year of the nineties was notable too for Andrew's return from an educative two-year spell with Jack and Lynda Ramsden in Yorkshire, bringing with him one of their best horses – a grand old handicapper called Top Cees.

Although all the horses were running under my licence, Andrew was now responsible for just under half of them round in the back yards. He had ridden Top Cees most days at Breckenborough and knew the old rascal extremely well. The horse had slightly dodgy tendons and could only be trained or indeed run on ground which was good or softer. Andrew planned his campaign in minute detail, so that when the nine-year-old gelding won a one-mile-five-furlong handicap at Ayr in mid-September, after the weights for the Cesarewitch had been published, it was not a valuable enough race to earn Top Cees a penalty in the big race. I could see just what he had learned from the Ramsdens; and apart from the cunning, there came the jockey also. Kieren Fallon rode Top Cees at Ayr and then to a famous victory in the Cesarewitch on Newmarket's July course. Andrew's interview after that event was almost as emotional as the fabled speechless one at Epsom a few years later!

Our best horse that year, however – by a long way – was a brown colt by Selkirk called Trans Island. Gordon Smyth, the old trainer who had won the Derby with Charlottown, had bought this horse himself as a yearling and managed him for an old friend of his in Hong Kong. This four-year-old quality colt won three very valuable and high-class races within three weeks in the autumn, ending up with the Group II Prix du Rond Point at Longchamp. A prestigious win at the Arc de Triomphe meeting, just as Andrew was coming into his own and providing considerable assistance to our operation, was a notable way to enter the new millennium.

During the 1990s – and indeed long before that – I had realised that being able to train a large string of racehorses successfully depended on various different factors. The most important of these by far was having a workforce that, in terms of both quantity and quality, was able to cope.

John Porter was obviously well aware of this more than a hundred years before me, and was shrewd enough then to appreciate that to acquire good staff in the first place and then to keep them meant housing them in top-class accommodation and looking after them properly in every other way. Peter Hastings-Bass had also been very diligent about the welfare of his staff, and had both upgraded the hostel for the single lads and built six new cottages between the stables and the stud yard for the married men.

When Emma and I first moved down to Park House in

December 1978, we had divided the house into two halves, giving ourselves plenty of room in the front half while also providing three extra flats and four very nice bed-sitting-rooms for staff in the back half. I had further upgraded the hostel, and in particular converted the large old dormitory into six separate bedrooms which left space to install extra showers and bathrooms. As soon as we could afford it, I built four new three-bedroomed cottages in Hollowshot Lane, so that in total we had twenty cottages for married men (who live in them rent-free), six flats, and bed-sitters in the hostel and back half of Park House for sixteen single people. All twenty cottages have been upgraded in my time and all now have central heating.

In 1972 I was fortunate enough to find a wonderful couple, Harvey and Joyce Watts, to look after the boys, and gradually also some girls too, in the hostel. Harvey and Joyce were marvellous with the youngsters, not only feeding them superbly and catering for all their domestic needs but also, to a certain extent (and with my assistance and encouragement!), exerting a fair degree of discipline. Between us we tried to ensure that the youngsters were tidy and polite, went to bed at a reasonable hour and were always up at the right time in the morning. Those who were riding in races were helped with their fitness and diet, and of course with transport to and from race meetings. In the 1970s and 1980s I used to give as many of our apprentices as possible the opportunity of riding in races. Even those who were going to end up as grooms had, for the most part, at least one ride in a race, and throughout my training career we kept 'apprentice' horses, who belonged to us, especially for this purpose.

The consequence of this policy – of looking after the staff's domestic comfort as well as giving them the opportunity to ride in races – is that nearly all my best apprentices have stayed on as full-time stable lads; at least half of our current staff have been at the yard for twenty years or more. I am proud that over the years we have produced many good apprentices who have gone on to become successful senior jockeys, and that Kingsclere has always had a reputation for caring about its workforce. Wages are, of course, crucial; but in my view the long hours worked without a break are even more so. Originally our lads worked two weekends in three; then in the 1980s and 1990s it became every other weekend; and finally, in the past two years we have been able to arrange for the whole staff to work only one weekend in three. This, I think, has made a big difference to their lives.

Harvey and Joyce were with us for seventeen years and I have never been sadder to see a couple retire. Their place was taken by another pair, Martin and Lyn Brown, whose tenure with us was possibly shortened slightly by the sense of humour of probably my best ever apprentice jockey – Martin Dwyer.

Our tiny young apprentice from Liverpool did not see eye to eye with Lyn, who did most of the cooking. Somehow he had found out that she had a phobia about spiders, and one day, having contrived to capture several of the creatures from the bathrooms, he dispersed three or four of them at strategic points around the kitchen just before Lyn came in to prepare the evening meal. Hearing the screams and swearing as she discovered them – and even realising that it might mean no meal for anyone that evening – he strolled into the kitchen, said to Lyn, 'How did you miss this one?' and threw an especially large spider towards her.

There followed a complete temper tantrum from our cook, who for a while locked herself in the pantry and eventually issued an ultimatum: either she was going or this 'horrible young Scouse' was. Fortunately, perhaps, for Will Farish, Andrew Balding and Casual Look, I decided that our young apprentice was a better long-term prospect than our cook at that time!

The hostel was then taken over by Denise Smith, who has fed and catered for the occupants extremely well since 1994. As for Martin Dwyer, of course, he has gone on not just to win the Oaks on a Kingsclere-trained filly, but to become one of the very best riders in England. Nothing would give me more pleasure than to see him become champion jockey one day – and I certainly would not bet against it.

12

Outside Interests

It may sound obvious, but to be a successful trainer of racehorses, one has to be more than merely dedicated. The day begins in the summer at about 5 a.m. and one gets to bed some time between 11 p.m. and midnight. The whole morning is taken up with the organisation needed to exercise about a hundred horses. There is a short break for breakfast, which is usually interrupted by various phone calls and spent scouring the *Racing Post* to help decide on the runners for the following day.

Before the advent of the mobile phone the trainer could grab a nap in the car on the way to the racecourse, assuming that he had someone else to drive. Even then, though, most of the time driving or being driven was spent looking through the racing papers and turning the pages of *Raceform* or *Timeform* to decide about future runners. Nowadays in the car the mobile phone is constantly engaged, talking to owners, jockeys, or one's secretary. In the middle of the summer I would frequently go to two meetings, one in the afternoon and one in the evening.

Some of the larger trainers, particularly at Newmarket, often did not go racing themselves, feeling that their time was better employed at home, and I can understand that. My own feeling was always that if our owner was going it was important for me to be there too, and because what happens on the track is the end product of all that work at home then I wanted to be there in any case.

It is not too hard to see how easily the whole business becomes an all-consuming passion, and how little time there is for anyone or anything else in this hectic way of life. The winners, if and when they come, act like a high-powered fuel that keeps one going longer and working harder. The winner-less periods, when nothing seems to go right, just cause a depression that makes life difficult, especially it seems for one's nearest and dearest.

Thankfully, during most of my years as a trainer there was an off season when the horses had a longish break and so could the trainer. During the summer, unless one had a runner abroad, Sundays were sacrosanct and the trainer, along with the half of his staff who were not working the weekend, had a day off. Sadly for the present-day trainer, this situation is rapidly changing, and soon there will probably be Flat racing and jumping every day of the year, except possibly Christmas Day and Good Friday.

In the winter months I could relax and enjoy myself. I used to go foxhunting regularly in my first few years at Kingsclere, and ever since 1975 I have been drag hunting almost every Sunday and occasionally midweek as well. The foxhunting in our area, mainly because of the high proportion of land given over to arable crops rather than grassland, could never be as exciting as the sport in some of the better known hunting areas. I did qualify Milo with our local pack, the Vine and Craven, for his hunter chasing, but after him we used to send the odd point-to-pointer to my old chum Terry Biddlecombe to be qualified. Terry, retired from his brilliant career as a National Hunt jockey, was living with his first wife, Bridget, in a little village near Gloucester called Corse Lawn where he had a small livery yard and specialised in having some pointers. His local pack of hounds was the Ledbury.

In the late 1960s I had in the yard a big chestnut by Acropolis named Academy, who had been bought as a yearling for Bill (Earl) Cadogan. The colt was soon gelded, and then he injured his knee quite badly one day when completely bolting with one of our riders up on Watership Down. The owner was very patient, but when finally at the age of four Academy had proved himself to be very moderate as well as unsound, Lord Cadogan gave him to his trainer.

The following year I sent Academy to Terry to get qualified for point-to-points. I told him all about the troubles the horse had had, and particularly to be careful who he put on him as the horse was still a fierce puller. After hearing nothing for several weeks – not unusual for Terry – when I rang to enquire how he was going the reply came back: 'Great, he's as quiet as a pussy cat, Bridget's been hunting him in a snaffle and you ought to come and have a day on him yourself.'

I was amazed by this news but thought it would be fun and asked if Emma could bring a horse of hers and have a day as well. We arrived at the meet a tiny bit late and I scarcely had time to get on Academy (or Spots, as Terry had nicknamed him) before we had found a fox and were away with almost indecent haste. I certainly had not had time to pull my leathers up or even to tighten the drop noseband, which was much too loose to be any help to the bit in the horse's mouth. Going at a fairly decent gallop up a narrow lane, and riding with much longer stirrups than I was used to and with just a snaffle in the horse's mouth, I soon realised that I was not in control of the situation. At least while we were in the lane I was able to cover him up in behind some other horses so that he could not actually go past them.

When we got to the top of the hill and into a large grass field I thought, Great, I can let him gallop now, and perhaps he will settle better once he has worked off a bit of steam. At the far end of this field there was a big hedge which, although large, looked very jumpable. I was approaching it at a pretty rapid pace when I suddenly noticed that no one else was jumping it; they were all queuing to go through a narrow gate in the corner of the field. What a load of wimps, I thought, it doesn't look that big – besides, I had no option but to jump it as I was going much too fast to pull up and go through the gate. I set Spots at the hedge and at the last moment realised why no one was jumping it – I could see a single strand of barbed wire about three feet high stretching right across and about six feet out in front of the hedge.

Whether my bold horse saw the strand of wire or not I don't

really know, but I asked him for a long one and with a mighty leap he cleared both wire and hedge comfortably. I just about had time to gloat and think, Well, they probably consider I'm a show-off, but what a horse this is! The next moment my poor brave horse was landing right on top of a single strand of wire slightly further out on the landing side. We turned arse over end and I took a really good tumbling fall. Poor Spots was a shade winded, so that I was able to get up and at least catch him before he galloped off loose. I could almost hear the chuckles as everyone went by me, obviously thinking, That'll teach him to show off.

The pause at least gave me a chance to pull my leathers up and tighten the drop noseband before I got back into my saddle. Emma was with me as we set off again. Before long we were cantering along a tarmac road and, in spite of my stirrups and bridle being adjusted, I realised once again that I was a complete passenger. The only way I could stop Spots was to stuff his head right up the backside of another horse and shout at the lady rider, 'Would you please help me out by pulling up!' Thank God she did, and I waited there stationary until Emma caught up. I said to her, 'Look, I know we have only been out about twenty minutes, but I am completely out of control and will have to take him home. If by any chance I can find that wretched Terry and we put a stronger bit in his mouth I may just see you later, but you stay out and have some fun.'

Ten or fifteen minutes later I had been walking quietly along the road when we came to a narrow but very attractive-looking grass lane on my right. I looked along it and it appeared to stretch slightly uphill for about a mile – and then, way over on the right, I could see all the other riders standing below a hill. They looked to be two or three miles away and I imagined that our very good fox had gone to ground.

I thought, I can't go home yet, having come all this way – and besides, what will Terry say? Ill-advisedly I decided to trot up this lane, taking my time, but gradually making my way over to join the rest of the field. I had trotted for about two hundred yards when Spots broke into a steady hack canter. I still thought, I've got you, you bugger – at which point Spots took charge again and suddenly we were into a strong canter and very soon thereafter a full gallop. The end of the long grassy lane came very rapidly, at which point I swung him round right-handed in a wide turn towards where the others were gathered. There looked to be nothing but grass stretching out between me and the seventy-odd riders, and I was thinking that if I let him really put his toe out he might just tire a bit and I could perhaps be back in control by the time I reached them.

The assembled followers of the Ledbury Hunt had nothing else to do but to stand and watch this single rider on his chestnut horse approaching them at speed. My wife, of course, realised at once who it was, but I doubt anyone else did. What looked like a simple long stretch of grass turned out to be three separate fields divided by two wide dykes. The first one was about twelve feet wide and we met it on a good stride. My horse, who if ignorant was very brave, took off and cleared it in style. We were rapidly getting nearer to the other riders when suddenly we came to the second dyke. This one was wider still and though my poor steed tried his best to jump it, it was much too wide even for him and he literally 'breasted' the far side of it. I, of course, went straight over his head and did about three somersaults before I came to a halt and was able to sit up and see where I was.

The man standing next to Emma exclaimed to her: 'My God – it's that man again!' I did go home then, and I made sure I never rode Academy out hunting again or even in a point-to-point.

The Berks and Bucks Draghounds were first formed by Roger Palmer in 1974. My Uncle Ivor's son David Balding was living over here at the time, and both he and Emma went to one of the very first meets, which was held fairly nearby at Appleshaw, both riding hirelings from Mary Ravenscroft's livery yard near Basingstoke. I was simply an observer, trying to keep up with proceedings partly on foot and partly in the car. I had never seen a drag hunt before and was keen to find out all about it.

At one point, about halfway through the hunt, I had found out where they were going and drove on in front to get by a jump next to the road. I hopped out of the car and stood right next to this somewhat unattractive post and rail obstacle. Roger Palmer, the Master who was hunting hounds, came into the fence right behind the hounds. His horse met it all wrong and took quite a nasty fall. Roger lay for dead on the landing side of the jump and I just had time to stop the rest of the field and catch his horse. Health and safety officers would have had a fit as I rolled Roger over on to his back and took his hunting cap off. I probably slapped his face to help him come round and as he recovered consciousness his eyes rolled and he uttered the words, 'Send someone after the hounds.' I soon had him standing and legged him up on to his horse. To my amazement, a few minutes later he galloped off after his precious hounds as if nothing unusual had happened! I thought then: This chap must be OK if the first thing he thinks about when he comes round from a nasty fall are his hounds.

The next thing I knew was that I had been recruited as a joint master of the Berks and Bucks, and Emma and David had bought their two hirelings from Mary Ravenscroft. It was so different from formal foxhunting and seemed to all of us just enormous fun. I even persuaded brother Toby to come out on one occasion. He and his horse managed to get stuck in a large field when his mount refused to jump out, and Toby ended up having to leave his horse there for a few hours before a key to the gate could be found. Cousin David was for several years what was known as a 'line organiser'. His building of fences was quite unique and the obstacles were still easily recognisable when I came to look after his meets a few years later!

I was a joint master and field master of the draghounds for the best part of the next twenty-five years. It became my winter obsession as I went around the local countryside visiting farmers to persuade them to let us come across their land, constantly planning routes we could take and helping to build fences. At my busiest I organised six different meets, and on those Sundays, and occasional Wednesdays, I was also responsible for providing the 'runners'. These were my youngest apprentices who had been convinced by the trainer that running across about a six- or eight-mile stretch of country through hedges and ditches, pulling behind them a foul-smelling ball of stockings attached to a rope and carrying a canister of the special scent, was extremely good for their eventual chances of making the grade as a jockey!

I could dwell on my experiences out drag hunting for some considerable time, but I will confine myself here to one or two occasions that were painful at the time but amusing afterwards. Other field masters will know that it is not easy to find the perfect horse to lead the field: one that will never stop at a fence and yet will pull up quickly, does not kick hounds or other horses, and is bomb-proof in traffic is a rare beast. As most of mine were Thoroughbreds who were going to run in point-to-points in the spring, I was not always suitably mounted. One advantage of building the fences myself was that I knew the horse I would be trying to jump them on the next Sunday!

I have to say that in all those years I never once got to know any single hound by its name. That side of the drag hunt was entirely Roger Palmer's prerogative. I admired enormously the way that over the years Roger actually bred and perfected his own pack of black and tan draghounds. I admit, however, that I considered the hounds to be something of a necessary nuisance, and was always cursing the stragglers who were constantly slowing us up.

If there is a temptation to get even the slightest bit pompous as a field master I hope I resisted, because I soon learned that embarrassment or minor disaster was always just around the corner. One time we were due to meet locally at Baughurst, which was a meet I did organise and was always one of our most enjoyable, with particularly friendly farmers and lots of good hedges to jump. We had a new fence builder and I had shown him exactly where to trim a fifteen-foot-wide strip in the middle of a big hedgerow and to put a couple of rails across on the take-off side.

I was a bit worried about this new big jump and drove with Clare to look at it on the Saturday evening on our way back from Sandown races. I drove across the field and down to the jump, and inspected it closely with my car headlights on. It looked big but quite inviting – and then suddenly I noticed an old post in the middle of the jump which the fence builder had missed and, although hidden in the hedge still, was pointing straight out in the direction we would be coming. With Clare's assistance we eventually managed to pull it out and I was pleased that I had bothered to go and look at the jump.

The next day the hunt went well until we reached this same new jump. I was on one of my very favourite horses, called Johnny, whom I had originally bought as a failed eventer from Nicky Coe. Normally he was brilliant, but he did have this horrible habit of ducking out left at the occasional jump he didn't fancy. So I got two of my bolder friends who were well mounted to come either side of me as we galloped into this new big hedge. I thought there was no way my horse could escape jumping it, but I have to admit that I had been thinking quite a lot about that fence and some of my doubt must have communicated itself to my horse. At the take-off stride he viciously put the brakes on. We were going too fast for him to be able to stop altogether and he blundered straight through it so that we both took a pretty nasty fall. The uncanny thing was that where he went through the hedge was exactly where Clare and I had removed the post. I learned later that I had broken a bone in my left arm, but I always reckoned that the post would have gone straight into my poor horse's chest.

We usually had our Christmas meet at Kingsclere on the Sunday that was nearest to Christmas Day. We always got our biggest field that day and a good cap to help our hunt staff. Some years there would be as many as seventy or eighty riders. On one such occasion in about 1990 I had planned our whole hunt meticulously as usual, and we had four different lines going all around our side of the road and also on my mother-in-law's farm the other side. There were lots of free-standing jumps over there and this route led us through a wood and eventually up to the downs.

This year, for some reason, Roger was unable to hunt hounds, so his place as huntsman was taken by Jeff Hobby, who whipped in for years and then became a joint master and whip. Clare, who knew where we were going and was well mounted, was deployed to take Jeff's place as the only whip. We set off down on the grass beside the farm road. As usual I let the hounds get a good quarter of a mile ahead before we started so that we would not be held up by the stragglers along this good row of fences. We turned left at the bottom of the road, crossed a bridge and then started a row of fences beside our six-furlong summer plough gallop.

Jeff and Clare knew exactly where we were supposed to go, but Jeff's sight is not too good and he could obviously not see that we were following just one single hound who was on the scent. I could see that we had lost the whole of the rest of the pack, but despite shouting as loud as I could at my daughter and Jeff, I could not get them to hear that we should stop. I imagine they were thinking the hounds had gone so fast that the one hound was a straggler and they had to go faster than ever to catch them up.

Normally my good friend Dave Pitcher likes to jump the big rubber tyres at the end of this run of fences upsides, as if we were in a point-to-point. On this occasion I was going so fast in pursuit of Clare and Jeff that Dave was not able to catch up with me and at the second of the series I was not concentrating on my take-off stride. My big, bold horse, Croupier, got too close, turned right over and fell on top of me.

I suppose I was knocked out for a few moments, because I can remember thinking as we were about to hit the ground: Oh shit, this is the fall I have been dreading all my life! As I came round I could not move my legs at all, and my first thought was: Oh dear God, no – I must have severed my spinal cord. Then I opened my eyes and could see to my great relief that the reason I could not move my legs was that Croupier was still lying across them.

People arrived and got my poor horse up (he was winded), and I was gradually able to sit up. I was in considerable pain, but there was no way a vehicle could reach us where we were, so eventually I was hoisted into the saddle and Croupier and I walked slowly back to the farm. What transpired was that just after our apprentice had dragged his foul-smelling sock down the farm road and turned left, as he was supposed to, my mother-in-law had gone for a walk with her dogs. She had started on the same route but at the bottom end of the farm road she had turned right and walked back up to her house. Her dogs had obviously got the scent on the bottom of their feet and the main group of hounds had followed them – and just as I was having my fall, Priscilla had about ten couple of draghounds baying and scratching at her windows!

I was driven to hospital where I was found to have six broken ribs and a broken collarbone. I had never dared to admit to

Dave Dick that up until that moment I had not broken my collarbone!

Drag hunting was not always falls and disasters – in fact it gave myself, Emma and Clare enormous pleasure for many years. The meets at places such as Bucklebury, which Roger organised, at Johnny Manners's farm at Highworth, and at Great Missenden, where Chris and Suzanne Collins are the hosts, are superb, and some of the big hedges we jump have become legendary. We have made a great many good friends, and both the Hunt Dinner and the Aniseed Ball, which Emma organised for many years, are sparkling social events.

When I retired as joint master a few years ago the hunt members gave me some wonderful presents, including a lovely painting by Charles Church of all of us in full cry across a line of fences at Baughurst which I know well. I was moved upstairs to be president of the drag, but still organise and act as field master at our own meet at Kingsclere twice a year. Andrew's apprentices will still be told that running the line is a vital preparation for success as a jockey and that Martin Dwyer was one of our best runners!

There was one subject on which Roger Palmer and I totally failed to agree and that, strangely enough, was the question of hunting caps versus crash helmets. It might seem to be against my nature to prefer the latter, but there had been an incident earlier in my career as a trainer which had totally changed my attitude towards safety. In our youth Toby and I, and all our jockeys and lads, had always ridden, even when schooling over fences, in nothing more than a cap on our heads – often turned round so the wind would not catch the peak and blow it off. Even when Micky Lynn was killed it did not really change my attitude.

When in 1976 the Jockey Club suddenly decreed that all riders in racing stables, including the trainers themselves, must ride out in crash helmets, I can remember thinking, What is the world coming to? We are all going soft! However, thank God, I went along with the new ruling and on the designated day we all, including myself, rode out in these quite smart-looking little blue crash helmets. About a week later I had just legged up our best young rider, Alison Catterall, on to a two-year-old in our new tarmac-covered Mill Reef yard. Almost as soon as I let go, the colt reared up and Alison slipped out the back door, landing on her back on the tarmac. I can still hear the sound of her head hitting the hard surface now, and it horrified me. She was knocked out cold and didn't come round for about five minutes; I know that if she had not been wearing that helmet she would have been dead. At that moment my attitude towards crash helmets (and now body protectors) altered. I have never let anyone ride out here since without a properly fitting crash helmet with a chinstrap.

I remember Andrew Wates telling me about his wife Sarah's near-fatal fall, when her hunting cap slipped off before her head hit the ground. I always tried to insist that our riders who came out drag hunting wore crash hats with a black velvet cover rather than hunting caps. There was, however, never a chance that I was going to alter Roger's view. His mind was firmly made up that as huntsman he would always wear a proper hunting cap with no chinstrap!

Point-to-pointing was my favourite of all the sports in which I took part. After my owners insisted on retiring me from riding in hunter chases in about 1983, I had several more years riding between the flags. The twelve stone and in some cases twelve stone seven pounds weight limit suited me much better; but above all it was the informality of the occasion and the fact that the races, with the horses and riders involved, were not published in the newspapers that I most liked. There was so much else to enjoy besides. Many times the four of us went as a family: Emma would prepare the picnic and bring the horse with Clare and Andrew in the horsebox; I usually came later in my car, but in time to walk the course accompanied by two children who were longing for the day they could replace me as the jockey. We had countless such happy days at Tweseldown, Larkhill, Barbury and Kingston Blount in particular, but occasionally we went further afield.

I had several good horses over the years and one superstar: a bay gelding called Ross Poldark, whom I acquired one day when a friend of ours called Glyn Johns brought the horse drag hunting at Kingsclere. Glyn was well known in the music world and a close friend of Mrs Penny's owner, Eric Kronfeld. He couldn't hold one side of this horse and was frequently passing the field master and having to take wide turns to pull up. He did not stay out for all the lines as he was exhausted after the first, but he waited and came back for tea afterwards. There I said to him, 'I like the way your horse jumped, but noticed he was pulling quite hard – what are you going to do with him?' Glyn said that he would be happy to sell him, and as Emma needed a drag horse at the time I bought him on the spot at what I thought was a very reasonable price.

Ross Poldark had been stabled with a chum of ours called Roger Stack, who is well known in the hunter showing world and in racing, and he recommended the horse highly. Emma had seen him perform with Glyn and said she knew she wouldn't be able to hold him either, thank you all the same; so I suddenly had a new draghunting horse for myself. After my first outing on him I realised that the horse must be a Thoroughbred, although we had no papers for him; I had not sat on anything that gave me that sort of feel since Milo.

I had had a couple of disastrous attempts at the Melton Hunt Ride in previous years and thought that this time I had the perfect horse for it. I had arranged with a good young friend of ours, Ashley Bielby, that I would bring Poldark up the day before the big cross-country race for both of us to stay the night with him and his family. Ashley, who had won it the previous two years, walked me right round the course; as early as the third fence I did not agree with the line he was going to take and thought I could go a slightly shorter route by jumping one hedge on an angle. The ground was quite soft and they had obviously had plenty of recent rain. It then poured with rain all that night.

When about fifty of us lined up at the start the next morning I noticed that I was the only idiot to be wearing light racing breeches and boots; I was even stupid enough to be using my favourite racing saddle, which weighed about four pounds made up with girths and stirrups. I got a good start and was leading comfortably when we came to the third fence on the angle. The slight dip in front of it had filled up with rainwater overnight so that it looked like a mini water jump in front of the hedge. Poldark ducked out sharply to his right at the last moment and of course

I went straight into the water on my back. I suppose I might have survived had I been using a hunting saddle. I managed to hold on to the reins in spite of lots of riders galloping by me on either side and jumping the fence. Once I had remounted I was easily last, but I turned my horse round and jumped the obstacle straight on this time – and for the next mile and a half had the most exhilarating ride I have ever had across country. I just could not believe how many riders I was passing effortlessly, and my horse was jumping superbly.

I had got up to about fifth place, within easy range of the leaders, when Poldark refused again at a big fence with a wide ditch facing it. I got over that at the second attempt too, but eventually pulled up when he stopped a third time, by which time my light racing saddle had slipped right back.

Emma was waiting rather anxiously for me at the end of the race and could not understand, when at last I arrived, why I should have a big grin on my face. When I had finished telling her the embarrassing bits of the story, I said, 'This horse is a machine – I haven't sat on anything like him for years. We are going to have to run him in point-to-points.' We managed with Roger Stack's help to get a passport for him from Ireland, and very soon we were at Tweseldown and running in the open race at the Army point-to-point in February 1982. I had phoned my big brother and told him that if he wanted to take some money off the Tweseldown bookmakers he had better come. Eric Kronfeld, who was staying with us at the time, also came, as did my pal Dave Pitcher. As we were saddling Toby said, 'Why on earth are you running in the open, why aren't you making a certainty of it and running him in the maiden?' I said he had recently worked better than a novice we had that had won a maiden hurdle at Fontwell a few days ago and, with me riding, Poldark must have been giving that horse two stone!

Apparently Ross Poldark, who of course had never run in his life and was now aged eleven, opened at 20–1. Eric tells the story that he was approaching the bookmaker with five tenners in his hand when Toby, in his haste to get the 20–1, barged in front of him and knocked him over. By the time he got up, Eric said, the best price available was 5–1!

The race was no contest – we made all the running and won comfortably. I ran Poldark just once more that season, about a month later, when he won at Tweseldown again. In the meantime, of course, he was leading the field in all our drag hunts.

The following season he won another open at Tweseldown in early February on his first start – and by now I was beginning to dream of my long-time ambition to win the Foxhunters at Aintree. I have always had an obsession with Aintree. In my view the Grand National course provides the greatest test for man and horse together that exists. I had ridden winners over hurdles and over fences on the Mildmay course, but I had never won a race over the big obstacles, though I had got round on a couple of occasions in the Foxhunters before I started training; and I knew by now that I would never fulfil my lifetime ambition of riding in the National itself. Every year I have been to the National I have always walked the course. Just looking at those superbly built fences and walking on that wonderful turf has given me an enormous buzz; and here at last was my best chance of actually riding a winner there.

At the end of February Ross Poldark won his first start over the bigger fences in a maiden hunter chase at Leicester, and went on ten days later to beat good horses in a two-and-a-half-mile hunter chase at Folkestone. After three races pretty quickly on top of each other, and the odd drag hunt in between, I should have given him a break and not run him again before Aintree. However, stupidly, I ran him in another hunter chase at Lingfield only ten days later; for the first time in his racing life he seemed a shade lifeless and was narrowly beaten. I was very disappointed and angry with myself, but still determined to go to Aintree with him.

The family all suffered as I reduced my weight to the lowest I had been for many years in order to ride at twelve stone with a decent saddle. I went for runs in my sweat suit, leaving a trail of clammy wet underwear to be washed by Emma, and as I ate and drank less and less so my temper became more frayed. Even the lads in the yard were aware of what was happening.

The night before the Foxhunters we all went up and stayed in a hotel near Aintree. Luckily we were joined by my old chum Tony Lewis, Andrew's godfather; who helped keep the evening reasonably light-hearted as everyone was becoming more nervous. Unfortunately the racing press had eagerly picked up the story of the royal trainer riding around the Aintree fences at the venerable age of forty-four, so that, unlike my point-to-points, this event was not only live on television but also getting a lot of publicity nationally.

I wish there was a happy ending to relate, but in hindsight the trainer had got both himself and his horse well over the top. Poldark jumped beautifully and we led until after the last, when we both tired quite badly on that long run-in and faded to finish fourth. I can remember being massively disappointed – but perhaps it was not too bad an effort from two relative old-timers.

My lovely old horse missed the next season with tendon trouble acquired out hunting. So he was fourteen when, in 1985, I determined to have one more crack at Aintree. He had won another men's open at Tweseldown as a prelude to Aintree, but a slight mistake at the open ditch – third in the Grand National but fifth in the Foxhunters – saw jockey and horse separated. Again it was a major disappointment, because I felt we were both better prepared on this occasion – and I had even managed to avoid being knocked off at the Chair earlier by Brod Munro-Wilson's wild swing in my direction with his left arm as he 'hailed a cab' jumping upsides in front.

Poldark and I won a couple more point-to-points, including our Berks and Bucks members' race at Kingston Blount, but my favourite memory of him later on was when Clare, aged sixteen, was having her first ride in a point-to-point on him, also aged sixteen. It was the Easter Monday Vine and Craven meeting, and both Guy Harwood and I had come to Hackwood Park for the ladies' open, where our daughters were riding against each other, rather than going to Kempton where we both had rather more important runners on the Flat.

The conditions were appalling after torrential rain, and cars were stuck everywhere trying to get into the course. The stewards at the meeting even came and asked Guy and me if we felt it was safe to race. Knowing that our girls were on two very experienced jumpers we both said, 'Yes, of course, it's perfectly safe,' and the meeting went ahead. There was a third runner but Amanda (now Perrett) and Clare had a wonderful race with each other, with

Amanda finishing just ahead on her slightly younger horse. On pulling up she was thrilled to have won, but knew she was in for a bollocking from her father for allowing Clare to get up on her inside at the last bend! Both fathers were extremely proud of their daughters and also of their wonderful old horses, who had taken them safely round in those desperate conditions.

I often wondered what heights 'Poldarkle', as our family used to call him, might have reached as a chaser if we had found him four or five years earlier. He was without doubt the most brilliant jumper of a fence that I ever rode, and I do not think I was ever happier in my life than when bowling along in front making the running on him in those point-to-points at Tweseldown.

At one stage there were three of us all riding in point-to-points, and Clare, Andrew and I even rode in the same race at Kingston Blount. Emma, as always, was there to pick up the pieces and massage the damaged egos!

There was one very happy day a few years later when a lovely horse called King's Treasure, who had been given to me by Paul Mellon, won a good hunter chase at Stratford. Emma supervised his training and rode him daily herself from the stud yard, and Andrew was his jockey. Clare and I were both members of the 'Tunnel Vision Partnership', in whose name he ran, and we were both present to greet our winner.

With the considerable help and expertise of my friend David Morton, we created a hunter trial/team chase course up on our patch of the downs about twenty-five years ago. There was not a hedge in sight on the downs when I first came to Kingsclere, but we planted thorn shoots behind all the solid rails and over the years this course has become perhaps one of the best of its kind. It extends to just over two miles, going up one side of our famous old valley gallop, through the ring at the top and back down the other side, finishing where it started. There are three separate courses with fences of all different sizes, and a small and much shorter hunter trial course for youngsters. The ground in all weather conditions is amazingly good; I can only remember once having to cancel a team chase when it was decided that the ambulances could not get round the course.

For many years Emma had the hassle of running the team chase – I hope that the twice she finished on the winning team herself made up for the many hours she spent organising the event. She was on her old home-bred favourite Stuart when the four of us as a family team won the Cubhunter section one year. She says that Andrew, Clare and I treated her very much like the fourth person, who is of no importance, the whole way round, and even shut the gate of the 'pen' in her face. But in fact we tied with another team and her faster time in fourth place made all the difference, enabling us to collect the spoils!

In the summer months, right up until these last five or six years, my Sundays were nearly always spent playing cricket. I loved it and used to look forward to it all week. For quite a few years I used to run our own side at Kingsclere, and we had occasional enjoyable visits from the South Wales Hunts team captained by A. R. Lewis himself. Tony even brought a few of his championship-winning Glamorgan side to stay with us one weekend. I always found the professional cricketers whom I met to be the most charming and good-natured sportsmen I encountered. My brother-in-law's wife, Sue, also used to bring a team, normally strengthened by a couple of well-disguised county players, for a needle match on our home ground. After a few years the difficulty of maintaining our own pitch became too much and I concentrated entirely on country house cricket, which meant Arundel and Highclere. There was one other long-standing and hugely enjoyable annual match at Headley, where for many years I played for the Wates family XI against the local village side.

At Arundel, because I knew all the Duke and Duchess's daughters so well, I usually captained their XI against their father's team. Many of our side would spend the weekend at the Castle, which was always a treat in itself, as was playing on that beautiful ground. In my very first year of captaining the Daughters' XI I was batting as well as I had ever done, and I had been in for quite a long time when, after we lost a wicket, a new batsman came in with a message for me from the Duke himself: 'It's high time you declared.' I thought we probably had enough runs and dutifully declared at the end of the next over. This was before the days of proper scoreboards, so I had no idea how many runs I had scored personally. I was more than a little peeved later at the Duke's request, for not only did his side get the runs quite comfortably, but I found out from the scorer that I was on ninety-eight not out! I never did score a century. Great friends like the two Wates brothers, Michael and Andrew, Robin McCall and Mike Hooper usually played in these games. My final game at Arundel, in a team captained by the great Colin Cowdrey, showed me all too late how a really good skipper could make the game fun and interesting for all eleven players.

Playing regularly for many years at Highclere for Henry Porchester's XI was also a great joy. The cricket was always very competitive, and no one more so than our non-playing but very enthusiastic host himself. As my own batting became less productive and I gradually moved further down the order, I began to enjoy a second career, as it were, as a very slow off-break bowler. On one occasion I was playing for Henry's side against Jim Swanton's vaunted Arabs XI. I managed somehow to take three wickets and had the unusual experience of Jim himself watching me bowl from all different angles before proclaiming to all and sundry that I was a 'chucker'! The thought of my very slow off-breaks, which never turned, being worthy of such intense inspection because they might be delivered with a bent arm, amused me enormously.

My final game at Highclere might interest other middle-aged players who are wondering if it is time to retire gracefully. Playing a good young South Wales Hunts XI, we batted first; I came in about no. 6 and had scratched around for about twenty minutes for four singles before I was clean bowled. When it was our turn to field, my skipper, Harry Herbert, kindly said that I could have a bowl, which happened, unfortunately, when the better opposition batsmen were still in. My first ball was hit for six a long way over where my deep mid-wicket was posted. I immediately lost all confidence and had trouble even pitching the ball as my next five balls went for a further twenty runs. When Harry said, 'Thanks very much, Ian,' at the end of that first over, I was moved out to my favourite position of long off, where I had plenty of time to see the ball coming.

Being an old full back I rather enjoyed the odd high catch

coming in my direction. So very shortly afterwards when just that happened I moved forward off my boundary rope with some confidence. I suddenly realised to my horror that I had gone too far in, and as I stretched up as far as I could the ball went straight through my hands and over the boundary for six. The young South Wales Hunts supporters behind me were full of exaggerated sympathy, saying, 'Oh, *bad* luck, but of course the sun was right in your eyes, poor chap!' We all knew the sun was well behind us and not hindering anyone's vision – and I knew then that it was high time to spend my Sundays playing golf!

Not long after I came to Kingsclere Herbert Blagrave, who was president of Southampton Football Club, persuaded the directors, who were all fairly ancient, that they should have a new young director who was very sports-minded. I became that new young director and diligently attended board meetings at the Dell every Thursday morning. The chairman of the board was a marvellous old gentleman called George Reader – an ex-schoolmaster who had been a world-class referee and knew the game backwards. Our manager, Ted Bates, was another football expert whom I liked and admired enormously. Both of them were highly respected by everyone in the game. Our star players at that time were Terry Paine and Mick Channon, both of whom loved racing, and I got to know them both quite well.

I was still playing rugger most Saturdays, so I did not get to see our team play as often as I should have done. I took the opportunity of going to some of the more famous grounds, though, and enjoyed visits to Highbury very much when we played Arsenal. With Denis Hill-Wood as chairman and Bertie Mee as their manager these were always very friendly occasions, whatever the result of the match.

I also had one memorable visit to Old Trafford when Matt Busby was manager of Manchester United. The team coach was leaving too early on the Saturday morning for me to be able to travel on it, as this was also our busiest work morning. The secretary at the Dell asked me for the number and make of my car as this would make it easier for me to park if I was going to arrive just before the match started. As usual I left late and frightened Emma to death on the hectic journey to try to get there on time. When finally we got to the right road, I saw from some way off an enormous policeman in his full uniform with a long swagger stick at his side standing in front of what looked like the rear of the grandstand. He was motioning for me to drive right up to him. When I pulled up and let my window down he said to me, 'Are you Mr Balding, Sir?' I immediately thought, with my usual guilty conscience, that someone must have caught me speeding and phoned through to the Manchester police. Then he said, 'Would you please park right here, Sir?' Suddenly I realised with relief why I had had to give my car details.

Matt Busby himself was interested in racing and, like the true gentleman he was, he made a big fuss of Emma and showed us both around the relatively new stadium with great pride. He had been responsible for a great deal of the design and ideas behind it.

A few years later, when we had many more horses, it became impossible for me to get to the Thursday morning meetings, and I felt I should make way on the board for someone who could spend more time with the club. I must admit that I had also become disillusioned with the way the game was going and in particular with how spoilt the players were getting. Nevertheless, Andrew and brother Toby have always been serious Saints fans as much as I have, so we still have very good season ticket seats at the new St Mary's ground and I much enjoy going to the games there and to the odd match at Stamford Bridge when Bob Michaelson takes us. I remain very grateful to Herbert Blagrave, who not only got me involved with the club but also took me as his guest to Wembley on that fantastic day in 1966 when England beat Germany in the World Cup final. It was an amazing occasion and I shall always be grateful that I was there.

One of the most interesting involvements I have had outside the world of horses and racing has been as a member of Council at Radley College. In 1986, when Andrew was in his last two years as a pupil at Radley, much to my surprise Dennis Silk, who was Warden at the time, was deputed to ask if I would like to join the board of governors. I was highly flattered, but could not help wondering what use a racehorse trainer who was notoriously lacking in academic qualifications could possibly be to them. At this time I was the only member of Council who had a son currently at the school, so I did perhaps have access to some useful inside information. The chairman of the twenty-strong board was David Rae Smith, a big man in every sense and a very distinguished one. My hearing has never been that brilliant, and in my first few meetings when I felt that, as the new boy, I should sit in the seat furthest away from the action, I could hardly hear a word that Dennis and David said, as both had especially quiet voices. I gradually learned to get to the meetings early so I could sit nearer to them, but in such eminent and wise company it took me quite a while to gain sufficient boldness to ask a question or to make a comment.

David eventually became an owner of ours and, with his wife, 'Johnny', enjoyed one very special day at Newmarket when in 2001 the horse they share with their son Alan and with John and Pauline Gale, Distant Prospect, won the Cesarewitch. The result that day was a triumph, in fact, for a former senior prefect at Radley: for although the trainer's licence was still in my name, Andrew had masterminded the preparation of both the winner and the second, Palua. David was succeeded as chairman of Council by another good friend of mine, Mike Melluish, who has also become a part-owner at Kingsclere.

On the occasion of Radley's 150th anniversary in 1997, when the Queen and Prince Philip came to open the fabulous new Queen's Court academic building, all the governors stood in line and were introduced to them both. Her Majesty was not surprised to see me as I had mentioned the visit in one of our evening conversations, but Prince Philip's jaw dropped when he saw me and he said with astonishment, 'What on earth are you doing here?' I think I said something about there being rather a lot of ignorant racehorse trainers who went through Radley and they needed someone to look after their interests!

Mainly, I suppose, because he had known me for such a long time, Dennis always took quite a keen interest in racing and was himself president of the Tattersalls Club at Radley, a small group of about thirty enthusiasts of the Turf. Dennis took them all one time to Goodwood for an evening meeting. Willie Carson's son

Ross was at Radley at the time, and Dennis sent him into the weighing room before the first race to get the champion jockey to come out and talk to the assembled group of Radleians. Willie of course, as always, was great company, but after a while he said, 'Look, I'm in the first race, I had better go and change.' The Warden said, 'Willie, before you go, you better tell us what is going to win the first race.' Willie replied, 'I haven't got a clue I'm afraid, but I'll quickly go in and ask the other jocks, they will tell us.' After a few moments he came running back out and with a big smile said, 'Apparently I'm going to win it' – and he did!

For his leaving present the Warden was given a £100 voucher with Ladbrokes by the Tattersalls members. It was not a wise present as it has helped to turn my old friend into something of a betting fanatic. I have a suspicion that he studies the form almost as closely nowadays as his and my old hero, Jack Meyer, used to!

Running a large boarding school is in many ways like running a big racing stable: the headmaster is like the trainer, his parents are the equivalent of our owners, the pupils like the horses and his common-room members similar to our staff. The other remarkable likeness is that the cost of having a child at a large independent boarding school has always resembled the cost of having a horse in training – horribly expensive.

I have always much enjoyed my involvement at Radley and on one occasion at least I felt I might have served a useful purpose. Radley and Marlborough had a very well-publicised disagreement a few years ago on the cricket pitch. Both schools felt that the other was to blame, and so strong was the feeling that future fixtures of all games looked likely to be cancelled. As the only old Marlburian on the Radley Council I was deputed to try to make peace with the Marlborough headmaster. I am happy to say that the two schools were soon playing games against each other again and relations since then have been amicable.

It has been an enormous pleasure to have been a member of such a distinguished group of men for a long time now, and I have much enjoyed watching Radley over the years becoming an even better school in every way, as time goes on.

*

The holidays that Emma and I have taken over the years – usually in January and February – have become the lifeblood of our rather hectic existence. Those two or three weeks spent with our closest friends have been great revivers. Many years ago we decided that for Clare's and Andrew's sakes we should all take up skiing. It was rather late in life for Emma and I to become experts, but we did enough to enjoy holidays at various places in Europe with Werner and Bee Aeberhard and their children as our guides. At Aspen, Colorado, George and Nina Strawbridge had us all to stay at different times and I always adored the times spent on Aspen Mountain in particular. I was seen to have one or two rather spectacular falls there.

One year George invited Andrew and myself to go helicopter skiing with them in the deep powder of the Bugaboos. That challenge certainly satisfied my lust for excitement and we had several pretty hairy moments. My old Cambridge mate, Rogie Dalzell, even persuaded me in my late forties to go and do the Cresta Run in St Moritz for a couple of years running. I had considerable difficulty navigating the notorious bend called Shuttlecock and had one or two dramatic exits there. Finally the best English 'rider' there at the time, Grant Boyd Gibbons – a son of my father's polo-playing friend Boyd – was kind enough to explain to me how to negotiate this bend, and the two or three times that I got to the bottom at a decent speed made it all seem almost worthwhile – I say 'almost' because the very early cold mornings while on 'holiday' that the beginner had to endure and the unnecessary schoolmasterly abuse that we received from the somewhat pompous MC in the tower slightly spoiled the enjoyable bits. I must admit I was very envious of the experts who were coming down from 'top' at great speed, and they made me wish I had started in my youth.

In recent years since Michael Wates first made me take a set of golf clubs to Barbados, our holidays have mostly been based around golf courses in Barbados, South Africa and even Argentina, where we were accompanied by Michael and Caroline, Andrew and Sarah Wates, and Anga and Vivi Lillingston. Apart from the golf we went on a five-day riding trip to Jane Williams's place near

Baraloche, which was a great experience. The horses were brilliant – and they needed to be to negotiate some amazingly challenging countryside.

In recent years I have come to regret that I did not play golf sooner or have lessons at an early age. Like nearly everyone else who starts in middle age, I have become addicted and ever more frustrated that I did not play when younger. Perhaps in retirement I will find time to play enough to get decently handicapped and become able to beat some of my golfing friends, like the horribly gifted John Francome! The day that he hosts at our own home club of Sandford Springs for the children's sport charity SPARKS is just one of many such enjoyable days during the summer months. Our two main bloodstock sales companies, Tattersalls and Doncaster, make an effort to cater for their many enthusiastic golfing clients. Tattersalls have a superb day at Woburn, and DBS (Doncaster Bloodstock Sales) have a three-day outing revolving around Muirfield which provides a great summer break especially for the National Hunt trainers. Both have competitions which offer rewards for the true bandits among the racing clan.

The holidays I treasure above all are those we spend with my little sister Gail and her husband David in Aiken, South Carolina. Not only do Gail and I go out most mornings riding in the unique Hitchcock Woods, but thanks to their friendship with Bobby Goodyear, who is one of the oldest members at Augusta National Golf Club, I always seem to have the opportunity to play there, usually with David, my nephew Andrew and Bobby himself. It is a very special treat and, although I find myself wishing I was a better golfer, the home of the Masters is an inspiration in itself.

Aiken is perhaps the one place that I know of where I would most like to spend the winter months. It was always the winter playground of wealthy Americans, and families like the Hitchcocks and Bostwicks have helped to mould it into what it is now, with polo, drag hunting and other horsey sports such as showing and carriage driving. There is a training track on the edge of the town where a lot of trainers winter their horses, and a steeplechase course on which they still have one big day's racing. In addition there are great facilities for golf, squash and lawn tennis – and on top of all that they have one of the few real tennis courts in the country. Ten minutes recently on this court with a strangely shaped racquet in my hand was enough to convince me that this sport will soon become my new winter passion.

Over the years I have tried to give some of my own time and energy to various committees within racing. For many years I was a trustee of the Stable Lads' Welfare Trust – now quite rightly embraced by Racing Welfare, along with all the other various racing charities. The trust first evolved when the redoubtable little Welsh ex-bookmaker Wilfred Sherman started up the moribund Stable Lads' Boxing Association again. For a while it depended on the sponsorship and organisation on the big night of the Anglo American Sporting Club. It was fascinating to see little Wilfred verbally taking on the boxing heavyweights Micky Duff and Jarvis Astaire at our committee meetings. Neil Durden-Smith, who was the secretary, and I had to keep the peace – but the finals, usually at the Hilton Hotel, used to be one of the most enjoyable of all racing's social occasions. I always had great admiration for the lads who took part and it was no surprise to me that a lot of the better and braver boxers went on to make jockeys. One of the factors that helped to hasten the end of the stable lads' boxing was a request to take part from two of our girls. We couldn't let them; but what a sell-out that would have been!

I was a member of our National Trainers' Federation (NTF) Council for more years than I care to remember, and for a long time was one of our representatives on the wages committee. For quite a few years the lads were represented by the powerful Transport and General Workers' Union, and it was fascinating to find ourselves negotiating with the likes of Moss Evans and Ron Todd. I recall an occasion when the latter was saying that the lads' annual holiday should be extended from two weeks to three and thereafter by at least a further two days each year. While we were in agreement with the annual holiday increasing from two to three weeks (it is now four weeks) I asked him what would happen with his theory in many years' time – did he envisage an era, for example, when they worked for six months and holidayed for six months? He wouldn't answer my question and just pulled his union card out of his pocket and told me why and how he had first come by it!

While no one thinks that our stable staff are overpaid, I personally feel that the Stable Lads' Association has done a good job for them over the years. The lads and girls in all the top stables nowadays are very well looked after generally and certainly are paid a good deal more than the minimum figures that are always quoted.

The NTF has a very important role to play in the complicated world of racing politics, and happily we currently have a very intelligent and industrious former trainer as our chief executive in Rupert Arnold. I did my stint on the industry committee for a while, but it was much too political for me and I did not like it at all. On the other hand I much enjoyed my two years on the race planning committee, which was much closer to my heart.

For several years I have been a director of Salisbury racecourse under the excellent chairmanship of Michael Wates. I have found it interesting and enjoyable having always been very fond of the racecourse. Not being beholden to any shareholders, we have been able to run it for the benefit of the racegoers, owners and trainers.

It saddens me enormously that, much though we all love our great sport, it seems impossible for the various factions to unite under one umbrella for the sake of the common good. I remember once asking Arnold Weinstock if he would consider lending his considerable talents and getting involved to this end. He laughed and said, 'No, thank you very much, racing is my hobby and I want it to remain that way.' I didn't blame him; but racing desperately needs a man of his stature to unite us and thereby ensure a prosperous and secure future.

13

Slipping into Retirement

A s one gradually slides into the mentality of retirement, it seems that there is more time to reminisce, and I have found myself thinking about some of the more remarkable characters I have met over the years.

Before I came to Kingsclere I had not met any members of the royal family, or indeed anyone who might be termed a member of the aristocracy. I was soon to meet someone who, of all the aristocrats I have ever met, was easily the most aristocratic. Hugh William Osbert, Viscount Molineux, was the 7th Earl of Sefton and an important owner/breeder here when I came in 1964. I have already indicated that of all the owners I took over from Peter Hastings-Bass he was the only one I found the slightest bit difficult. He was a very large man and probably in his early sixties at that time. Priscilla told me that he had been very handsome in his younger days and was well known for having many lady friends. His wife was a sweet American lady of about half his size known as Foxy. Lord Sefton's family home was Croxteth, where he also had his stud farm; it bordered on the slightly better-known Derby family estate, Knowsley, both being on the outskirts of Liverpool.

Lord Sefton had already been Senior Steward of the Jockey Club and was still one of the most important figures of that august body. He expected attention from his trainer and I always had to phone him at 10 a.m. sharp every Sunday morning, when he would spend at least half an hour discussing the future plans in every detail of the six or eight horses he had here. He was a steward at Newbury racecourse, and for the two-day meetings at our local track he very often stayed at Park House on the Friday night. He himself would be flown down in his plane and land on the racecourse in time for lunch in the Royal Box. His driver would arrive in his Rolls-Royce with his luggage halfway through the afternoon and drive him to Kingsclere after racing. I once remember one of our other guests having the temerity to ask him what sort of car he drove. His lordship didn't even hesitate as he replied, 'Oh, one of those things we all have,' in his somewhat exaggerated public-school accent.

On one occasion as I was standing in the paddock with him watching the horses walking around we could see the jockeys leaving the weighing room and making their way towards us. He said to me, 'Oh, God, here come the enemy – you realise, of course, that we are all entirely in the hands of these ghastly little men!' All the jockeys who rode for him were always addressed as 'Piggott' or 'Smith' or 'Breasley', and our own stable jockey was thrilled to bits when Lord Sefton finally after several years addressed him as Geoff rather than 'Lewis'!

In spite of his obvious arrogance Geoff and I admired him a lot and were always thrilled if we ever had a winner for him. Not long after Emma and I were married we were invited to stay, along with Priscilla as well, at Croxteth for the Grand National meeting and I was quite excited about the prospect. In those days it was a mixed meeting, and Lord Sefton had not only owned Aintree racecourse but was senior steward at the meeting as well. He and Foxy and his house party were loaded into three large Rolls-Royces and driven into the racecourse at high speed with the help of a police escort.

When Emma and I first arrived at Croxteth with Priscilla, I had driven up the long, tree-lined drive and parked in front of a very formal entrance to this enormous mansion. We were at once greeted by Foxy and two butlers who took our luggage away, and taken in to a big drawing room where we and the other house guests had tea. After this, Foxy took Emma and myself up to show us our room. Our 'room' turned out in fact to be three rooms: first, a large bedroom with a big double bed in it on which Emma's long evening dress was already laid out; then a spacious bathroom where the tub itself looked to be seven feet long; and finally 'my' room, which was smaller, with a single bed on which my dinner jacket was arranged along with bow tie, socks and shirt.

After dinner, when all the ladies departed straight after the dessert to have their coffee in a different room, the port and cigars were passed around and our host told us chaps some amusing and quite saucy stories. Eventually Emma and I went upstairs to bed and I was mildly surprised to see that the big double bed was turned down on one side only, with Emma's nightie laid out neatly on it. I went through the bathroom and to my dismay saw 'my' little bed also turned down with my pyjamas tidily set out.

I went back to Emma's room and said, 'Surely they must realise we have only recently been married and would like to share the same bed.' She replied with a smile, 'You bloody well sleep in your room where you are supposed to be!' I managed to sneak my way back into the double bed after a while.

Next morning there was a knock on our door promptly at 8 a.m., when we had asked for a pot of tea and a *Sporting Life*. Emma sat up and said, 'Go on, quick! Get back into your own bed!' – and, conditioned I suppose by years of similar situations and a natural guilty conscience, I got up and ran, and was back in 'my' bed before her door even opened!

Hugh Sefton was an unlucky owner – his horses were always second in photo-finishes and just as we seemed to get one ready for a big race at one of his favourite meetings so it would meet with a setback. After seven or eight years at Kingsclere I recall him being really distraught when he told us he was going to move his horses to try and get a change of luck. Much more sadly, he and Foxy never had any children; the title died with him and Croxteth was left to Liverpool City Council.

Even more unfortunately for racing, he had previously sold Aintree Racecourse to the current tenant at the time, Mirabel Topham, who eventually wanted to sell the whole site for building.

He always regretted the sale enormously and had to spend a small fortune on a court case to prevent her from selling to developers. It meant in the end that Racing plc, led by Sam Vestey, had to find £4.25 million to buy the course from Mrs Topham and to preserve it for racing for ever. Lord Sefton could so easily have just given it to the Jockey Club in the first place.

Arnold Weinstock, the great entrepreneur and managing director of GEC, became an owner of ours in 1983. He too was never very lucky here and unfortunately his horses were with us during several years when we had some of our worst doses of the dreaded 'virus'. I always liked him enormously, and Emma said that he possessed more charisma than any other person she had met. On one occasion when he came to see his horses we were all sitting in the kitchen and somehow missed seeing his car arrive. Suddenly the front doorbell rang and Clare, who was about twelve at the time, jumped up from the table with normal childlike enthusiasm and rushed out, saying, 'I'll get it!' Arnold himself told me later how the conversation went. Apparently Clare looked at him and said, 'Who are you?' to which he replied, 'My name is Arnold Weinstock, and who, may I ask, are you?' 'I'm Clare Balding,' came the confident reply, and they then had a two- or three-minute discussion before they came in to join the rest of us. As he was leaving later Arnold said to me – and he meant it – 'Please be sure and let me know if that young lady ever needs a job!'

There was another occasion when he happened to be here at the same time as the celebrated Australian tycoon Robert Holmes à Court, who also had a horse here then. It amused Emma and me to see these two mega-powerful entrepreneurs walking around each other rather like male tigers and hardly addressing a word to each other. We were sitting in the drawing room when it started to rain and Robert, who had come in a Bentley convertible, said, 'I had better just go and put my roof up.' After a few minutes he came back and said in some dismay, 'I am embarrassed to say I can't seem to get my roof shut, can anyone help?' I am worse than useless in such circumstances, and was delighted when Arnold said, 'Yes, let's see if I can help.' After about twenty seconds he found the right button to press and the roof shut at once. They were immediately best friends and we could hardly separate them after that.

One other time Arnold's son, Simon, had come separately and he and I were standing in the main courtyard outside the stables waiting for his father. A few minutes later Arnold arrived in his Bentley and parked near us. The radio or CD was playing very loudly and he waited, sitting in the car, until that particular piece of opera had finished before he got out to join us. Then he smiled at us both, knowing we couldn't have failed to hear the last passage of stirring music, and said to Simon, 'Any idea what that was?' Simon replied, 'Sounded like Verdi to me.' Arnold smiled again and looked at me with eyebrows raised. I had recognised one of my favourite excerpts of *La Bohème* and was rather chuffed to be able to say Puccini and even to know which 'variety' it was this time! He gave me a look of surprise mixed with approval.

Arnold was, of course, a great lover and sponsor of classical music, and anyone fortunate enough to have attended his memorial service at the Guildhall will forever have fond memories of this remarkable man. I was at Newbury the day that Islington won her first race; he was enough of a horseman to recognise then that here was the best filly that he had ever bred, and I have a strong feeling that from somewhere above he will have been able to enjoy her famous victory at the Breeders Cup meeting.

Way back in 1979 a rather different type of owner came our way. This was the now very recognisable voice of BBC rugby football, Mr Ian Robertson. Ian had been capped for Scotland at fly half and later became an extremely successful coach to the Cambridge University team. We had quite a lot in common, and when he expressed an interest in taking part in a small way I let him take my half share in a very useful three-year-old we had at the time appropriately named Twickenham. He shared the horse with Ben Michaelson (Roger and Bob's father), who had bought a half share in the horse originally as a yearling. Ian's syndicated half share included several rugby-minded friends of us both, and over the next few years the horse was a great success, winning several decent handicaps.

Our next venture, involving a colt named British Lion, was not so successful. Ian persuaded some very famous ex-internationals to come in on this one and I should have guessed we might not have a superstar when, in a publicity stunt that Ian organised, the renowned Scottish full back Andy Irvine appeared to go every bit as fast as the horse in a hundred-yard sprint! After several disastrous runs over a two-year period, we had lost all confidence in our horse and entered him in a claiming race at Thirsk. Ian was too embarrassed even to tell his friends that our steed was taking part in such a lowly event and Barry John, the ex-Welsh fly half and a member of our syndicate, said that he nearly drove through the M4 barrier when he heard the name British Lion announced on the radio as the 20–1 winner of the 3.30 at Thirsk!

I had long since realised, of course, that the real reason Ian wanted a small share in one horse in the yard was so that he would not be reticent in asking his 'senior' trainer – poor Gavin Pritchard-Gordon was always referred to as the 'junior' trainer – for all the privileged information about the stable's runners. If nothing else, Ian can be said to have been incredibly loyal over the many years of our association. The BBC rugby correspondent never seems to admit to backing many losers or missing many winners, in spite of his senior trainer being one of the worst tipsters of all time. Luckily he has a very friendly bookmaker who seems to give him far better information, even on our horses! It never ceases to amaze me, nevertheless, that he keeps coming back for more, even though I do sense a sigh of relief from him nowadays when I pass him over to Emma or Andrew, who is now known by Ian as 'the boy wonder'.

On one occasion I leased Ian an old dual-purpose horse, Cheka, which Paul Mellon had given me. We were all at Bath where I was running a useful horse called Waterlow Park, who belonged to a very nice Scottish couple, the Kennedys, in a two-mile handicap. He was quite a warm favourite and I had encouraged Robert Kennedy to have a few quid on him. We also ran Cheka in the race to give one of our more obscure apprentices a ride, and he was at odds of 25–1. Ian had brought some of his rugby-playing partners and, unbeknown to me, they were all standing together a few steps behind the Kennedys and myself on the open-roofed stand above the members' enclosure.

Waterlow Park, confidently ridden by our stable jockey John Matthias, took up the running with about two furlongs to go and quickly went about five lengths clear. I was beginning to congratulate the Kennedys when suddenly I saw a horse coming out of the pack and finishing pretty fast. I was not very familiar with my own colours in the summer months and was used anyway to Cheka running in P.M.'s black with a gold cross. It took me a few moments to realise who this fast-finishing horse was – and then, hearing some rough-sounding rugby players behind me starting to shout, 'Come on Cheka!', realised that my worst nightmare was now being played out. Cheka got up in the dying strides to beat Waterlow Park by a neck. Robert Kennedy, understandably, was not best pleased and his horses are now doing very well with Mark Johnston training them!

The beaten horse that day just about got his own back a couple of years later when Ian insisted on being allowed to have a ride one day. I put him on Waterlow Park, now owned by me, who was as quiet a ride as we had on the place and the regular mount for all the youngest apprentices. I suggested to Ian that he might be safer to restrict himself to trotting, but if he insisted on having a canter he could go quietly round our starting-gate field gallop inside the schooling fences. Old Waterlow must have relished carrying a complete novice on his back and came round this four-furlong stretch at a pretty decent gallop. Ian was able to steer him wide of the schooling fences and even managed to stay put when the old horse came to a rapid halt in the far corner of the field. The rider has always been very proud that he didn't fall off that day, but it has not escaped wider notice that he has never asked to ride again since!

There is no doubt in my mind that the best Flat jockey I have ever seen was the incomparable Lester Piggott. He had his first ride for me in my very first season in 1964, when I still held only a temporary licence. We had a half-brother to Silly Season, a year older, called Moonlighter. He was still a maiden in September as a three-year-old, having been second a couple of times in very lowly company, and was very one-paced. I was going through the runners for a one-mile-five-furlong maiden the next day at Newbury in the paper when I realised we would have to run as the opposition looked pretty moderate. Geoff had several rides booked for us up north and when quickly searching for a possible jockey I noticed that L. Piggott was not jocked up on anything else in that race. With some excitement I rang his number and was even more elated when his wife Susan said, 'Funny you should ring, Lester has just asked me to phone you about that horse.'

The next day I saw Lester as he came on to the racecourse, made sure he knew who I was and told him the horse was very one-paced but pulled quite hard. I didn't like to tell him that the horse had rather a bad mouth and that Geoff usually took him down last, very slowly, with his head pulled sideways over the running rail. I suggested that if he could find someone else to go a real good gallop it could suit us very well. When he came into the paddock and I asked him if he thought there would be a good gallop he said, 'I think this Hicks will go on.'

Lester came out on to the track first, trotted down in front of the stands, turned round and then on a nice long rein cantered quietly down to the mile and five start. It was a lovely piece of horsemanship and the horse looked very happy and relaxed. In the race 'this Hicks' (G. Hicks, claiming seven pounds) went very fast and Moonlighter sat in second place some way behind the leader. As they turned into the long Newbury straight Lester gradually moved closer to the leader and at the two-furlong marker took up the running. He had several of those disdainful peeps over his shoulder and without coming off a tight rein the horse won by about ten lengths.

I was over the moon and hurried to greet our winner. When Lester dismounted he turned to me and said, 'He's no good, you know – you should sell him.' I was dumbstruck, having already begun to think we had a valuable prospect. I stupidly ignored Lester's advice, but of course he proved to be absolutely right – Moonlighter never looked like winning again!

A different side of the great man's character emerged a couple of years later. He had ridden a winner for us somewhere and in those days there was no deduction from prize money for the lad who looked after the horse. As a consequence the jockeys used to give the travelling head lad a tenner for the lad. We were accustomed to Geoff always being very generous to the lads, but Bill Jennings had been chasing around after Lester for a couple of weeks trying to get this present for our lad. Finally he caught up with him one day as he came out of the weighing room at the end of racing to go to his car. As the great jockey increased his walking pace Bill was virtually running beside him, saying, 'Lester, you remember that winner you rode for us a couple of weeks ago? Would you like to give me a fiver for the lad?' Lester kept walking and mumbled, 'I can't hear you – you'd better come round to my good ear.' Still jogging to keep up, Bill got a bit braver this time and shouted, 'Lester, remember the winner you rode for us – how about a tenner for the lad?' Lester looked at him, smiled and said, 'I think you'd better come back round to the five-pound ear!'

What I admired so much about Lester, apart from his brilliance as a jockey, was his total comprehension of the whole system – and this, of course, was also well before the days when jockeys had agents. He appeared to control where half a dozen different trainers ran their horses. He may have had one deaf ear and a slight speech impediment, but that man understood the racing calendar better than any trainer.

He rang me one Sunday and said, 'Are you going to send that old horse up to Haydock next week?' That 'old horse' was a six-year-old called Arctic Judge belonging to Bud McDougald, and I had entered him in a conditions race without really looking closely at the conditions. I had noticed in the calendar that he was easily top weight with ten stone twelve pounds because he had won quite a few races recently and the penalties were cumulative. I had one brief look at the race and thought, Silly me, what a waste of money to have entered. So my reply to Lester was, 'No, I haven't even considered it – he has too much weight to carry.' He asked me to get the relevant calendar and go through the race with him horse by horse, which I did. He knew every single horse and what they were all like. 'This one won't run because I ride it at Chepstow the previous day, that won't because I know it's coughing, this one doesn't try' – and so he went on. Finally he said, 'He'll win, you know – you'd better send him.' Amazed, I said, 'OK, if you ride him I'll send him.' Arctic Judge, ridden by L. Piggott, won at Haydock that August with ease.

I could easily write a whole chapter on Lester, but suffice it to say that in my lifetime he was the only person in racing that I could consider without doubt to be a genius. The top jockeys who rode with him did not all exactly love him, because they knew that at any given time he might jock them off their best rides. They all admired him hugely, though, and knew that in terms of ability he was out on his own.

Scobie Breasley was a tough Australian who was good enough to come over here and run Lester close in the jockeys' championship several times, and even win it on four occasions himself. He was a more natural size and weight for a jockey than his great rival and was also a fabulous horseman. He hated going round horses, and if ever you had missed watching the first half of a race for any reason you knew exactly where to look for Scobie – he would for sure be scraping paint off the inside rail, not far behind the leaders. If he had a failing it was that too often he would get stuck on the inside and would sit still and leave the horse for another day.

He only ever rode one winner for us – a filly of Paul Mellon – and Scobie appeared hardly to move a muscle on her as she won very comfortably. However, when they reached the winner's enclosure I noticed that his face was dripping with sweat. He was certainly not out of breath as he told us about the race, but I always reckoned that he must have been squeezing so hard with his legs that the effort made him sweat.

Scobie went on after his riding career to train at Epsom for several years. He was always enormously respected by everyone in racing and when he attended the Derby at Epsom in 2003 as the racecourse's guest of honour I was very happy to have the chance for a good chat to him and to his great old friend who was there as well, Geoff Lewis. Scobie was still much saddened by the recent loss of his wife of over sixty years, May. We had a laugh, though, at the famous story of what happened when they both attended a smart lunch given by the Jockey Club at Newmarket. Scobie was still training at the time and May had been seated next to the Senior Steward. To make conversation he asked May idly if Scobie ever had a bet these days. 'Oh no,' she said, and then added, with typical Australian tact, 'he hasn't had a bet since he gave up riding!'

Steve Cauthen had proved his ability in the States, of course, before he came to England. Our higher weight range and far more attractive lifestyle for a jockey suited him admirably and he adapted to our different style of riding very quickly. Steve, probably as much as Lester, had a clock in his head and was a master of front running. He proved it many times but never better than on Slip Anchor when winning the 1985 Derby. Steve was a golden boy who found the right lady and retired at the right time. While he lived in England his strong, graceful style of riding was a pleasure to watch and he became a true gentleman of the Turf whom everyone idolised.

Pat Eddery, like Scobie, was blessed with being the perfect size and shape for a Flat race jockey. Of all the top jockeys I have watched over the years I think that Pat probably made the fewest mistakes. He very rarely ever seemed to be in the wrong place in a race. I never admired his style in a finish, where he would bump up and down very hard on the horse's back every other stride, but it was enormously effective. Pat was the true professional in every sense and I would imagine that you could count the times he was late for anything in his life on the fingers of one hand. It says everything for his popularity that all the jockeys came out of the weighing room to applaud him into the winner's enclosure when he won the Sussex Stakes on Reel Buddy in his last year of riding.

Yves Saint-Martin rode a winner for us one day at Chantilly in 1983. I was there and saw him win three other races as well on the same afternoon, all with different riding tactics. At the time he was far superior to any of the other French jockeys and on the world stage he was as good as anyone. He too had a superb physique and always looked very much part of his horse.

Of our current champions, Kieren Fallon and Frankie Dettori have ridden many winners on our horses, and both, with their very different riding styles and personalities, would rank with the very best I have ever seen. Frankie at the time of Lochsong almost became part of our family. Clare and Andrew both adored him and his bubbly enthusiasm is infectious. Emma gave him a boxer puppy called George a few years ago and he and Catherine often ring to tell us of his latest exploit.

Of the National Hunt jockeys I have known, some of whom I have been privileged to ride with in schooling sessions at Kingsclere, I would rate John Francome, Tony McCoy and Richard Dunwoody as the best. Many years ago Fred Winter was the best of his era; Stan Mellor (rather like Willie Carson with Lester) was the only one good enough to run him close and even beat him in the championship. Peter Scudamore and Jamie Osborne are two other top-class riders who rode for us from time to time.

The style of riding has altered so much over the years that it would be unfair to compare some of my youthful heroes with today's champions. However, I have a photograph of Martin Molony jumping a fence on Silver Fame in 1952, and I cannot believe that even now, fifty-odd years later, anyone could possibly look better. I once tried vainly to follow him across country when hunting with the Limerick, and I don't suppose anyone ever did that better than he did either.

It is hard to try to compare other trainers, because obviously one does not see them at work every day in the same way one sees jockeys perform. One can only really look at their records and make assumptions. Having been at Ballydoyle many years ago and known Vincent O'Brien during his great years, I would always consider that he was equivalent to Lester but in the training ranks. To have won all the top National Hunt races in a relatively short period and then give it up and do the same thing on the Flat shows that he was both brilliant and versatile.

His successor at Ballydoyle, Aidan O'Brien, is obviously very talented and is also delightfully unaffected by his tremendous success rate. He, like his predecessor, is a superb horseman and also pays enormous attention to detail. He is very fortunate, however, in that he does not have to worry about acquiring horses himself, or anything much else except the actual preparation of very good horses for all those top races.

I have always admired Dermot Weld, who has competed extremely well with both O'Briens over many years with far less ammunition. His record of travelling horses and winning major races on every continent is second to none. I do not mean it in any sinister way at all – I am just envious – but it must be a great advantage to both him and Mark Johnston to be qualified vets.

I would always consider my close friend Dick Hern as one of the great trainers during my time. I know that Dick trained his horses very hard; they were always out at exercise for long hours and were galloped well. There were horses he trained, such as Brigadier Gerard and Boldboy, who I am certain would not have been as successful anywhere else. Dick, with his wonderful sense of humour, was as good company as anyone I know, and I was touched when he left me in his will a beautiful painting of Bustino by Peter Biegel.

Noel Murless and his son-in-law Henry Cecil were both marvellous trainers and I suspect that Noel's daughter, Julie, who never had the same horsepower as her father or husband, would probably have been just as good if she had had the resources really to have made a go of it on her own. Michael Stoute is the modern-day virtuoso of Newmarket and is obviously a complete master of his art. I sometimes wonder if both he and Henry, a few years ago, might have had too many good horses in their yards at the same time to give all the horses the fullest benefit. There are times when it has appeared that the odd one has not run in an obvious race because an equally good horse in the yard in different ownership is scheduled to run. It would, I imagine, be a lovely problem to have!

Luca Cumani is a very intelligent trainer and in spite of being an Italian in England has done extremely well. He has had the benefit, of course, of a beautiful English wife to translate for him and charm the owners! Luca was a fine amateur rider in his time and won the Moët and Chandon Trophy at Epsom for us one year. Of the many other very good English trainers I have always admired John Dunlop greatly, because apart from training just under two hundred horses extremely successfully, he has found the time and vigour to lend his considerable talents to support charities and committees both within and outside racing.

David Elsworth is a trainer with 'green fingers' for the development and preservation of some great old champions. To have achieved what he has with Desert Orchid and Persian Punch under both codes speaks volumes for his all-round ability. He has a wonderful eye for a yearling, too, and has had to go out and buy most of his horses himself.

I have always respected the Easterby family. Peter was a brilliant trainer under both codes; the handover to Tim on his retirement was achieved with amazing efficiency and is something that Andrew and I have tried to emulate. Tim seems every bit as successful as his father. Peter's brother, Mick, is something else – one of racing's true characters, whom both Emma and I like enormously. I can remember Robert Sangster telling me that he loved having a horse with Mick, but that the only time he came to see it, it took Mick about twenty minutes to find it! I can well believe it, because many years ago we went up there and spent a hilarious morning with him. The main purpose of our visit was for me to try a young horse whom Mick had convinced me would make a super point-to-pointer. During the ride I was standing with Mick as half a dozen horses approached us at a canter on a dirt gallop. I asked him as they went by what they were – expecting, as one normally would, to be told the age, sex and breeding of each individual. After about half of them had passed, Mick said, 'Oh them's the Flat 'osses.' A few seconds after the last one had gone he said, 'Oh no, sorry, them's the jumpers!'

After the ride he invited us to look at the yearlings he had recently bought at the sales. There were at least a dozen of them, still with their sales stickers on their rumps, turned out in this one field which could only be described as stock proof. The driver said, 'Hold tight, we'll see if any of these buggers can go!' He then proceeded to chase them round the field in his car, tooting his horn as he went.

Just as we were leaving he said, 'What about this 'oss then?' To be honest I didn't really like him, but needless to say ended up buying him! The first time I took him out drag hunting he 'bled'. After a few easier days, trying to qualify him without pushing him hard enough to make him bleed again, I took a gamble and ran him in a maiden point-to-point at Tweseldown. We had only gone about a mile when blood started coming back all over my colours and breeches and I quickly pulled him up. I was never able to run him again. The horse had a smart name but was always known by us as Mick.

The real Mick let almost eighteen months pass before he finally enquired, ''Ow's that 'oss then? D'you ever do any good with 'im?' I smiled and said, 'No, Mick. I'm afraid he was quite a bad bleeder.' The reply came back, 'That's funny – d'ya know, all my buggers are bleeding at the moment too!'

My old football friend from Southampton, Mick Channon, has done brilliantly. He has been brave enough to spend his own money buying and refurbishing West Ilsley, and it will be no surprise to me if Mick fulfils his own ambition to become the leading trainer in the land. He will always have Mark Johnston to contend with in that same ambition. I am full of admiration for Mark, who somehow finds time to write very well in various publications and to give his time in playing a big part in the National Trainers' Federation as well.

I took Andrew with me one day when we went down to spend a morning with Martin Pipe. It was fascinating, and it's not difficult to see why he is so successful. His regime of short, sharp, hard work and strict control of the horses' diet helps to ensure that his runners are fitter than anyone else's. His success rate has been phenomenal and he must be as good a trainer as there is now or has been.

I have written at length about the best horses I have trained, but I often think about my old favourites just as much. They naturally were geldings who were around for a lot longer than the colts and fillies, and one had time to get to know and appreciate them more. I suppose my all-time favourite was Paul Mellon's old soldier, Morris Dancer. He won twenty-five races in all, the last of them at the age of twelve. He had an amazing record of travelling to Paris, winning there five years in a row. In his early days he was something of a savage and even in his advanced years he was never very pleasant, especially to strangers. Many was the time that he was late pulling out in the morning. When Bill Palmer or I went into his box to find out why, we would discover that a young apprentice had not been allowed by the old horse to get near enough to put his tack on. We would laugh and put it on for them with no problem at all.

I recall Geoff Lewis, who rode the old boy in most of his twenty-five victories, visiting one weekend and seeing the name

Morris Dancer on the stable door. Without saying anything to me he opened the door and went in. I smiled as I heard him say, 'Come on my old m-m-mate, come and say hello' – and then a few seconds later he came flying out of the stable shouting, 'You rotten old b-b-bastard!'

After his racing days were over, we used Morris Dancer as Bill's or my hack for several years. I even took him hunting on one hilarious occasion with the Vine and Craven. He refused to jump anything at all except some puddles, and all he wanted to do was attack any of the genuine hunters that I got too close to. I was not encouraged to take him out a second time.

Like so many of our old favourites he was totally retired for his last few years, up in those lovely paddocks behind The Lynches. One sad day at the age of twenty-five he took no interest at all when we moved him from one paddock to another and we knew the dreaded day had come. Bath racecourse ran a race named in his honour for many years and P.M. sponsored it, of course, for nearly all that time.

I have said previously that I never thought that Idiot's Delight had much chance of making the grade as a stallion. Emma and I were offered a free nomination to him and it shows what high esteem I held him in when I suggested we send Emma's lovely, but very un-Thoroughbred, hunter mare Ellie May. The offspring was gelded as a foal and named Quirk after my stepfather. He became one of our favourite family hunters. Clare and Andrew rode him in many hunter trials and he went with them to Pony Club camp, where he was apt to cause a certain amount of chaos and confusion. Emma rode him in the team chase on several occasions and drag hunted him frequently.

I was never allowed to ride him much then, but when he retired from hunting he was for several years my summer hack. He became famous at Kingsclere for being Lochsong's boyfriend. In her last couple of years the famous sprinter became rather mulish and refused to go near the gallops unless Quirk and I led her. She adored him and often when she got to the top of the gallop refused to move until he reached the end, rather more slowly, a minute or two later. She would certainly have been a problem to train without him.

At the end of our exercise in the summers we always stop with the whole string in the corner of the field so that they can have a pick of grass and get down and have a roll. So that I could wander around to look at each horse more closely and chat to the lads, I used to leave Quirk on his own, and he would nearly always give us some amusement. He would usually jog or even canter off to a different part of the field to have a pick of grass on his own, but would always come back as we started to go in. Sometimes he would get down and roll with his tack on and occasionally would give his own rodeo show to show me he had not had enough exercise that morning. He was very fond of our dogs and would often nuzzle up to them; and he loved chasing the deer off the gallops before the racehorses got there. Quirk was an amazing character and had a real sense of humour, if a horse can have such a thing. He is still with us, aged twenty-five, and looks remarkably healthy, acting as usual as a nanny to some of our foals and yearlings on the stud.

Grey Shot was bred by Jeff Smith at Littleton Stud and came here as a yearling in 1993. He was iron grey in colour then; now, of course, over ten years later, he is white. On the Flat he was a very game front-running stayer and won several good races, such as the Goodwood Cup and the Jockey Club Cup at Newmarket. We took him to Australia for the Melbourne Cup at the end of his four-year-old season, which in hindsight was probably a year too soon. He had to travel all that way on his own with just his faithful lad, Dylan Holley, for company. The Aussies looked after us superbly and their big day is for sure one of the great sporting occasions in the world. Dylan and Grey Shot are both loners and they loved the whole three-week trip.

At the end of his five-year-old year I persuaded Jeff Smith and his manager, Ron Sheather, that Grey Shot ought to go hurdling. He won his first race over hurdles in Jeff's colours, but the owner is no real lover of the winter game and I soon negotiated a sale to Robert Hitchins. Grey Shot became a very good hurdler, running well more than once at Cheltenham, and when he won the Kingwell Hurdle at Wincanton we thought he should take his chance in the Champion Hurdle. He ran disappointingly and I felt then that if he was to reach the highest grade in the winter game it would probably be over fences. He won twice in his usual exciting front-running style, but a horrid fall at Sandown at the Whitbread meeting curtailed his career.

He had a long recuperation, like many of our invalids, down in Devon on the farm of our old vet John Gray and his wife Mo. Since he has returned to Kingsclere the 'white wonder' has become my current summer hack. He loves it and would happily stand and watch the others galloping all day. Ears pricked always, he never misses a trick and will watch the deer and cattle mooching about on the adjoining farm half a mile away in between times. He still loves to jump the odd fence, too.

Three or four years ago an old owner, Peter Oldfield, sadly no longer alive, gave me a retired racehorse whom I had once trained for him, called Diviner. Andrew tells me that the only time he looked like winning a race was when he rode him one day in a bumper at Warwick. They finished second and apparently I gave the jockey quite a bollocking as I felt they should have won! Diviner immediately became my winter hack and my drag hunt horse, and I can say categorically that he is the best I have ever had. He is the schooling companion for all our few jumpers now and has even won various hunt races with his ageing owner aboard. I ran him in our Berks and Bucks members' race at Kingston Blount a couple of years ago and he gave the promising young jockey James Davies, who was apprenticed to me at the time, his first win over fences.

Not so long ago I was invited to go hunting with the Middleton Hunt in Yorkshire as a small reward for speaking at the Gimcrack Dinner the previous evening. Camilla Halifax said that I could ride up with the huntsman Frank Houghton-Brown, just behind the hounds. I had a feeling some of my Yorkshire friends were waiting for me to be disgraced by my horse refusing at a fence, or perhaps even kicking a hound. Diviner was brilliant and never put a foot wrong all day, for which I was very grateful.

A few weeks later I was a guest again, this time with the South Notts Hunt by courtesy of their retiring master Richard Brooks, who supplies us with Eurobale. I took Diviner up again and recall our standing outside a particular cover for some little while at the start of the day. We did not have much to do but look at this very big grey-stone wall which was obviously going to be our first fence when the fox finally emerged. The longer we were there, the bigger the wall seemed to get. Richard was on a fine, big, handsome hunter and I thought I would be sure to jump it right behind him to get a good lead. When the moment came, Richard jumped it well – but someone cut in just in front of me and fell off on the landing side. Diviner had a good excuse to stop or run out, but he jumped the wall superbly and then neatly sidestepped the rider on the ground.

Sadly, our day did not last long because the fog came down and we had no option but to call a halt. Just as I was boxing up in the car park ouside the pub where we met, a lady came up to me and said, 'Excuse me, are you Mr Balding?' When I said yes, she went on: 'Well, I felt I had to come and find you just to tell you that I couldn't get over the way your horse jumped that first stone wall. It gave me a terrific thrill and I just hope it did you too.' That incident made my whole journey worthwhile, and while I have such a good horse I intend to do as much foxhunting and drag hunting as I can. Diviner has a beautiful mouth and is just about the perfect ride for a retired trainer who still likes to jump the odd fence. I have become extremely fond of him.

Throughout my life I have always had dogs around me, and as with the horses there have been special ones among them. Until very recently we always had lurchers, and my favourite of all of them was a wonderful dog called Bertie, who in the late 1970s won the Lambourn Lurchers Championship two years running and became a great sire. Every day without exception Bertie would come with me when we rode out, and when he died I missed him horribly.

Favourite horses and favourite dogs bring me around finally to favourite people. We have always been a close family. From my earliest days I always adored my big brother Toby, and our family and his have been very close. I have the greatest respect for his achievements in the world of horse racing – not just for the many big races he has won, nor for the countless hours he has given to the owners' and trainers' committees, but also and especially for his boundless enthusiasm for the sport. I have said already that his work days and schooling sessions are events of improvised flair rather than meticulous planning. They were always designed to be fun for the visiting owner, even if that occasionally entailed his horse being chased up the gallops by a selection of enthusiastic dogs!

The many good trainers and top jockeys who have been through the Fyfield academy are testament to his ability to be able to pass on some of that skill and passion. Happily in 2002 there was a lovely surprise party, superbly organised by some of those graduates, at Elcot Park for Toby and his wife Caro, to which all their old friends and acquaintances came in numbers. With a video of some of the great moments and a couple of speeches it was, we all thought, the sort of happy gathering that only usually happens at funerals! But it demonstrated in just how much affection my big brother is held in our world of racing. Their recent move from Fyfield to Kimpton Down is just the stimulant that he and Caro needed and will provide a wonderful platform from which to hand over to the next generation.

Our own family of four have always got on remarkably well. United perhaps by a love of horses and dogs as well as each other, we celebrate, commiserate and, most importantly, laugh together. Andrew demonstrated his priorities very early on when at prep school he was asked to name the seasons of the year. His reply, 'Flat and jumping', was instant. While at Radley he showed quite an appreciation of art, and in fact draws very well. He remembers being severely rebuked for not taking his subject seriously enough on one occasion. His class were sitting in a circle sketching a nude male model. When the art mistress came around to see his progress, she said, 'Andrew, why are you being so coy about drawing his private parts?' The reply came, 'Well, it's very difficult, Miss, because that particular part keeps changing shape.'

Andrew had an enjoyable and very educative year at Fyfield where his uncle Toby always affectionately referred to him as 'Minder'. Also there at the time were Tony McCoy, Barry Fenton and Emma Lavelle who are still great friends of his. From there he went for two vital years to Jack and Lynda Ramsden. On returning from the Ramsden academy I remember chiding him for not riding out more often or even coming drag hunting with us occasionally. His reply was, 'Well, Dad, you may have been a frustrated jockey all your life, but you've got to realise that I've been a frustrated trainer all mine.' When I gave him the two back yards to manage on his own he soon showed his prowess by winning the Cesarewitch twice in three years and then the Mill Reef Stakes at Newbury. When he then won the Britannia Stakes at Royal Ascot with Pentecost, still officially under my licence, I knew it was high time to hand over.

Like me almost forty years ago, he has been very lucky to take over some good horses, wonderful owners and superb staff – but with Casual Look and Phoenix Reach in particular, he too has shown that at least he has not 'messed up' a couple of good horses! Actually, he has made a brilliant start and quickly shown that he has a real instinct for getting the best out of the horses in his care.

The confident young lady Clare Balding, whom Arnold Weinstock would happily have employed, was quick to make her mark in the racing world. At Cambridge she was one of the first women to achieve the prestigious post of President of the Union. She approached the racing world with equal enthusiasm; indeed, her determination to become leading lady amateur rider on the Flat nearly got her in trouble when she badly crossed and almost brought down the Princess Royal on one occasion at Beverley. She was fortunate that we had some useful old geldings in the yard at that time that proved to be perfect for those ladies' races. Her sensitive and quiet style suited them extremely well and in some cases revitalised their enthusiasm for racing.

Clare will always be grateful to Cornelius Lysaght for her first opportunity to make her way in the media world. In the early days she was inevitably referred to frequently as my daughter, and I remember well her saying to me at one time, 'Dad, I'm fed up with constantly being called Ian Balding's daughter – I can't wait until you are known as Clare Balding's father.' Needless to say, that happened all too soon; and in 2003 she was thrilled at the accolade bestowed by her peers in racing journalism, who voted her Racing Journalist of the Year at the Horserace Writers' Association annual lunch – the first woman to be so honoured. Clare has become an outstanding and much admired broadcaster and I am extremely proud of her. She was fortunate that she inherited from her mother a good brain and a very quick mind.

After Casual Look's victory in the Oaks, she was worried that the infamous 'speechless' interview with her father and brother was unprofessional. Her only mistake, perhaps, was not to approach her mother in the first instance, who as usual could probably have made more sense than the rest of us put together. All our good friends and relations know just what a remarkable lady Clare's and Andrew's mother is. It was at the Horserace Writers' Association Luncheon in 2002 when I was presented with the much-treasured Clive Graham Award that I tried to say just how much she meant to me. I had been thinking at the time a lot about my life and how incredibly lucky I have always been. I did not say it then, but I think I had realised at last just what Jack 'Boss' Meyer meant when I heard him that evening all those years ago describing me as 'one of God's own' – I suspect what he meant was that I was someone on whom God has smiled. Never was he smiling more generously than when he guided Emma Alice Mary into my path.

Index

Note: 'IB' denotes Ian Balding. 'The' (when an integral part of a horse's name) is not transposed.

Tagula (horse) 212
Taj Dewan (horse) 122
Tanner, Tony 30-31
Tarleton, Georgie 27
Taylor, E.P. 167
Thatcher, Margaret x
The Argonaut (horse) 153
The Brigand (horse) 2, 119
The Lynches 105-6
The Quiet Man (horse) 32-3, 52-3
Thomas, Brian 65
Thompson, Derek ('Tommo') 152
Thompson, John ('J.R.T.') 25-6
Thompson, Ken 169
Time Charter (horse) 181
Time (horse) 83
Todd, Danny 11
Todd, John 11
Todd, Ron 242-3
Tom Fool (horse) 97
Tommy (pony) 15
Top Cees (horse) 214-15
Topham, Mirabel 246-7
Tory, Michael 51
Trans Island (horse) 215
Tree, Jeremy 57, 78, 180
Trickle (horse) 140
Tross, Martha 185
Troy (horse) 149
Tryon, Lady 92
Turnell, Bob 76, 103
Turnpike (horse) 167
Turpin, Randolph 14
Twickenham (horse) 213, 248

United States 7-12, 21, 165, 169-71, 181, 183, 184-5, 186, 203-4, 240, 241-2

Valkyrie (pony) 162
Vanian, Souren 180
Vestey, Sam 247
Vick, Lionel 80-81
Vigors, Charlie 183
Vigors, Sarah 183
Vigors, Tim 207

Waddell, Gordon 62, 65-6, 68
Wade, Mike 68
Wait For The Will (horse) 140
Waldron, Philip 118, 128, 130, 131, 179
Wallabies (rugby team) 52
Ward, Pam 13

Ward, Tony 5, 136
Warner, John 128
Warrior (horse) 162
Waterlow Park (horse) 249-50
Wates, Andrew 70-71, 72, 161, 228, 235, 240
Wates, Caroline 240
Wates, Michael 235, 240, 243
Wates, Sarah 228, 240
Watts, Harvey 216, 217
Watts, Joyce 216, 217
Weedy, Micky 177
Weinstock, Arnold, Lord 180, 187, 243, 247-8
Weinstock, Simon 187, 248
Weld, Dermot 255-6
Wells, Anne (*married name* Peate) 35-7
Welsh Note (horse) 185
Welsh Pageant (horse) 121
Westminster, Duke of 95
Weston, Galen 8
Weyhill 34-5, 44-5
Whitbread, Bill 34, 39, 44-5
Whitechapel (horse) 158
Whitman, Christie Todd 11
Whitney, C.V. ('Sonny') 21
Whitney, Jock 12, 16, 18-19, 32, 34, 44, 45, 53, 54, 57, 74, 81, 83, 139-40
Wigan, James 175
Willcox, John 68
Willder, Jeremy 28, 161
Willder, Penny 161
Williams, Barry 4-5
Williams, Evan 96
Williams, Gill 96
Williams, Jane 240-41
Williams, Peter ('Cazzy') 144, 148, 149, 150
Willis, Margerite 79
Willmot, Bud 168
Winter Fair (horse) 119, 120
Winter, Fred 255
Winter Gale (horse) 49-50, 70
Woolley, Steve 149
Wragg, Geoff 203
Wright, Peter 184

You'd Be Surprised (horse) 140
Young, Bill 186
Young, Lucy (*married name* Ruspoli) 186

Zaefferer, Adriana 163
Zafonic (horse) 150